"To help all, especially young people of limited means, to a greater knowledge, love and care of the countryside, particularly by providing hostels or other simple accommodation for them in their travels, and thus to promote their health, rest and education."

To book a Youth Hostel visit

www.yha.org.uk

or call your chosen Youth Hostel.

During the next two years you'll be able to book more and more Youth Hostels on-line or by calling 0870 770 8868. News of this and other developments will be sent to you with the members' magazine, Triangle, mailed to all members in the spring and autumn.

For up-to-the-minute opening dates, prices and information

0870 770 8868

Welcome TO YHA

Your membership

You already enjoy the benefits of individual YHA membership, but are you aware of all we have to offer, including…

Family membership: Joining as a family makes economic sense – when one or both parents join, children between 5 and 17 are enrolled free. Turn to page 8 to see how you and your family can enjoy a holiday with YHA and its child-friendly facilities.

Life membership: Invest in YHA membership for life and choose to pay in a single sum or five annual instalments.

Group membership: This enables formally constituted groups and organisations to stay at Youth Hostels worldwide. Your membership card can be used for groups of five or more (ten or more outside England and Wales). To learn more about what YHA can offer groups, turn to page 10.

International membership: The International Youth Hostel Federation (IYHF) sets minimum standards for hostels throughout the world. Because your YHA membership card is also a Hostelling International membership card, you can stay at these hostels worldwide. If you are visiting England and Wales from abroad, you can either buy at home or International Membership on arrival.

What do you get?

Your individual YHA membership is valid for one year from the date of joining. It entitles you to:

● Stay in any of the varied Youth Hostels in England, Wales, Scotland and Ireland as well as over 4,500 Youth Hostels worldwide.

● Take advantage of substantial discounts at local attractions, shops and other organisations to save yourself money. Simply ask staff at your chosen hostel about discounts available in the area.

● Receive Triangle magazine, which is packed with news and ideas to help you get the most out of your stays.

● Receive a discount on travel insurance from Columbus Insurance. Call 0845 076 1030 and quote offer code 'YHA Go!', or visit www.columbusdirect.net/yha (note: discounts and offers are provided by third parties and many include a right to withdraw the offer).

● Take part in hostel-based activities and make new friends. See page 24 for further details.

● Make a difference by volunteering. There are opportunities to offer practical skills or professional advice. It is also possible to contribute to the governance of YHA.

The accommodation

YHA accommodation has changed considerably over the years, but one thing that has remained is the distinctive character of each location. From remote farm cottages in spectacular countryside to rambling Victorian mansions and modern purpose-built Youth Hostels, no two are the same. YHA is also developing its accommodation network through YHA Enterprise. This scheme encourages other accommodation providers to join the YHA network. YHA currently offers the following types of accommodation:

Youth Hostels

You will stay in comfortable bunk-bedded rooms, sharing with people of the same sex. Guests may be able to book a room to themselves. You will be given laundered bed linen to make up your bed, pillows, duvets and blankets. At most hostels, you will find a sitting area, self-catering kitchen, drying room and cycle store. Many offer a much wider range of facilities including a full meals service – check the individual hostel entries in the directory to see what each offers.

The daytime access section also lists the minimum access you can expect during the day and if you arrive without a reservation – more than this may be available, so please check when booking. Above all, we hope that your YHA stay is fun and enjoyable.

If you have ever stayed at a Youth Hostel, you'll know that they offer clean and comfortable accommodation at low prices, a chance to meet people and access new places and experiences. So read on for over 200 great places to stay in England, Wales and the Channel Islands.

Camping Barns

Converted farm buildings or Camping Barns offer self-catering accommodation. Facilities vary, but sleeping platforms, tables for eating and preparing food, cold running water and a flush toilet are available.

Bunkhouses

Similar to Youth Hostels, Bunkhouses have bunks plus shared cooking and daytime facilities. Bedding is not always provided; guests are advised to check when making a booking. Four bunkhouses are included in this guide: Bishopdale in England and Blaencaron, Dolgoch and Tyncornel in Wales.

YHA Campus

YHA now offers acccommodation in university towns and cities throughout July and August. Single, en-suite rooms and self-catering kitchens are available in university halls of residence or student villages. If you are booking more than seven days ahead call 0870 770 8868. Check the campus page on www.yha.org.uk

YHA Guest House

YHA Guest Houses offer bed and breakfast accommodation in town and countryside locations. You can expect comfortable, attractive accommodation, often with en-suite bathrooms, not to mention a hearty breakfast.

Our promise to you

YHA England & Wales has adopted the worldwide Hostelling International Assured Standards. All hostels displaying the Hostelling International sign will provide these standards:

Welcome

Our staff are committed to welcoming you. From the staff at our smallest hostels to YHA's chief executive, nearly everyone has participated in the tourism industry's Welcome Host training schemes in customer care. Most Hostel receptions will be open 8-10am and 5-10pm as a minimum. Your enquiries will be dealt with promptly and bookings can be made in advance.

Comfort

Your bed will be comfortable and linen provided. There will be hot showers, toilets and washbasins. The hostel will be well lit and noise levels kept to an acceptable level.

Cleanliness

High standards of hygiene and cleanliness will be met throughout the hostel.

Security

YHA staff will do all they can to ensure your personal safety and the security of your belongings. Where appropriate, Youth Hostels provide secure lockers. (You may find it useful to carry a small padlock).

Privacy

Most accommodation is in rooms shared with people of the same sex, although private rooms can be reserved. Proper privacy levels will be provided in toilets, showers and wash areas.

Go! FOR GOOD FOOD

"Round off a great day with a mouthwatering local dish."

Enhance the enjoyment of your break with a choice of eating options... and a true taste of the region you are visiting.

It's part of the experience

YHA believes that the food you eat during your stay enhances your experience of the place you are visiting. We know you care about where the food you eat comes from so we endeavour to get as many of the ingredients as possible from within 30 miles of the Youth Hostel you're staying at.

We cater for different diets

We aim to provide a flexible meals service which offers a choice of delicious healthy food and which can satisfy any special dietary requirements. You'll also begin to see a difference in the type of YHA dining experience you can enjoy depending on which hostel you stay at, from

bistro and café style to more traditional fare.

You can self-cater too

Guests who prefer to cook for themselves will find convenient and clean self-catering facilities available at all but a small number of our Youth Hostels. A simple selection of groceries is usually on sale at reception.

Enjoy a drink

Many of our Youth Hostels have alcohol licences, so you can enjoy a glass of beer or wine with your meal, and some of the larger hostels now have fully licensed bars, often selling local beers and ales. You may also, at the manager's discretion, take your own. If you prefer a non alcoholic brew, Cafedirect's Fairtrade tea and coffee is available at almost all Youth Hostels.

Special menus for kids

When you come on a family break you can take time out from the cooking. Better still, some hostels also offer a special menu for children under 10. Be sure to ask when you book.

We cater for special events

If you're renting a hostel for a special occasion then you won't want to worry about preparing meals. So let us do the cooking instead. At some Youth Hostels, a meals service is available for celebratory meals or you can choose full catering during your break, with flexible meal times agreed in advance.

"Spend time with the family as we take care of all your needs."

Whether you want a break in the country, a traditional seaside holiday or an overnight stay in the city, there is a family-friendly Youth Hostel that's ideally suited to your needs.

You can book a family room

We have well over 100 Youth Hostels which are ideal for families, all with small, private rooms at affordable room prices. Expect a comfortable bunk-bedded room with a wash basin, storage space, bed linen and duvets. Many Youth Hostels offer rooms with en-suite facilities and some with double beds. You will also get your own key so you can come and go as you please. We also have family bunkrooms (marked **FBR** in each hostel entry), which are simpler and can be booked by families for their private use, although facilities and levels of access may vary.

If you are unable to book a room for your family, you can stay in single sex dormitories shared with other people. Children need to be at least five years old. Those aged 5-13 must share the same dormitory as a parent or guardian of the same sex.

Let us cook...

Choose a hostel with a meals service and forget about doing the cooking. Many hostels also offer a special menu for under-10s.

...or self-cater

We also understand how important it is to be flexible when travelling with children, which is why, at most Youth Hostels, there is the option of self-catering. If you need a night off, then book an evening meal at the Youth Hostel.

You can travel light

If you've got a young child, you know how much stuff you need take with you just to get out of the house. But with YHA, you can leave much of it at home and travel that bit lighter. More than 80 Youth Hostels cater for families with children aged three years and under, offering cots, highchairs, towels, baby baths and baby alarm – just ask your chosen hostel for availability and don't forget to pre-book. There are laundry and clothes-drying facilities too.

There's plenty of entertainment

All Youth Hostels offer a selection of activities, from board games to kite making, keeping the children amused

and giving you time to relax. For more organised entertainment, why not book an activity break at one of our activity centres where outdoor pursuits include climbing and watersports (see page 24) or choose a special interest holiday advertised in Triangle, the YHA magazine.

You are in the great outdoors

With many Youth Hostels set in some of our finest countryside, you can give your kids freedom to explore. For example, YHA Poppit Sands overlooks a Blue Flag sandy beach where dolphins often swim, while YHA Sherwood Forest is surrounded by acres of ancient woodland. Other hostels enjoy acres of grounds, allowing plenty of room for outdoor games.

It's relaxing!

Leave all the hard work to us. The only thing we ask is that you tidy up after yourselves.

We'll help you plan your break

Our staff know their local areas well and will help you find the best activities for your family, making sure you get the most out of your stay.

It's great value

Choose a YHA family membership and your kids join free. Reduced rates are also available for single-parent families.

Ian Walmsley from Salford discovered a family holiday with a difference...

My family and I recently stayed in a Youth Hostel for the first time and now we wish we'd done it sooner. Our first experience of hostelling at YHA Derwentwater in the Lake District was made even more special by the friendly and helpful staff. The team were always on hand to assist us and we were made to feel very welcome. The staff really did make our whole trip. We had such a great time that we have decided to continue hostelling and have already changed our holiday plans for the year.

Go! *AS A GROUP*

"Choose from our range of stimulating group opportunities.

Many Youth Hostels are perfect for groups of every age, from school children to adults, while our residential breaks and special packages offer exceptional value. For further information please contact groups reservations on 0870 770 8868.

- Educational
- All age and ability groups
- Youth & Community
- Guides and Scouts
- Duke of Edinburgh Award

It's great value

A group membership card allows you and your group of five or more to stay at Youth Hostels. All we ask is that you are a formally constituted group and, if your group includes young people under 14, there is an adult leader of each sex. For larger groups taking full board, we offer one leader place free for every ten paying participants. To help get the most out of the trip, group leaders can take advantage of a free planning visit to the Youth Hostel after booking a full board break for their group.

We value safety

At YHA we know how important it is for groups – particularly children – to feel safe and secure when away from home. All staff work to the most exacting standards in matters of health, safety and security and are trained to deal with emergency situations. Our hostels are fully risk assessed and YHA is also registered with the Criminal Records Bureau to assist in the recruitment of new staff and volunteers. Many of our hostels offer exclusive use for your group, provided your group is of a suitable size. To enquire, call your chosen hostel or Group Reservations on 0870 770 8868.

Let us do the organising for you...

Whatever your group is hoping to achieve through their residential stay, YHA can help. Whether it's National Curriculum linked Education visits or Guide and Scout badge breaks and Duke of Edinburgh award schemes, Key Skills and positive parenting courses or activities for adults, a Youth Hostel is a superb, fun location for all kinds activities. We offer more than 100 fully

organised and packaged breaks. For information on any of these contact 0870 770 8868. Alternatively, just relax and see the sights, as you can on many of our group Explorer packages, or use us as a base for your own activities.

No problem...

Whether your group includes wheelchair users or those requiring special diets, we have locations that can meet your needs. We also run programmes tailored to help disadvantaged or special needs groups. For details contact the groups reservations team

...and with funding

We are committed to providing accommodation for less privileged youngsters. Three YHA funding schemes – Give Us A Break, Provident Action for Creative Kids with generous support from Provident Financial, and the Diversion Partnership Fund – help groups, particularly schools and youth organisations, meet the costs of a Youth Hostel break. If your group might be eligible, call 01629 592696.

We'll entertain you

Groups have access to free and low-cost self-led or organised activities designed to provide safe recreation, educational support or just to fill gaps in a programme.

"Hire the whole hostel to share with your friends."

Need a venue for a large gathering? Ask about Rent-a-Hostel, the scheme that allows you to have an entire Youth Hostel to yourselves.

The location will be totally unique

Rent-a-Hostel offers you the unique opportunity to stay in a wide range of buildings, each with their own character. Whether you would prefer sea views or mountain vistas, a central town location or a forest retreat, we have a hostel that's perfect for your needs. Our more unusual properties include a former chapel, a remote mountain hut, a 17th century water mill, a former lifeboat station and a spectacular shooting lodge. Use your imagination to add the finishing touch to that special occasion.

You will have exclusive use of the hostel

You, your relatives, friends or colleagues will have the Youth Hostel all to yourselves. With your own key, you can come and go as you please. Please bear in mind that YHA staff do live on site at many locations.

We can cater for any number of people

No matter how big your group, we're pretty sure we have a hostel which is just the right size for you. If you've got activities in mind, whether it's sight seeing with the folks or team-building with colleagues, we can also find the right place

for you. Our knowledgeable staff will be happy to help you make your choice to ensure you find the hostel that best meets your needs.

You will get great value for money

When you rent a Youth Hostel, you pay for the whole building and not for each bed, offering you unbeatable value for your money.

You still travel light...

All bed linen, kitchen equipment and cleaning materials are provided and many hostels have a selection of board games and cots and highchairs for toddlers. In fact, all you need to bring are towels, your toothbrushes and yourselves!

...and you don't have to cook

If you're celebrating something special then you won't want to

worry about preparing meals. So let us do the cooking instead. At some Youth Hostels, a meals service is available for one-off celebratory meals or you can choose full catering during your break, with flexible meal times agreed in advance.

Making a booking is simple

Rent-a-Hostel is generally available between September and Easter but some locations can be rented for periods during the spring and summer months. The scheme is particularly popular at weekends, during school holidays and over the Christmas and New Year period so it's advisable to book early to avoid disappointment. And it really couldn't be simpler. Just decide the area in which you'd like to stay and how many people will be in your group. Then call the Rent-a-Hostel Booking Office on 0870 770 8868 or email rentahostel@yha.org.uk where staff will advise you of suitable Youth Hostels.

To discover which hostels are available to rent, refer to the individual hostel entries in the directory section of this guide. You can also book Youth Hostels in England, Wales, Scotland and Ireland via www.rentahostel.com

To discover which hostels are available to rent, refer to the individual hostel entries in the directory section of this guide or call 0870 770 8868 for more information. You can also book Youth Hostels in England, Wales, Scotland and Ireland via www.rentahostel.com

Jane Tarver 50, from Bingley, celebrated her 50th birthday YHA-style...

My husband Joe had arranged to take me away for my 50th birthday – but as it was a surprise I was kept guessing until the last minute. As I knew it was a self-catering weekend, I began to think of possible YHA destinations. I have been a member of the YHA since I was 18 so I know them all pretty well!

We had collected my daughter from York and my son was already with us, so when we finally arrived at YHA Lockton I was really looking forward to my birthday celebrations. It was even better that YHA Lockton is an old school building as I studied this subject as part of my degree.

The hostel was fully booked, but I hadn't seen any other hostellers. I'd forgotten about the mystery of the empty beds when suddenly two of my cousins walked in! They were soon followed by more friends. This continued into the next day, where more friends and family joined us until the hostel could take no more. We visited the village of Thornton-le-Dale, picnicked, and visited a local pub where everyone sang 'Happy Birthday'. This is definitely one birthday I won't forget in a hurry!

Go! IT ALONE

"Set off on an adventure and leave the folks at home."

Each year, Youth Hostels become a stepping stone for thousands of young people. The experience offers a first taste of independence and, more importantly, a whole lot of fun.

It's a secure environment

From the age of 14 you can stay at a Youth Hostel without your parents. Because Youth Hostels provide safe and secure accommodation, as well as assured standards of cleanliness, privacy, comfort and welcome, we offer the perfect place for young people to get their first taste of freedom, while providing peace of mind for their parents and guardians.

It's affordable

Youngsters on a break can choose full or half board, self-catering or mix and match for a range of inexpensive, but hearty meals. Whatever your needs and budget, you'll find an affordable solution with YHA.

We'll guide you around the world

If you're planning a world tour for your gap year, it's good to know that a YHA membership card is accepted at 4,000 Hostelling International Youth Hostels across the globe. YHA can also provide you with excellent tips on how to stay safe on your travels. We've teamed up with the UK Foreign

and Commonwealth Office to promote or to give plenty of excellent tips on being well-prepared before you make your journey: having adequate travel insurance and contact details for British embassies; as well as providing advice on passports, visas, money, health and drugs. For more information, visit www.fco.gov.uk

For useful tips on safe travel, visit the Foreign Office website www.fco.gov.uk and click on the Know Before You Go link. The site has information tailored to the needs of all travellers, including backpackers, young people and sports travellers with guidance on passports and visas, insurance, money, health and drugs.

" I first stayed in Youth Hostels with friends when I was around 16. It was very exciting to be independent and I really enjoyed the friendly atmosphere. It made such a positive impression on me that I ended up running a hostel!

Here at YHA York we see quite a lot of young people both from the UK and the rest of the world, travelling with their friends or on their own for the first time. They always have a fantastic time – York is a great place to visit. All staff are very welcoming and can advise on things to do. We are a very safe place to stay. There is always someone available to help, including during the night in case of an emergency. We also have night security. Like most hostels, as well as providing meals we also have a well-equipped self-catering kitchen. I'd advise any teenager to try hostelling, it's a great way to make friends and see the world! "

"YHA makes your stay enjoyable whatever the circumstances."

YHA is for everyone and we are working to remove the barriers that prevent anyone from getting the most from their YHA stay.

We're improving accessibility

With such a diverse range of buildings, we need to look at each Youth Hostel to examine how accessible it is and what improvements if any need to be made. For example, handrails, tactile signage, hearing assistance systems or specially adapted en suite bedrooms for wheelchair users may be required. We are assessing each Youth Hostel against the standards set by VisitBritain's National Accessible Scheme and through the YHA For All appeal, you can help us to carry out this vital work.

We have included standards for all new hostels

New Youth Hostels have been designed with access in mind, while we have made improvements to many of our older buildings. Please speak to the Youth Hostel of your choice to discuss your specific requirements to see if it's the right place for you. We'll do our best to meet those needs. If your first choice Youth Hostel is not appropriate, we'll endeavour to find one that is in the area you want to visit. We recommend these Youth Hostels if, for example, wheelchair access is required:
Northumberland: Wooler, Kielder. **Lake District:** Arnside, Borrowdale, Duddon Estuary. **Yorkshire & South Pennines:** Dentdale, Stainforth. **Peak District & North West:** Hartington Hall, Ilam Hall, Liverpool, Manchester, Sherwood Forest. **Heart of England:** Coalport, Leominster, Oxford. **South West England:** Lizard Point. **South East England:** Medway, Littlehampton. **East of England:** Blaxhall, Lee Valley Village, Wells-next-the-Sea, Sheringham. **London:** Rotherhithe, St Pancras, South Kensington. **Wales:** Broad Haven, Conwy, Manorbier, Trefdraeth, Idwal Cottage. **Channel Islands:** Jersey.

There is good accommodation for every budget

Whether you're staying full or half board or even self-catering, YHA is within just about everyone's budget. With no single supplements in sight, Youth Hostels are ideally placed to provide accommodation for people making the journey on their own.

You can save money as a student

If you are a student aged 18 and over, not travelling as part of a group, you can claim a reduction on the Youth Hostel's overnight charge on production of a valid student identification card from your university or an ISIC, EURO<26, NUS card or Connexions card.

You can take advantage of concessions

Adult members of YHA not travelling as part of a group and who can show they receive means tested benefits related to low income will be entitled to a concessionary overnight price.

There are big discounts

Many organisations offer discretionary discounts to YHA members including local attractions, travel, entry to properties and special deals on clothing and equipment.

For all the latest YHA news visit www.yha.org.uk

Go! ON FOOT OR BY BIKE

"You discover much more on foo or from the saddle of your bike."

Use Youth Hostels as your base to discover the best of Britain's countryside, coast and cities.

It's making the most of the countryside

Many Youth Hostels and Camping Barns enjoy to-die-for locations in incredible tracts of countryside, including Areas of Outstanding Natural Beauty and National Parks. With such scenery on your doorstep, you can't help but enjoy days of walking the surrounding footpaths or cycling the bridleways nearby. Some Youth Hostels, such as YHA Edale, in the Peak District, and YHA Okehampton, on the edge of Dartmoor, offer specialised breaks. You can find details in Triangle or at www.yha.org.uk

You can choose to be led by experienced, friendly guides...

To take all the hassle out of a walking break, book a YHA Walking Holiday. We offer a wide choice of routes, all selected to sample the finest landscapes in England and Wales. You will be guided by a qualified YHA leader in small groups of no more than 12. And these exclusive breaks are fantastic value for money.

...or guide yourself

Stay with YHA and it's easy to explore under your own steam too. The YHA Booking Bureau can book a number of single nights at various hostels on your behalf – all you have to do is provide the leg-power between overnight stays. There are many recognised inter-hostel routes – you can buy both the

YHA AND THE NATIONAL CYCLE NETWORK

8,000 miles of the National Cycle Network (NCN) now wind their way across the UK with an increase to 10,000 miles in 2005. Co-ordinated by Sustrans, the sustainable transport charity, it is a superb network of traffic-free routes, quiet lanes and traffic-calmed roads, offering a wonderful means of travelling through countryside, coast, towns and cities by bike or on foot. Many Youth Hostels are located on or close to the network. What's more, our staff can always point you in the direction of the nearest cycle hire shop, so even if you don't have your own bike, you can explore these routes to your heart's content during your stay. Visit www.sustrans.org.uk to view the nearest National Cycle Network route to you via interactive mapping and for a selection of free and retail maps and guides. Or call 0845 113 0065 for more information.

The following is a list of Youth Hostels within five miles of the NCN:
- **Northumberland & North Pennines:** Alston, Edmundbyers, Greenhead, Newcastle-upon-Tyne, Ninebanks, Once Brewed
- **The Lake District:** Ambleside, Arnside, Black Sail, Buttermere, Carlisle, Cockermouth, Derwentwater, Elterwater, Grasmere, Hawkshead, Helvellyn, Honister Hause, Kendal, Keswick, Langdale, Patterdale, Windermere
- **Yorkshire & South Pennines:** Beverley Friary, Boggle Hole, Grinton Lodge, Keld, Kirkby Stephen, Mankinholes, Osmotherly, Scarborough, Whitby, York
- **North West cities & Peak District:** Chester, Crowden, Dimmingsdale, Hartington Hall, Ilam Hall, Langsett, Liverpool, Manchester, Matlock, Ravenstor, Sherwood Forest, Shining Cliff, Youlgreave
- **Heart of England:** Bradwell Village, Coalport/Coalbrookdale, Malvern Hills
- **South West England:** Bath, Boscastle, Boswinger, Bristol, Cheddar, Dartington, Exeter, Exford, Golant, Land's End, Litton Cheney, Okehampton, Penzance, Perranporth, Portland, River Dart, Salisbury, Slimbridge, Street, Tintagel, Treyarnon Bay
- **South East England:** Alfriston, Arundel, Blackboys, Bradenham, Brighton, Broadstairs, Burley, Canterbury, Dover, Eastbourne, Hastings, Hindhead, Jordans, Littlehampton, Margate, Medway, Oxford, Portsmouth, Sandown, Streatley-on-Thames, Tanners Hatch, Telscombe, Totland Bay, Truleigh Hill, Winchester
- **East of England:** Blaxhall, Cambridge, Epping Forest, Great Yarmouth, Hunstanton, King's Lynn, Lee Valley, Lincoln, Wells-next-the-Sea
- **London:** City of London, Earls Court, Hampstead Heath, Holland House, Rotherhithe, St Pancras, South Kensington
- **Wales:** Bangor, Brecon, Broad Haven, Bryn Gwynant, Capel Curig, Capel-y-Ffin, Cardiff, Conwy, Corris, Idwal, Kings, Lawrenny, Llanbedr, Llanberis, Manorbier, Penycwm, Pen-y-Pass, Poppit Sands, Pwll Deri, Rowen, St David's, Trefdraeth, Trefin

Go! ON FOOT OR BY BIKE

guidebooks and maps from the Booking Bureau.

Take a trip of a lifetime

It's every serious walker's and cyclist's dream to complete a long-distance route at some stage in their lives. Whether you decide to embark on a National Trail, a classic route such as the Coast to Coast, or devise your own epic route, you will find conveniently-located hostels on the way. Long-distance routes are also available in the range of YHA Walking Holidays.

It's perfect when you're travelling light

If you're striding or pedalling between hostels, you will want to travel light. Stay in a camping barn and you don't need to pack a tent. Choose a Youth Hostel and leave your sleeping bag at home too. See the next section of the guide for travelling to Youth Hostels by public transport. On a YHA Walking Holiday, we'll transport your luggage between hostels,

leaving your days hindered by nothing more than a day pack.

You can expect a warm welcome

We know that, after a full day's walking or cycling, you want to relax. So choose a hostel offering a full meals service and you can enjoy a three-course breakfast, picnic lunch and evening meal. Self-catering facilities allow you to prepare flasks, and cycle stores will keep your bike safe. So you'll have plenty of time to swap experiences with fellow hostellers in a sociable atmosphere.

Hostel-based walking routes

Most Youth Hostels have easy-to-follow circular and inter-hostel walking routes, carefully researched and drawn by Martyn Hanks. Walks start from the hostel doorstep and vary to suit all ages and abilities. Just ask at the Youth Hostel you are at or call 0870 770 8868 for more information.

The Ramblers

YHA & THE RAMBLERS' ASSOCIATION

YHA has for many generations worked alongside the Ramblers' Association to open up the country-side for the enjoyment of all sections of society. Were it not for the Ramblers' dedication to protecting our footpaths, encouraging walking and campaigning for greater access on foot to the countryside together with the YHA's provision of affordable places to stay, thousands of people would have been denied the opportunity to enjoy the hidden secrets of Britain. It is thanks to over 60 years of Ramblers' campaigning that it will soon be possible for the public to walk through four million acres of uncultivated, open country. That is why, as a member of the YHA, we would also encourage you to become a member of the Ramblers' Association*. Doing so enables you to participate in regular walks and a range of local activities, while helping to protect the places you love for future generations to enjoy.

Benefits include a free Ramblers' Yearbook, quarterly magazine, discounts at outdoor clothing stores and membership of your local walking group which provides its own walks programme and social activities. Visit **www.ramblers.org.uk**, email **ramblers@london.ramblers.org.uk** or call **020 733 8500** and quote 'YHAG'.

SELECTED WALKING BREAKS

YHA offers an exciting range of walking breaks to suit both seasoned hikers and newcomers. Here's just a taste of what's on offer.

Byways of Borrowdale

Suitable for... all walkers seeking a relaxed break with a guide.
Where you'll walk Borrowdale is one of Lakeland's finest valleys with classic views of mountains and fells. But you don't have to climb high to appreciate this imposing landscape – this two-day break leads you along quiet valley byways to wonderful vistas.
Where you'll stay Stay in a tranquil, riverside location at YHA Borrowdale during this centre-based break.

The White Peak Way

Suitable for... reasonably fit walkers wanting guided hikes but no hard climbs in the ever-changing scenery of the Peak District National Park.
Where you'll walk The White Peak takes its name from the white limestone which has created a distinctive landscape of river valleys in the Peak District National Park. You will explore its picturesque dales and market towns on this 90-mile route.
Where you'll stay From the gothic splendour of YHA Ilam Hall to the 17th century style of YHA Hartington Hall (below), enjoy a range of unique accommodation on this circular walk.

• For details of the full range of breaks, visit **www.yha.org.uk** or call **0870 770 8868**. For booking and information, please call **0870 770 8868**. Find details of other walking breaks at **www.yha.org.uk**

"Staying with YHA: it's good for you, good for the planet."

Our commitment to helping everyone to a greater knowledge, love and care of the countryside means that we promote sustainable and responsible tourism.

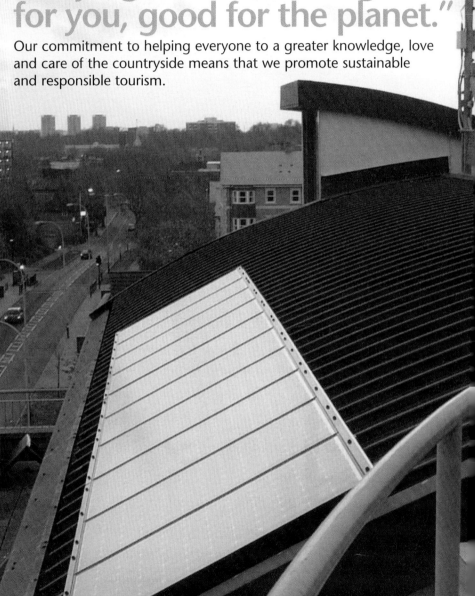

We promote public transport

Inside this guide, you'll find out how to travel to Youth Hostels by public transport. We can point you in the right direction of the nearest rail station and advise you on which buses to catch. Under our Empty Roads initiative, we are launching a website in Spring 2005 with even more detailed information about public transport services, cycling and walking to Youth Hostels. We are already aware that many members prefer to use public transport to reach Youth Hostels and we're working to make it easier for people to do so.

We practise what we preach at our Youth Hostels...

We've always been committed to the principles of sustainable tourism, so we have to make sure our Youth Hostels match that commitment. We are constantly looking at ways of reducing energy consumption and waste, conserving resources, promoting recycling and protecting local environments. In the North Pennines, for example, YHA Langdon Beck has been blazing a trail for 'green' hostelling, harnessing renewable energy such as solar and wind power. In the Lake District, remote YHA Ennerdale is powered by a hydro-electric system and YHA Lockton, in the North York Moors, is going to be redeveloped as an 'eco-hostel'.

...and in the local environment

We also aim to contribute to worthwhile environmental initiatives. For example, Lakeland Youth Hostels have joined the

Lake District Tourism and Conservation Partnership. This initiative is raising money to restore badly-eroded footpaths. Through

action such as this, YHA aims to practise what we preach, which is to promote a greater love, care and understanding of the countryside.

...and not just in the countryside

Many Youth Hostels have won awards or earned recognition for their environmental work. And it isn't limited to the countryside: solar panels were installed at YHA Rotherhithe and YHA St Pancras to launch the Renewable Energy Action for London project.

We're reducing food miles

Our catering policy promotes local food, thus reducing food miles and pollution levels.

"Take an exhilarating break that challenges you."

The YHA boasts two dedicated activity centres where you can try new sports, improve old skills or simply have great fun. Here's why you should visit them.

You will be spoiled for choice

You could try caving or canoeing, watersports or winter mountaineering, archery or abseiling. Then there's orienteering, raft building, navigating, night hiking, climbing... and that's just the start. Visit our website to find the one that gets the adrenalin pumping or just satisfies the soul. Join a course that concentrates on improving your talents in one particular area or opt for a break that combines a wide variety of activities. Some stays lead to recognised qualifications, others teach you universally useful skills such as first aid. Your only problem will be finding time to do everything you want to do.

We will work around you

Come by yourself, bring friends and colleagues or stay as a family and we will do our best to cater for your needs. Some multi-activity programmes are designed with families in mind, with a wide range of activities to appeal to all family members. Courses that improve specific skills will appeal to the individual, and you will meet new friends. Book as a group and our staff will work closely with you to design a break that targets your objectives.

You don't have to be Superman (or Superwoman)

With such a wide range of courses, we offer beginners a taste of a new sport as well as help already accomplished folk to hone their skills. You don't need to have any previous experience and rest assured – our friendly, experienced instructors know how to help you achieve your potential without pushing you past your limit.

Fantastic locations

Both our activity centres are set in incredible locations. YHA Edale sits on the flanks of Kinder Scout in the heart of the Peak District while YHA Okehampton is on the edge of Dartmoor National Park, within easy walking distance of the most remote area in southern England.

It's great value

The set price you pay includes all expert instruction, food, specialist equipment, accommodation, transport and VAT during your stay.

You'll experience real challenges...

You won't just learn how to paddle a canoe on our activity breaks. Trying a new sport involves a leap of faith as you venture into new territory. As you conquer your fears and

master a fresh skill, you will build your confidence and develop your teamworking and communication skills. All in all, it will be a rewarding adventure.

...in a completely safe environment

All our instructional staff hold relevant national governing body qualifications, including first aid, and are subject to on-going training and monitoring procedures. All staff are trained to operate to approved health, safety and security standards and can deal with emergency situations at any hour should they occur. Our equipment is continually inspected and maintained to ensure its safety and both centres are registered by The Adventure Activities Licensing Authority. Rely on us – you're in safe hands.

Other hostels offer plenty of breaks too

Whether you want to learn to surf at YHA Treyarnon Bay, kayak at YHA Windermere or try a paintball fun day at YHA Poppit Sands, a wealth of individual hostels have tailored activity breaks. Details of current courses can be found in the members' magazine, Triangle, or visit www.yha.org.uk and follow the 'stay at YHA' link. With so much to choose from, there is something for everyone.

For details contact YHA Edale (0870 770 5808), YHA Okehampton (0870 770 5978) or Customer Services (0870 770 8868).

Go! GET INVOLVED

"Support YHA and make the most of your skills."

YHA is a charity that has always wanted the support of its members. Here's how you can play your part and make a difference.

The choice is yours

YHA offers you plenty of opportunities to make the most of your talents. You can volunteer to help with fundraising, publicity, hostel wardening, conservation and countryside work, professional advice, tour guiding... the list is endless. Through the VALVE (Valuing Volunteering and Enterprise) scheme, supported by the Community Fund, we're developing all kinds of volunteering opportunities for everyone. Call 0870 770 8868 for an information pack.

YHA supports you too

In return for all your efforts, we will give you the level of supervision, training and support you need. As well as your efforts being invaluable to us, we promise they will be rewarding too.

You'll shape the future

YHA members govern YHA through its Board of Trustees. Board members come from a wide range of backgrounds, forging an excellent combination of skills and expertise. If you feel you would like to contribute to governing YHA, please write to the National Secretary at YHA National Office, Trevelyan House, Dimple Road, Matlock, Derbyshire, DE4 3YH. You can also become involved by attending a regional meeting – see Triangle or visit www.yha.org.uk.

We value your opinions

If you have a point to make about YHA or simply an entertaining hostelling tale to share, please get in touch by contacting Triangle magazine. If you'd like to speak to us directly, call our customer services team on 0870 770 8868.

YHA is a charity

Which means it wants your help to raise funds to continue its work, whether it be upgrading premises or giving youngsters a chance for a holiday on the Give Us A Break scheme.

MEMBER'S STORY

Tony Rees found out about volunteering through a friend, and has never looked back.

Just two short months after attending an induction training course at Manchester Youth Hostel, I was running my first youth hostel, Meerbrook! It was a perfect week and I enjoyed absolutely every minute.

I'm now into double figures with the Youth Hostels that I've run. I have enjoyed meeting and helping members who have visited and look forward to receiving the programme each November so I can plan my next year's walks.

It is very rewarding to be able to put something back into an organisation that has given me so much pleasure and enjoyment over so many years.

"Escape modern life with a break miles into the country."

If you need a break from modern living, take time out for tranquillity at a hostel or camping barn miles away from the noise of the city.

FOR A REMOTE HOSTELLING BREAK, HEAD TO THESE HOSTELS AND BUNKHOUSES

- Black Sail (p47)
- Blaencaron (p96)
- Dolgoch (p104)
- Ennerdale (p52)
- Hindhead (p156)
- Marloes Sands (p109)
- St David's (p112)
- Steps Bridge (p148)
- Tanners Hatch (p162)
- Tyncornel (p114)

28

It's a chance to escape modern life…

Imagine leaving civilisation behind and travelling to your chosen hostel on foot or by bicycle, surrounded by hills and without a street light in sight. Tranquillity reigns. But you don't need to travel a long way to guarantee a memorable experience. YHA Tanner's Hatch is in the Surrey Hills Area of Outstanding Natural Beauty. It's a mile's walk from the nearest car park to the door, enough to ensure total rural isolation without incurring any blisters.

…and make the most of the outdoors

Small hostels nestle in some of Britain's finest stretches of countryside and enjoy stunning views, making them perfect for walkers, cyclists and nature lovers. You could, for example, wake up to a vista of untamed seas in YHA Perranporth, a former coastguard station set on Cornish cliff-top. With miles of footpaths and bridleways in

the area, some running right past the hostel's front door, you can immerse yourself in the outdoors for a healthy, and relaxing break.

You'll love the challenge

If you never leave home without your mobile phone, a break in a remote hostel will allow you time to appreciate what's really important in your life. Just remember to take a torch and a sense of adventure.

You'll meet like-minded friends

The real charm of these smaller hostels is their friendly, relaxed atmosphere. Many of the

smaller hostels are without a television, so expect to spend your evenings chatting to new-found companions in front of open fires in cosy lounges and sharing stories over dinner.

Camping Barns offer even more variety

You don't need to be a YHA member to use Camping Barns – converted farm buildings offering simple, self-catering accommodation. You could find yourself staying in a former cornstore or cattle byre, with a choice of countryside on your doorstep. Facilities are generally basic with a shared sleeping area, food preparation area, cold running water and a toilet, although many offer hot water, heating showers. It's like camping, except you will enjoy a weatherproof roof over your head. Just look for the Camping Barn colour-coded circle in the directory to find barns in North Yorkshire, the Forest of Bowland, Lake District, North Pennines and Hadrians Wall, Peak District, Kent, Exmoor and Dartmoor.

"Choose from over 4,000 Youth Hostels in 60 countries."

An extensive network of Youth Hostels across the globe means a safe and comfortable place to stay wherever your travels take you

Youth Hostels are everywhere

As a member of YHA you are automatically a member of the International Youth Hostel Federation. With over 4,000 hostels in 60 countries, whether you're embarking on a month's trip to experience Europe or a year's odyssey around the world, you'll find a range of Youth Hostels in the locations you need. As you would expect, all the hostels have their own character. You could find yourself staying in a Swiss Youth Hostel that's situated inside a train or booking a skiing holiday in a hostel at the heart of the Andean mountains in Chile. To see the exciting range of hostels, visit www.hihostels.com or buy the Hostelling International Guides (Volume One details Europe and the Mediterranean while Volume Two covers Africa, America and Asia) by calling **0870 770 8868**.

It's easy to book

Simply book online at www.hostelbooking.com or call 0870 770 8868.

You can depend on us

In a new country of different cultures and language, you can sleep easy knowing that Hostelling International Youth Hostels offer assured standards of safety, privacy, comfort, welcome and cleanliness. You always know what to expect when travelling the world as a YHA member because all Youth Hostels must meet the International Youth Hostel Federation's safety and security standards. Just look for the Hostelling International logo, which assures you of comfortable, safe and clean and accommodation.

Staying in touch

How are you going to stay in touch? YHA is offering member bonus call time worth £6 as soon as you activate *online* your YHA Global Phonecard account – a great way to stay connect while on the road and save to 70% on your international calls back home! To activate the service (and receive your online bonus) visit **www.yha.ekit.com** or call our freephone number in the UK – 0800 376 2366 – then press 0# for our 24-hour Customer Service.

How to book

With our flexible booking system and affordable costs, the perfect Youth Hostel is just a single call away.

YHA aims to provide comfortable, affordable accommodation. That's why, although prices vary between hostels according to their facilities and location, you will always get great value for money. Some hostels provide private rooms and family rooms, charged on a per room basis.

Call your chosen hostel to check current charges and availability. You can book by using a YHA credit card and help YHA at the same time. Every time you use your YHA card Bank of Scotland will make a donation to YHA. Call 0800 731 2239 and quote 13BD. Here's all you need to book...

Booking ahead

We always advise that you book ahead. Times of year when Youth Hostels are open vary. In popular cities and tourist areas Youth Hostels may be open all year round. At other locations Youth Hostels may only be open during the main season. There may be one of two nights during the week or longer periods when they are not available. Always check ahead to ensure that the Youth Hostel is open and that beds are available. Further information is available on www.yha.org.uk or call 0870 770 8868.

Booking is easy

Call the Youth Hostel of your choice to check availability and your accommodation will be provisionally reserved. Although larger hostels can handle enquiries throughout the day, if you have chosen a smaller hostel it's best to call before 10am or after 5pm. You can book via

www.yha.org.uk or write to, email or fax your chosen hostel. If your booking is less than £100 you will be asked to make full payment when you book to secure your full stay. If your booking is in excess of £100 you will be asked to pay a minimum £100 deposit with the full payment for the remainder to be paid eight weeks before your arrival date.

You can pay at most Youth Hostels by credit or debit card or send a cheque made payable to YHA. Up-to-date prices and details of when Youth Hostels are open can be found on www.yha.org.uk or by calling 0870 770 8868.

On a long-distance route

Let us help you book your trip. Simply call the Booking Bureau (0870 770 8868) with details of your itinerary and we will book your accommodation and any meals you require for you. For further details please see page 33.

One hostel to the next

Once you are on the hostelling trail, most hostels are able to book ahead for you using our booking system. Just ask at the reception desk about the Book A Bed Ahead scheme, giving details of your chosen hostel(s) and dates you wish to stay.

Walking holidays and groups

Call 0870 770 8868.

An activity holiday

YHA has two dedicated activity centres. Call YHA Edale (0870 770 5808) or YHA Okehampton (0870 770 5978). Activity breaks are also organised at other Youth Hostels. Triangle, your YHA magazine, carries details or visit www.yha.org.uk

If you need to cancel

If you have to cancel your visit, please call the relevant Youth Hostel(s) as soon as possible. This is especially important in mountainous and remote areas – if you don't arrive at the hostel, police or rescue teams may be called out to look for you.

Getting a refund

Request a refund application form from the Youth Hostel or Customer Services (0870 770 8868). Send this with supporting evidence (include copies of booking forms, invoices, receipts etc) to YHA, PO Box 30, Trevelyan House, Dimple Road, Matlock, Derbyshire, DE4 3JX. Full terms and conditions of booking are on pages 176-8.

CONTACT US!

YHA would love to hear from you. If your stay in a Youth Hostel is perfect, let us know. If it isn't, tell us that too. Call, fax, write or email your comments.

Call: **0870 770 8868**
Fax: **0870 770 6127**

Write: YHA (England and Wales) Ltd,
Trevelyan House,
Dimple Road, Matlock,
Derbyshire,
DE4 3YH
Email: contactus@yha.org.uk
Visit: www.yha.org.uk

CONTACTS FOR HOSTELS ACROSS THE GLOBE

Australian **Youth Hostel Association**
Tel: (61) (2) 9565 1699 Fax: (61) (2) 9565 1325
Email: yha@yha.org.au Web: www.yha.com.au

Canada
Hostelling International
Tel: (1) (613) 237 7884 Fax: (1) (613) 237 7868
Email: info@hihostels.ca Web: www.hihostels.ca

France
Federation Unie des Auberges de Jeunesse (FUAJ)
Tel: (33) (0) 1 44 89 87 27 Fax: (33) (0) 1 44 89 87 10
Email: fuaj@fuaj.org Web: www.fuaj.org

Germany
Deutsches Jugendherbergswerk (DJH)
Tel: (49) (5231) 99 360 Fax: (49) (5231) 99 3666
Email: hauptverband@djh.org Web: www.djh.de

Republic of Ireland
Irish Youth Hostel Association (An Oige)
Tel: (353) (1) 830 4555 Fax: (353) (1) 830 5808
Email: mailbox@anoige.ie Web: www.irelandyha.org

Northern Ireland
Hostelling International Northern Ireland (HINI)
Tel: (44) (28) 9032 4733 Fax: (44) (28) 9043 9699
Email: info@hini.org.uk Web: www.hini.org.uk

Italy
Associazione Italiana Alberghi per la Gioventu (AIG)
Tel: (39) (06) 487 1152 Fax: (39) (06) 488 0492
Email: info@ostellionline.org Web: www.ostellionline.org

Japan Youth Hostels (JYH)
Tel: (81) (3) 3288 1417 Fax: (81) (3) 3288 1248
Email: info@jyh.or.jp Web: www.jhy.or.jp

Netherlands
Stay Okay
Tel: (31) (10) 264 6064 Fax: (31) (10) 264 6061
Email: info@stayokay.com Web: www.stayokay.com

New Zealand
Youth Hostels Association of New Zealand Inc (YHANZ)
Tel: (64) (3) 379 9970 Fax: (64) (3) 365 4476
Email: info@yha.org.nz Web: www.stayyha.com

Scotland
Scottish YHA (SYHA)
Tel: (44) (1786) 891 400 Fax: (44) (1786) 891 333
Email: info@syha.org.uk Web: www.syha.org.uk

South Africa
Hostelling International – South Africa (HISA)
Tel: (27) (21) 424 2511 Fax: (27) (21) 424 4119
Email: info@hisa.org.za Web: www.hisa.org.za

USA
Hostelling International – American Youth Hostels (HI-AYH)
Tel: (1) (202) 783 6161 Fax: (1) (202) 783 6171
Email: hiayhserv@hiayh.org Web: www.hiayh.org

How to use this guide

This guide has been specifically designed to help you choose the right hostel every time you book a stay. As well as a detailed entry for each Youth Hostel, Bunkhouse and Camping Barn, this guide offers a wealth of information to ensure you get full value from your YHA membership.

If you already know which hostel you wish to stay in: Turn to the index on page 174 and then to the hostel's individual entry. An index of Camping Barns is also on page 174.

If you know which region you want to visit: The directory is divided into regional sections. These are shown on the map on page 2 and indexed on page 174. At the start of each section there is a regional map showing the locations of all the Youth Hostels and Camping Barns. On the subsequent pages you will find detailed descriptions of the hostels and barns listed in alphabetical order.

If you know the type of hostel you want: Youth Hostels are wonderful places to stay and you'll be welcome at any Youth Hostel, Camping Barn or Bunkhouse. If you're travelling with your family or a group, your requirements may be more particular. To help you find your ideal hostel fast, each hostel entry has a colour-coded suitability marking. If you're looking for a hostel that is particularly suitable for families or groups, a Camping Barn, or you want to have a city, coastal or rural break, use these markings – a key at the top of every page shows you what colour represents each category.

Then simply flick through the directory to find hostels that match your requirements. A star rating is also included to allow you to assess the standard of accommodation on offer at most hostels. Between one and five stars have been awarded according to the Quality Standards for Hostel Accommodation set respectively by the English Tourism Council and Wales Tourist Board.

If you know what facilities you require: The guide has been designed to give you as much information about the hostels' facilities as possible. Perhaps you require a family room, education package, classroom or hostel to rent. Or do you need to reach the hostel using public transport or want 24-hour access to the Youth Hostel? Simply decide which facilities are essential to your stay and look through the directory to discover which fits the bill. You will also find a list of hostels that offer camping on page 29 along with some of those that offer facilities for the less able.

THE INDIVIDUAL YOUTH HOSTEL ENTRIES

Each Youth Hostel entry provides full details to help you decide whether the accommodation will suit your specific needs. Here's how to extract as much information as possible, using a sample directory entry:

1 BEST FOR RATING
The colour-coded boxes indicate the hostel's suitability for various types of stays. You will find the key at the top of every page.

2 STAR RATING
Most Youth Hostels have been awarded between one (lowest grading) and five (highest grading) ETC and WTB stars (Bed & Breakfasts are awarded diamonds). Camping Barns and Bunkhouses are also covered by this scheme: the three Bunkhouses in Wales have 1-star gradings.

3 CONTACT DETAILS
All the contact details you need to communicate with your chosen Youth Hostel are here.

4 DESCRIPTION
Read the description for a taste of the hostel, including attractions within easy visiting distance.

5 LOCATION
Find the exact location of the hostel with the Ordnance Survey (Landranger series) map number and six-figure grid reference.

6 GREAT FOR/YOU NEED TO KNOW
Is this hostel the right one for you? Make up your mind here, where we tell you any other facts we feel you should know before you visit.

7 ACCOMMODATION
The number of beds will tell you how large or small the hostel is. The size of the rooms will also let you know what to expect of your sleeping accommodation.

8 SPECIAL FACILITIES
Some hostels boast brilliant family rooms, offering families a room that's accessible throughout the day once you've booked in (for details turn to page 8). FBR means family bunk rooms. These are lockable rooms with no more than 8 beds that are available for exclusive use. If you are planning a group stay, you may want to know if the hostel has a classroom and/or education packages. This section also tells you if the hostel is available through the Rent-a-Hostel scheme (see page 12).

9 FACILITIES
The hostel's facilities are listed, including the minimum you can expect to be available in the daytime or if you arrive without a reservation (additional facilities may be available during the day to those with reservations - call your chosen hostel). Access to bedrooms is normally available after 5pm (family rooms unrestricted). Rooms must be vacated by 10am. In the evenings Youth Hostels are generally open until 11pm with lights out at 11.30pm, although larger hostels are more flexible.

10 RECEPTION OPEN
As soon as reception is open, you can book in.

11 MEALS
Discover whether the hostel offers a full menu of meals or self catering accommodation only. Please book your meals in advance (ask the hostel staff for last ordering times). Self catering kitchens will be equipped with a minimum of ring hobs, a grill, kettle and toaster, with pots, pans, crockery and cutlery provided. Storage for food should be available. The majority of hostels have ovens, microwaves and fridges. Some also have freezer space.

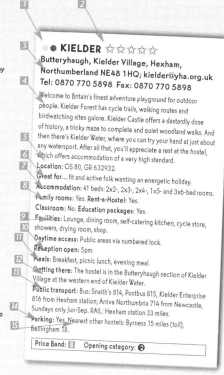

1   **2**

3 ● ● **KIELDER** ☆☆☆☆☆

Butteryhaugh, Kielder Village, Hexham, Northumberland NE48 1HQ; kielder@yha.org.uk

4 Tel: 0870 770 5898 Fax: 0870 770 5898

Welcome to Britain's finest adventure playground for outdoor people. Kielder Forest has cycle trails, walking routes and birdwatching sites galore. Kielder Castle offers a dastardly dose of history, a tricky maze to complete and quiet woodland walks. And **5** then there's Kielder Water, where you can try your hand at just about any watersport. After all that, you'll appreciate a rest at the hostel, **6** which offers accommodation of a very high standard.

7 Location: OS 80, GR 632932.

8 Great for... fit and active folk wanting an energetic holiday.
Accommodation: 41 beds: 2x2-, 2x3-, 2x4-, 1x5- and 3x6-bed rooms.
Family rooms: Yes. **Rent-a-Hostel:** Yes.
Classroom: No. **Education packages:** Yes.

9 Facilities: Lounge, dining room, self-catering kitchen, cycle store, showers, drying room, shop.

10 Daytime access: Public areas via numbered lock.

11 Reception open: 5pm.

12 Meals: Breakfast, picnic lunch, evening meal.

13 Getting there: The hostel is in the Butteryhaugh section of Kielder Village at the western end of Kielder Water.

Public transport: Bus: Snaith's 814, Postbus 815, Kielder Enterprise **14** 816 from Hexham station; Arriva Northumbria 714 from Newcastle, Sundays only Jun-Sep. RAIL: Hexham station 33 miles.

Parking: Yes. Nearest other hostels: Byrness 15 miles (toll), **15** Bellingham 18.

Price Band: 3   Opening category: 2

12 GETTING THERE
Concise directions are given here (there are maps at the back of the book for hostels that are difficult to find). These instructions are as clear as possible but maps of all Youth Hostels can be requested when you book and are available on our website.

13 PUBLIC TRANSPORT
We encourage our members to use public transport and a guide to services that will help you reach the hostel is given here. Once you arrive at the hostel, you will find more detailed information about the range of public transport in the area.

14 PARKING
Please observe any parking limitations shown here.

15 NEAREST OTHER HOSTELS
Explore the area by staying in a number of hostels. And don't forget that you can use the Book A Bed Ahead scheme to book other hostels during your stay.

Northumberland & North Pennines

From the natural wonders of the northern countryside to the exciting nightlife and shopping of Newcastle, there's something for all tastes here.

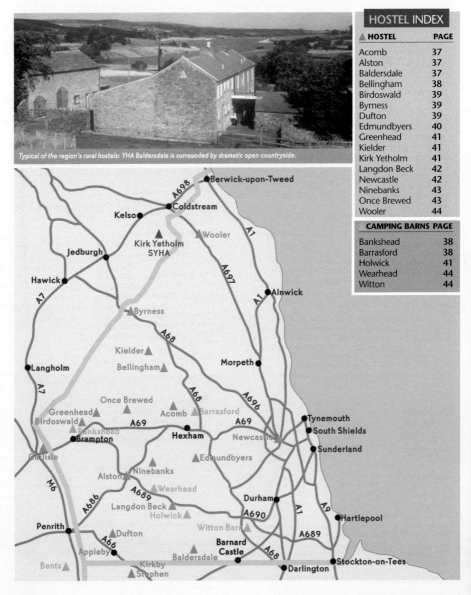

Typical of the region's rural hostels: YHA Baldersdale is surrounded by dramatic open countryside.

For all the latest YHA news visit www.yha.org.uk

● ACOMB

Main Street, Acomb, Hexham, Northumberland NE46 4PL; Tel: 0870 770 5664. For bookings more than 7 days ahead: 0870 770 8868

These converted stables offer simple accommodation close to the market town of Hexham with its fine abbey, museum and theatre. Better still is the hostel's proximity to breathtaking countryside. Follow winding lanes to pretty villages, enjoy the river and forest trails or take to the high moorlands of Northumberland and the North Pennines. Hadrian's Wall is also nearby.
Location: OS 87, GR 934666.
Great for... a comfortable, get-away-from-it-all active holiday.
You need to know... the toilets and showers are accessible from across the courtyard.
Accommodation: 26 beds: 1x12- and 1x14-bed rooms.
Family rooms: No. **Rent-a-Hostel:** Yes.
Classroom: No. **Education packages:** No.
Facilities: Lounge/dining room, self-catering kitchen, showers, drying room and cycle store.
Daytime access: All public areas via a numbered lock.
Reception open: 5pm.
Meals: Self-catering only.
Getting there: From the east/Newcastle take A69 to 1 mile past Bridge End roundabout, turn right on A6079, then first right at Acomb village sign. Follow Main Street uphill to hostel.
Public transport: BUS: Tyne Valley 880-2 from Hexham (pass Hexham station); otherwise Arriva 685 Carlisle-Newcastle-upon-Tyne, alight Hexham 2.5 miles. RAIL: Hexham 2.5 miles.
Parking: On-street only.
Nearest other hostels: Once Brewed 15 miles, Bellingham 15, Edmundbyers 16, Newcastle 20.

Price Band: A	Opening category: ②

● ALSTON ☆☆☆

The Firs, Alston, Cumbria CA9 3RW; alston@yha.org.uk Tel: 0870 770 5668 Fax: 0870 770 5669

Stay on top of the world in England's highest market town where steep, cobbled streets are surrounded by wild, solitary fells. Walkers and cyclists will love this modern hostel overlooking the South Tyne Valley on the Pennine Way and Coast-to-Coast cycle route.
Location: OS 86, GR 717461.
Great for... cycling and walking.
Accommodation: 30 beds: 2x2-, 2x4- and 3x6-bed rooms.
Family rooms: No. **FBR:** Yes. **Rent-a-Hostel:** Yes.
Classroom: No. **Education packages:** No.
Facilities: Lounge, self-catering kitchen, dining room, showers, drying room and cycle store. **Daytime access:** All public areas.
Reception open: Staff available before 10am and after 5pm.
Meals: Breakfast, picnic lunch, evening meal.
Getting there: At the south end of Alston (opposite Hendersons Garage), turn onto The Firs and take first right at top of bank.
Public transport: BUS: Caldew 680, Wrights 681 from Haltwhistle

station; 888 from Penrith station; 680 from Carlisle station.
RAIL: Langwathby 15miles, Haltwhistle 15, Penrith 19.
Parking: Yes.
Nearest other hostels: Ninebanks 8 miles, Langdon Beck 15, Greenhead 15 (17 by Pennine Way), Dufton 22 (by Pennine Way).

Price Band: B	Opening category: ②

●● BALDERSDALE ☆☆☆

Balderhead, Romaldkirk, Barnard Castle, Co Durham, DL12 9UP Tel: 0870 770 5684 Fax: 0870 770 5685

If you're walking the Pennine Way, you'll be glad to rest your weary feet at Baldersdale, nestling in a green oasis with open countryside all around. The hostel, an old stone farmhouse and adjacent barn, has 10 acres of grounds managed as an environmentally sensitive area, where the only sounds you'll hear are the calls of curlews and lapwings. The friendly small hostel atmosphere that awaits you will restore your spirits to explore nearby Teesdale and the interactive Killhope Mining Museum. When you return a well-earned pot of tea awaits. You can choose from our range of speciality and fair trade teas and relax in the sheltered garden with stunning views over Blackton Reservoir.

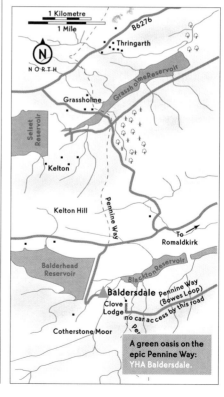

A green oasis on the epic Pennine Way: YHA Baldersdale.

Location: OS 91, GR 931179.
Great for... day walks, angling and birdwatching.
You need to know... it's difficult to access by public transport.
Accommodation: 37 beds: 1x3-, 1x4-, and 5x6-bed rooms.
Family rooms: Yes. **Rent-a-Hostel:** Yes.
Classroom: Yes. **Education packages:** No.
Facilities: Dining room, pool table, quiet room, activity room, TV, showers, drying room, cycle store and self-catering kitchen. Limited shop. Camping. Separate toilets and showers for campers.
Daytime access: All public areas.
Reception open: Staff available before 10am and after 5pm.
Meals: Breakfast, picnic lunch, evening meal.
Getting there: From Barnard Castle take the B6277 to Romaldkirk. Turn left at hostel sign to go through the hamlets of Hunderthwaite and Hury. After 5 miles turn left at sign to Balderhead Reservoir gate, go across reservoir dam, and at the end turn left. The remaining stretch (0.25 miles) is not surfaced. No car access from Cotherstone village via Clove Lodge.
Public transport: BUS: request bus service 73 from Middleton in Teesdale to Baldersdale Reservoir (tel: 01833 640213), 0.75-mile walk to the hostel; Arriva 95/6 to Middleton-in-Teesdale (connections from Darlington station).
RAIL: Darlington 27 miles.
Parking: Yes.
Nearest other hostels: Keld 15 miles, Langdon Beck 15, Kirkby Stephen 18.

Price Band: **B**	Opening category: **❷**

BANKSHEAD CAMPING BARN
campingbarns@yha.org.uk
Booking: 0870 770 8868
Arrival time: Mrs Ivinson, 01697 73198

This camping barn is a converted stone byre on a traditional family-run farm. It's an ideal stop-over while walking Hadrian's Wall and you'll enjoy outstanding views over the Irthing Valley.
Accommodation: Sleeps 10.
Facilities: Shower (coin-operated meter), toilet, hot water, cooking and recreation area with table and chairs, double burner gas stove, fridge, kettle, power points, crockery, cutlery, pans, oil-filled radiators on coin meter in recreation and sleeping areas, electric light. Food shopping service: phone owner 24 hours in advance to arrange.
Nearest pub: 2 miles. **Nearest shop:** 5 miles.
Location: OS 86, GR 586649.

Price Band: **G**	Opening category: **❸**

BARRASFORD CAMPING BARN
campingbarns@yha.org.uk
Booking: 0870 770 8868
Arrival time: Mr Milburn, 01434 681237

This converted stone coach house, now a camping barn, overlooks the North Tyne River. Walkers and cyclists will find it allows easy

Just a bike ride from Barrasford Camping Barn: Hadrian's Wall.

access to the breathtaking scenery surrounding Hadrian's Wall. For a camping barn, the facilities are very good with light, heat, a nearby shop and even a drying room.
Accommodation: Sleeps 8x2 in bunkbeds.
Facilities: Drying room, heating, electric light, toilets in adjacent building, hot water, cooking area and metered electricity.
Nearest pub: Next door. **Nearest shop:** 200 metres.
Location: OS 87, GR 919733.

Price Band: **G**	Opening category: **❸**

◌ ● BELLINGHAM ☆☆
Woodburn Road, Bellingham, Hexham, Northumberland NE48 2ED
Tel: 0870 770 5694 Fax: 0870 770 5694

This red cedarwood, purpose-built hostel sits on the Pennine Way, high above the little border town of Bellingham. But don't just make this a one-night stop while walking the epic long-distance route. Stay a while longer and you'll discover quiet lanes offering excellent cycling, and there's good walking on the Northumberland Moors too. Kielder Water, Europe's largest man-made lake, has watersports and miles of forest trails, with Hadrian's Wall nearby.
Location: OS 80, GR 843834.
Great for... an active, outdoor break.
You need to know... it's self-catering accommodation only.
Accommodation: 28 beds: 1x6-, 1x10- and 1x12-bed rooms.
Family rooms: No. **FBR:** Yes. **Rent-a-Hostel:** Yes.
Classroom: No. **Education packages:** No.
Facilities: Lounge/dining room, self-catering kitchen, showers, cycle store, grounds and camping.
Daytime access: All public areas.
Reception open: Staff available before 10am and after 5pm.
Meals: Self-catering only.

Getting there: Heading north, turn right off B6320 in town centre (signposted West Woodburn), continue straight up main road and hostel is 600 metres on left.

Public transport: BUS: Tyne Valley 880 from Hexham (passes Hexham station) RAIL: Hexham 16 miles.

Parking: Yes.

Nearest other hostels: Acomb 15 miles, Byrness 15 (via Pennine Way), Kielder 18, Once Brewed 18 (14 via Pennine Way).

> Price Band: **A**   Opening category: **②**

●● BYRNESS ☆

7 Otterburn Green, Byrness, Newcastle-upon-Tyne, Northumberland NE19 1TS;
reservations@yha.org.uk
Tel: 0870 770 5740 Fax: 0870 770 5740
Bookings more than 7 days ahead: 0870 770 8868

Two adjoining Forestry Commission houses have been converted to create a small, basic hostel that's ideal for exploring the northern part of the Northumberland National Park. Just five miles from the Scottish border, it lies on the Pennine Way in the foothills of the Cheviot Hills. From its doorstep, you can walk in practically every direction but don't miss out on a well-earned rest in the garden where red squirrels and roe deer are often seen.

Location: OS 80, GR 764027.

Great for... keen walkers who don't mind basic facilities.

You need to know... you should bring plenty of provisions as only limited supplies are available half a mile away.

Accommodation: 20 beds: 2x2-, 2x5- and 1x6-bed rooms.

Family rooms: No. **FBR:** Yes. **Rent-a-Hostel:** Yes.

Classroom: No. **Education packages:** No.

Facilities: Lounge/games room, self-catering kitchen, showers, cycle store and garden. **Daytime access:** To kitchen, drying room and toilet.

Reception open: 5pm.

Meals: Self-catering only. Packed lunches available.

Getting there: Turn off A68 at sign for Byrness.

Public transport: BUS: Munro's/National Express Edinburgh-Newcastle-upon-Tyne (passes close to Newcastle and Edinburgh stations). RAIL: Morpeth 34 miles, Newcastle 40.

NATIONALEXPRESS» Byrness lay-by 0.25 miles.

Parking: Yes.

Nearest other hostels: Bellingham 15 miles, Kirk Yetholm 27 (both by Pennine Way), Kielder 15 (by part-surfaced toll road), Wooler 28.

> Price Band: **A**   Opening category: **②**

●● DUFTON ☆

Dufton, Appleby, Cumbria CA16 6DB;
dufton@yha.org.uk
Tel: 0870 770 5800 Fax: 0870 770 5801

Where the mighty Pennines meet the gently rolling countryside of the Eden valley, you will find the historic village of Dufton and its

● BIRDOSWALD ☆☆☆☆

Birdoswald Roman Fort, Gilsland, Carlisle CA8 7DD; email: birdoswald@yha.org.uk
Tel: 0870 770 6124 Fax: 0870 770 6125

A new YHA location offering a memorable experience. Situated on the most continuous stretch of Hadrian's Wall, this well-appointed farmhouse conversion is within the Birdoswald Roman Fort Visitor Centre complex, so your night's stay includes your visit to this beautiful archaeological site. The hostel building itself lies within the ruins of the Roman Fort. Other Hadrian's Wall sites and attractions such as Lanercost Priory and Talkin Tarn Country Park are nearby.

Location: GR 615663 OS 86

Great for...a memorable historic and scenic experience.

Accommodation: 36 beds: 2x8-, 2x6- and 2x4-bed rooms.

Family rooms: Yes. **Rent-a-Hostel:** No.

Classroom: Educational facilities on site. **Education packages:** No.

Facilities: Self-catering kitchen, dining room/lounge, laundry facilities, showers and grounds. **Daytime access:** Limited. Please enquire when booking.

Meals: Self-catering only. Meal service may become available.

Reception open: 5pm.

Getting there: From Greenhead take the B6318 through Gilsland, turning left 1 mile beyond the village. From Brampton approach via Lanercost towards Gilsland. Follow tourist signs to

Birdoswald Roman Fort.

Public transport: the hostel is served from May to September by the Stagecoach AD122 service from Newcastle to Bowness on Solway.

NATIONALEXPRESS» Carlisle 14 miles.

Parking: Yes, overnight at hostel, daytime in nearby car park 100m.

Nearest other hostels: Greenhead 4 miles, Once Brewed 11 miles, Carlisle 16 miles.

> Price Band: **C**   Opening category: **②**

Historic: YHA Birdoswald is situated within a Roman fort.

Stay at YHA Edmundbyers and explore the lanes and footpaths of the village or spend a day at Derwent Reservoir.

newly refurbished hostel. This is an area of contrast: high moorland panoramas, gently rolling farmland, thickly wooded ravines and ghylls and wildflower meadows. On return to the hostel you will find home cooked food, a log fire and a secluded wildlife garden.

Location: OS 91, GR 688251.

Great for... lovers of wildlife; walkers of all abilities including families; and there are miles of traffic-free lanes for cycling.

Accommodation: 32 beds: 2x2-, 5x4- and 1x8-bed rooms.

Family rooms: Yes. **Rent-a-Hostel:** Yes.

Classroom: No. **Education packages:** Yes.

Facilities: Lounge, two dining rooms, self-catering kitchen, showers, drying room, cycle store, shop and garden.

Daytime access: All public areas.

Reception open: Staff available before 10am and after 5pm.

Meals: Breakfast, picnic lunch, evening meal.

Getting there: Leave A66 at Appleby, follow signs for Long Marton and Dufton, 3.5 miles.

Public transport: RAIL: Appleby 3.5 miles, Penrith 13.

Parking: Yes.

Nearest other hostels: Langdon Beck 12 miles (by Pennine Way), Kirkby Stephen 15, Alston 22 (by Pennine Way).

Price Band: B	Opening category: ❸

◉ ● EDMUNDBYERS ☆☆☆

Low House, Edmundbyers, Consett, Co Durham DH8 9NL; edmundbyers@yha.org.uk

Tel: 0870 770 5810 Fax: 0870 770 5810

This hostel is a former inn dating from 1600 with beamed ceilings and a cosy open fire, and has been refurbished to provide a comfortable and memorable place to stay. The village of Edmundbyers is surrounded by a 360-degree panorama of heather moorland. Active outdoor folk will be keen to explore the country lanes and moorland

of this Area of Outstanding Natural Beauty. It's only quarter of a mile from Derwent Reservoir which is ideal for watersports and trout fishing. All types of walker will be happy here — visit the picturesque village of Blanchland for a lowland stroll, or head on to the rugged uplands or to Hadrian's Wall for a day's hike.

Location: OS 87, GR 017500.

Great for... walkers; convenient for the C2C national cycle route.

You need to know... camping is available; no shop in the village.

Accommodation: 29 beds: 1x3-, 1x4-, 2x5- and 2x6-bed rooms.

Family rooms: Yes. **Rent-a-Hostel:** Yes.

Classroom: No. **Education packages:** No.

Facilities: Self-catering kitchen, lounge, dining room, showers, drying room, cycle store, disabled shower and toilet unit. Small but well-stocked shop.

Daytime access: Public areas via a numbered lock.

Reception open: 5pm. **Meals:** Self-catering only.

Getting there: The hostel is just off the A68 Darlington-Corbridge road, situated on the roadside just opposite the turning for the B6306 to Blanchland and Hexham.

Public transport: BUS: Stanley Taxis 773 Consett-Townfield, with connections on Go North East 719, 765 Durham-Consett (passes close to Durham station) or 45, 46, 770 Newcastle-upon-Tyne - Consett (passes close to Newcastle station); otherwise alight Consett 5 miles. RAIL: Hexham 13 miles. **Parking:** Yes.

Nearest other hostels: Acomb 16 miles, Newcastle 20.

Price Band: B	Opening category: ❷

◉ ● GREENHEAD ☆☆☆

Greenhead, Brampton, Cumbria CA8 7HG; greenhead@yha.org.uk

Tel: 0870 770 5842 Fax: 0870 770 5843

If you're planning on visiting the Hadrian's Wall World Heritage Site,

YHA Greenhead is very convenient. Mind you, the hostel has plenty of history of its own. It was built in 1886 as a Methodist Chapel, fuelled by the religious fervour of the village's mining population. The church gave its last service in 1972 and has been a hostel since 1978. Walkers of all levels will also find plenty of interest in the area.
Location: OS 86, GR 659655.
Great for... walkers with a head for history.
Accommodation: 40 beds: all 6-8-bed rooms.
Family rooms: Yes. **FBR:** Yes. **Rent-a-Hostel:** Yes.
Classroom: No. **Education packages:** Yes.
Facilities: Self-catering kitchen, showers, drying room, shop and cycle store. **Daytime access:** All public areas.
Reception open: 5pm.
Meals: Breakfast, picnic lunch, evening meal.
Getting there: From Carlisle take A69 to Newcastle. Turn off for Greenhead (19 miles), turn right at T-junction and hostel is on left opposite Greenhead Hotel. From Newcastle take A69 to Carlisle, turn right at Greenhead sign (45 miles), follow instructions above.
Public transport: BUS: the hostel is served from May to September by the Stagecoach AD122 service from Newcastle to Bowness on Solway; Arriva 685 Carlisle-Newcastle-upon-Tyne, passes Haltwhistle station. RAIL: Haltwhistle 3 miles.
Parking: Roadside only.
Nearest other hostels: Birdoswald 4 miles, Once Brewed 7, Ninebanks 16, Alston 17 (by Pennine Way), Carlisle 18.

| Price Band: **B** | Opening category: **❷** |

HOLWICK CAMPING BARN
campingbarns@yha.org.uk
Booking: 0870 770 8868
Arrival time: Mr & Mrs Scott, 01833 640506

If you've never stayed in a camping barn before, let Holwick be your first experience. After making the most of the walking all around, your return to the barn will be a pleasant surprise. The two field barns on Low Way Farm have heaters, gas cooking facilities and

YHA Kirk Yetholm is perfectly situated for hillwalking.

hot water, while there's a butcher's shop and café on the farm. For a camping barn, it's luxury indeed!
Accommodation: Sleeps 28 in bunkbeds in two areas.
Facilities: Sitting area, heaters, shower, gas cooking facilities (no oven), hot water, electric light and fridge (both on meter). Farmhouse café where meals can be ordered and butcher's shop. Breakfast and evening meal available by prior arrangement.
Nearest pub: 0.5 miles. **Nearest shop:** 3 miles.
Location: OS 92, GR 914270.

| Price Band: **C** | Opening category: **❸** |

● KIELDER ☆☆☆☆☆
**Butteryhaugh, Kielder Village, Hexham, Northumberland NE48 1HQ; kielder@yha.org.uk
Tel: 0870 770 5898 Fax: 0870 770 5898**

Welcome to Britain's finest adventure playground for outdoor people. Kielder Forest has cycle trails, walking routes and birdwatching sites galore. Kielder Castle offers a dastardly dose of history, a tricky maze to complete and quiet woodland walks. And then there's Kielder Water, where you can try your hand at just about any watersport. After all that, you'll appreciate a rest at the hostel, which offers accommodation of a very high standard.
Location: OS 80, GR 632932.
Great for... fit and active folk wanting an energetic holiday.
Accommodation: 41 beds: 2x2-, 2x3-, 2x4-, 1x5- and 3x6-bed rooms.
Family rooms: Yes. **Rent-a-Hostel:** Yes.
Classroom: No. **Education packages:** Yes.
Facilities: Lounge, dining room, self-catering kitchen, cycle store, showers, drying room, shop.
Daytime access: Public areas via numbered lock.
Reception open: 5pm.
Meals: Breakfast, picnic lunch, evening meal.
Getting there: The hostel is in the Butteryhaugh section of Kielder Village at the western end of Kielder Water.
Public transport: Bus: Snaith's 814, Postbus 815, Kielder Enterprise 816 from Hexham station; Arriva Northumbria 714 from Newcastle, Sundays only Jun-Sep. RAIL: Hexham station 33 miles.
Parking: Yes. Nearest other hostels: Byrness 15 miles (toll), Bellingham 18.

| Price Band: **B** | Opening category: **❷** |

KIRK YETHOLM ☆☆
Kirk Yetholm, Kelso, Roxburghshire TD5 8PG; reservations@syha.org.uk Tel: 0870 004 1132

An excellent centre for hillwalking, this Scottish hostel is close to the Cheviots and St Cuthbert's Way and at the northern end of the Pennine Way. Situated in beautiful surroundings, it's also within easy visiting distance of many historical sites including the Border castles and abbeys.
Location: OS 74, GR 826282.
Great for... those starting or finishing the Pennine Way and walking St Cuthbert's Way.

Accommodation: 20 beds.
Family rooms: No. **Rent-a-Hostel:** No.
Classroom: No. **Education packages:** No.
Facilities: Lounge, self-catering kitchen, showers, drying room, shop and cycle store. **Daytime access:** None until after 5pm.
Meals: Self-catering only.
Reception open: 5pm.
Getting there: The hostel lies 150 metres down the lane at the western corner of the village green.
Public transport: BUS: Swan 23 from Berwick-upon-Tweed station to Kelso then Munro 81, but on Sundays Busker's 223 through from Berwick-upon-Tweed. RAIL: Berwick-upon-Tweed 21 miles.
Parking: Limited.
Nearest other hostels: Wooler 14 miles, Melrose (SYHA) 24, Byrness 27 (via Pennine Way), Coldingham (SYHA) 28.

Price Band: £10.50 Adult, £8.25 U18 **Opening category:** ❷

● NEWCASTLE ☆☆

107 Jesmond Road, Newcastle-upon-Tyne, Tyne & Wear NE2 1NJ; newcastle@yha.org.uk
Tel: 0870 770 5972 Fax: 0870 770 5973

Newcastle is the friendly, distinctive and undisputed capital of England's northeast. Located on the city fringe, this hostel is ideally placed for exploring the area's attractions on foot, by car or using public transport. Enjoy the splendid attractions of Newcastle and the age-old splendour of Northumberland's coast and countryside.
Location: OS 88, GR 257656.
Great for... a busy city break.
You need to know... there are no drying or laundry facilities; breakfast is included in the overnight price.
Accommodation: 50 beds: 5x2-, 2x4-, 4x6- and 1x8-bed rooms.
Family rooms: No. **FBR:** Yes. **Rent-a-Hostel:** No.
Classroom: No. **Education packages:** Yes.

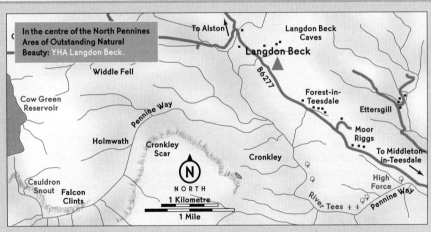

In the centre of the North Pennines Area of Outstanding Natural Beauty: YHA Langdon Beck.

To Alston
Langdon Beck Caves
Langdon Beck
Widdle Fell
B6277
Cow Green Reservoir
Forest-in-Teesdale
Ettersgill
Pennine Way
Moor Riggs
Holmwath
Cronkley Scar
Cronkley
To Middleton-in-Teesdale
Cauldron Snout
Falcon Clints
NORTH
High Force
1 Kilometre
River Tees
Pennine Way
1 Mile

● LANGDON BECK ☆☆☆

Forest-in-Teesdale, Barnard Castle, Co Durham DL12 0XN; langdonbeck@yha.org.uk
Tel: 0870 770 5910 Fax: 0870 770 5911

Those of you who have 'gone green' will appreciate the environmental efforts made in this hostel. There are recycling and alternative energy breaks, as well as weekend courses on the outdoors and the environment. And you'll certainly appreciate the environment while you're here – in the centre of one of Britain's largest Areas of Outstanding Natural Beauty, this is one of the highest hostels in England with magnificent views across the North Pennines landscape from the lounge.
Location: OS 91, GR 860304.
Great for... active families with an environmental conscience.
Accommodation: 32 beds: 1x2-, 1x2/3-, 4x4-, 1x6-, and 1x6/7-bed rooms.

Family rooms: Yes. **Rent-a-Hostel:** Yes.
Classroom: No. **Education packages:** Yes.
Facilities: Lounge/dining room, self-catering kitchen, showers, drying room, cycle store, laundry facilities and grounds.
Daytime access: Public areas, via numbered lock.
Reception open: 5pm.
Meals: Breakfast, picnic lunch, evening meal.
Getting there: The hostel is on the B6277, 7 miles northwest of Middleton-in-Teesdale.
Public transport: BUS: Alston 73 from Middleton-in-Teesdale (connections from Darlington station). RAIL: Darlington 33 miles.
Parking: Yes.
Nearest other hostels: Alston 15, Baldersdale 15 miles (by Pennine Way), Dufton 35 (12 by Pennine Way).

Price Band: B **Opening category:** ❸

A great base for both Newcastle and Northumberland: YHA Newcastle.

Facilities: TV lounge, games room, self-catering kitchen, dining room, showers and cycle store. **Daytime access:** All public areas.
Reception open: From 7am to 11pm.
Meals: Picnic lunches and evening meals also available.
Getting there: From the Metro (underground) by foot – under five minute walking on left side of Jesmond Road East (A1058). By car, access the A1058 (Jesmond Road) from central motorway (A167M), which is left from the northwest or right from the south (see map on page 172).
Public transport: BUS: frequent from surrounding areas. RAIL: Metro Jesmond 300m, Newcastle Central 2 miles. AIRPORT: 8 miles. FERRY: Bergen-Stavanger, Kristiansand-Gothenburg, Amsterdam.
NATIONAL EXPRESS》 St James Boulevard 2 miles. **Parking:** Yes.
Nearest other hostels: Acomb 20 miles, Edmundbyers 20, Osmotherley 50, Wooler 50.

Price Band: **D**   Opening category: **❸**

● NINEBANKS ☆☆☆
Orchard House, Mohope, Ninebanks, Hexham, Northumberland NE47 8DQ;
ninebanks@yha.org.uk
Tel: 0870 770 5974 Fax: 0870 770 6109

This small hostel offers a quiet retreat. Originally a 17th century lead miner's cottage, it stands in the peaceful valley of Mohope Burn in the North Pennines Area of Outstanding Natural Beauty. Walkers can explore secluded countryside and wild moorland, both of which are rich in wildlife, flora, fauna and industrial archaeology. The hostel is also near the C2C cycle route and close to Killhope lead mining

centre, the A686 (England's most scenic road) and Isaac's Tea Trail.
Location: OS 86, GR 771514.
Great for... walkers, cyclists and those seeking peace and quiet.
You need to know... it's a 5-mile trip to the nearest pub.
Accommodation: 26 beds: 3x4-, 1x6- and 1x8-bed rooms.
Family rooms: Yes. **Rent-a-Hostel:** Yes.
Classroom: No. **Education packages:** No.
Facilities: Common room, self-catering kitchen, showers, drying room, laundry, shop and cycle store. **Daytime access:** Public areas, via numbered lock.
Reception open: 5pm.
Meals: Self-catering only. Group catering by prior arrangement.
Getting there: Signposted from A686 south of Whitfield. The hostel is at Mohope, signposted from Ninebanks hamlet (see map on page 172).
Public transport: BUS: Wrights 889 Hexham-Alston (Tue, Fri only) (passes close to Hexham station); otherwise 888 Keswick-Newcastle-upon-Tyne (passes Penrith station), alight Ouston 1 mile. RAIL: Haydon Bridge 11 miles.
Parking: Yes.
Nearest other hostels: Alston 8 miles, Greenhead 16, Edmundbyers 26.

Price Band: **A**   Opening category: **❶**

● ONCE BREWED ☆
Military Road, Bardon Mill, Northumberland
NE47 7AN; oncebrewed@yha.org.uk
Tel: 0870 770 5980 Fax: 0870 770 5981

Few folk venture to Northumberland without walking a part of Hadrian's Wall and YHA Once Brewed is just half a mile from its most spectacular section, within easy walking distance of Vindolanda, where you can see how the Romans lived, and Housesteads Fort, the most complete Roman fort in Britain. Once you've had your fill of history, the hills of the Northumberland National Park await.
Location: OS 86, GR 752668.
Great for... visiting Hadrian's Wall, families.
Accommodation: 77 beds: mostly 2,3,4-, 1x5-, some 6- and 1x8-bed rooms.
Family rooms: Yes. **Rent-a-Hostel:** No.
Classroom: No. **Education packages:** Yes.
Facilities: Lounge, small self-catering kitchen, dining room, showers, toilets, dormitories, games room, laundry, drying room, garden and cycle store. **Daytime access:** All public areas from 2pm.
Reception open: 2pm. **Meals:** Breakfast, picnic lunch, evening meal.
Getting there: Hostel is on B6318 above Bardon Mill, next to NNP visitor centre.
Public transport: BUS: Stagecoach 185 from Carlisle (all year), Stagecoach in Cumbria 'AD122' from Hexham and Haltwhistle (passes Hexham and Haltwhistle stations) May-Oct; otherwise Northumbria 685 Carlisle-Newcastle-upon-Tyne, alight Henshaw, 2 miles. RAIL: Bardon Mill 2.5 miles. **Parking:** Yes.
Nearest other hostels: Greenhead 7 miles, Acomb 15, Bellingham 15, Ninebanks 16 (12 by path), Alston 23.

Price Band: **B**   Opening category: **❸**

WEARHEAD CAMPING BARN

campingbarns@yha.org.uk
Booking: 0870 770 8868
Arrival time: Mr Walton, 01388 537395

This farmhouse is a listed building and has been carefully converted to a camping barn. Just half a mile away from the Weardale Way, there are plenty of local walks in the area. Make sure you're a dab hand at lighting fires – coal is available at cost price for the open fire, which also heats the water.

You need to know... there's no electricity.
Accommodation: Sleeps 12 on the first floor.
Facilities: Cooking, eating and sitting area, toilet, open fire (coal available to buy).
Nearest pub: 1 mile. **Nearest shop:** 1 mile.
Location: OS 91, GR 851397.

Price Band: G   Opening category: ❸

WITTON CAMPING BARN

campingbarns@yha.org.uk
Booking: 0870 770 8868
Arrival time: Witton Estate, 01388 488322

A former barn and dairy, this camping barn is on the Witton Castle estate. You'll find plenty to do. The facilities include an outdoor swimming pool, public bars, games and television rooms, a shop and café in the grounds of the 15th century castle. For more rural entertainment, the Weardale Way is just half a mile away.
Accommodation: Sleeps 15.
Facilities: Cooking and eating area with cooker, toilets, electric light, wood-burning stove and shower.
Nearest pub: 0.5 miles. **Nearest shop:** 0.5 miles.
Location: OS 92, GR 155298.

Price Band: G   Opening category: ❸

Cyclists staying at YHA Wooler can ride part of the Steel Bonnet Route.

● ● WOOLER (CHEVIOT) ☆☆

30 Cheviot St, Wooler, Northumberland
NE71 6LW; wooler@yha.org.uk
Tel: 0870 770 6100 Fax: 0870 770 6101

Wooler makes an ideal base from which to explore the foothills of the Cheviots, Dunstanburgh Castle and Holy Island. Keen walkers will want to sample St Cuthbert's Way and the Ravenber long-distance walks that pass through the town, while cyclists can ride part of the 200-mile Steel Bonnet cycle route. Weather permitting, a boat trip to the Farne Islands will keep birdwatchers smiling.
Location: OS 75, GR 991278.
Great for... walkers, cyclists and birdwatchers.
Accommodation: 46 beds: 4x2-, 8x4- and 1x6-bed rooms.
Family rooms: No. **FBR:** Yes. **Rent-a-Hostel:** Yes.
Classroom: No. **Education packages:** No.
Facilities: Common room, self-catering kitchen, showers, drying room, laundry facilities and cycle store.
Daytime access: All public areas.
Reception open: Staff available before 10am and after 5pm.
Meals: Breakfast, picnic lunch, evening meal.
Getting there: Heading towards Coldstream on the A697, turn left for the town centre and then first left at the top of the hill up Cheviot Street. Go up road past Anchor Pub for 400 metres and then down drive on right-hand side marked YHA. If coming from Scotland, follow the signs for Wooler and, at the end of the High Street, turn right after the Bank of Scotland in Cheviot Street.
Public transport: BUS: Arriva Northumbria/Travelsure 464, Border Villager/Travelsure 267 from Berwick-upon-Tweed (passes close to Berwick-upon-Tweed station), Travelsure/IDM Travel 470/3 from Alnwick, with connections from Newcastle (passes close to Newcastle station). RAIL: Berwick-upon-Tweed 16 miles.
Parking: Yes.
Nearest other hostels: Kirk Yetholm (SYHA) 14 miles, Byrness 28 (by path), Newcastle 50.

Price Band: B   Opening category: ❷

The Lake District

For walkers, mountain bikers, climbers and those who simply seek peace and quiet, no region in England can match the appeal of the Lake District.

Stunning views: like so many Youth Hostels in the Lakes, YHA Honister Hause has a spectacular setting.

●● ARNSIDE ☆☆

**Redhills Road, Arnside, Cumbria LA5 0AT;
arnside@yha.org.uk
Tel: 0870 770 5674 Fax: 0870 770 5675**

If you love the Lake District but not its summer crowds, try YHA Arnside. This mellow Edwardian-Tudor house is positioned above the waters of Morecambe Bay and boasts great views of the Lake District mountains. It's a good touring base both for the Lakes and the western Yorkshire Dales and you'll find a variety of walks in the area. Birdwatchers will enjoy the RSPB reserve nearby and wildlife lovers shouldn't miss Arnside Knott, famous for its butterflies.

Location: OS 97, GR 452783.
Great for... a quiet base for wildlife wanders.
Accommodation: 72 beds: all 1-8-bed rooms.
Family rooms: Yes. **Rent-a-Hostel:** No.
Classroom: Yes. **Education packages:** Yes.
Facilities: Lounge with TV, sitting room, self-catering kitchen, drying room, games room, map room, showers, cycle store, cycle hire and garden. Accommodation now available for disabled guests.
Daytime access: All public areas.
Reception open: Staff available before 10am and after 5pm.
Meals: Breakfast, picnic lunch, evening meal.
Getting there: From south, leave M6 at J35 and take A6 to Milnthorpe. From north, leave M6 at J36, turn left and immediately left again onto A65 (Crooklands), then left on B6385 to Milnthorpe. Take B5282 to Arnside.

Public transport: BUS: Stagecoach in Cumbria 552 from Kendal.
RAIL: Arnside 1 miles. FERRY: Heysham to Isle of Man.
Parking: Yes.
Nearest other hostels: Kendal 12 miles, Hawkshead 18, Ingleton 19, Slaidburn 32.

Price Band: B   **Opening category:** ❷

BENTS CAMPING BARN

**Booking: 0870 770 8868
Arrival time: Dorothy Ousby, 017683 71760
(home) or 015396 23681 (farm)**

The building of this camping barn dates back to the 17th century. Walkers will find plenty to do here as the barn is close to the Howgill Fells, Sunbiggin Tarn and Smardale Gill Nature Reserve and on the Coast-to-Coast long-distance path.

Great for... the Coast-to-Coast, walking and enjoying the countryside.
You need to know... it's 1 mile from the village; there's parking at the farm and accommodation for tents nearby.
Accommodation: Sleeps 12 in bunk beds on first floor, mattresses are provided.
Facilities: Electric lighting, heating, power points (£1 meter), cooking facilities with cutlery and crockery.
Nearest pub: 2 miles. **Nearest shop:** 6 miles.
Location: OS 91, GR 708065.

Price Band: G   **Opening category:** ❸

● AMBLESIDE ☆☆☆

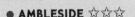

**Waterhead, Ambleside, Cumbria LA22 0EU;
ambleside@yha.org.uk
Tel: 0870 770 5672 Fax: 0870 770 5673**

Ambleside is in the very heart of the Lake District and a popular base for watersports, walking and climbing enthusiasts. This large hostel is just outside a busy village on the shores of Lake Windermere. The views from the hostel lounge and many of the waterfront bedrooms are outstanding. Need an extra degree of comfort? Premium rooms are available.

Location: OS 90, GR 377031.
Great for... outdoor people wanting a range of activities nearby.
You need to know... breakfast is included in the price.
Accommodation: 252 beds: 47x2-5- and 18x6-8-bed rooms.
Family rooms: Yes. **Rent-a-Hostel:** No.
Classroom: No. **Education packages:** Yes.
Facilities: Reception, lounges, games room, bar & coffee shop, TV room, luggage store, laundry, drying room, self-catering kitchen, showers, internet access, cycle hire, sailing school and cycle store.
Daytime access: All public areas.
Reception open: 7.15am to 11.45pm (24hr access March-Oct).
Meals: Breakfast, picnic lunch, evening meal. Hot buffet lunch by arrangement.

Getting there: The hostel is 1 mile south of Ambleside village at Waterhead on the A591 Windermere Road by Steamer Pier.
Public transport: BUS: Stagecoach in Cumbria services from surrounding areas (many pass close to Windermere station)
RAIL: Windermere 4 miles, King Street 1.
Parking: Limited. **Nearest other hostels:** Windermere 3 miles, Langdale 4, Grasmere Butherlyp Howe 4.

Price Band: D   **Opening category:** ❶

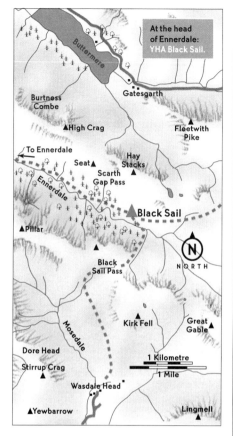

● BLACK SAIL ☆

Black Sail Hut, Ennerdale, Cleator, Cumbria CA23 3AY

Tel: 07711 108450

Black Sail is a legend, famous for being a remote and isolated shepherd's bothy at the head of Ennerdale, accessible only on foot. This location provides great access to the surrounding fells: Great Gable, Pillar, Red Pike and Steeple to name a few. It's on the Coast-to-Coast walking route and is renowned as a base for enjoying the mountains of the Lake District.

Location: OS 89, GR 194124.

Great for... hardcore walkers with a sense of adventure.

You need to know... there's no access to the hostel by car; YHA Black Sail now has an electrical supply (but no electrical sockets); credit cards are not accepted.

Accommodation: 16 beds: 2x4- and 1x8-bed rooms.

Family rooms: No. **Rent-a-Hostel:** Yes.

Classroom: No. **Education packages:** No.

Facilities: Sitting/dining room, self-catering kitchen, shower, shop, drying room and residential licence.

Daytime access: All public areas.

Reception open: Staff are available before 10am and after 5pm.

Meals: Breakfast, picnic lunch, evening meal.

Getting there: The nearest roads are the summit of Honister Pass or Gatesgarth in the Buttermere Valley. From either, it is a 2.5-mile mountain walk to the hostel. Alternatively, walk or cycle along the forest track in the Ennerdale Valley or take the mountain walk over Black Sail Pass from Wastwater.

Public transport: BUS: Stagecoach in Cumbria 77/A from Keswick, alight Honister Hause Hostel 3 miles, Apr-Oct only; otherwise 79 Keswick-Seatoller, then 3.5 miles. (For train connections see Keswick). RAIL: Whitehaven 19 miles.

Parking: No.

Nearest other hostels: Honister 2.5 miles, Buttermere 3.5, Ennerdale 4.

Price Band: B	Opening category: ❷

BLAKE BECK CAMPING BARN

Booking: 017687 72645

This 18th century camping barn is on the edge of the northern fells, close to Blencathra. The landscape up here is dramatic and you will no doubt be tempted to explore. Just as well, then, that Ullswater and Aira Force are only five miles away and Carrock Fell is nearby.

Great for... exploring the northern fells.

You need to know... there's an adjoining farmhouse and self-catering complex.

Accommodation: Sleeps 12 on first floor. Access is via external stone steps and mattresses are provided.

Facilities: Cooking/eating area, metered showers, two toilets, washbasins, wash-up area, electric light, hot water, radiators and cooking hob available for hire, metered electricity. Locked cycle shed and drying room.

Nearest pub: 2 miles. **Nearest shop:** 5 miles.

Location: OS 90, GR 367278.

Price Band: C	Opening category: ❸

● ● BUTTERMERE ☆☆☆

Buttermere, Cockermouth, Cumbria CA13 9XA; buttermere@yha.org.uk

Tel: 0870 770 5736 Fax: 0870 770 5737

If you're visiting the Lakes in high summer, Buttermere offers a quieter corner. Crummock Water and Buttermere are within a stone's throw of the hostel and Loweswater and the Vale of Lorton are within easy reach. Walks for all start from the doorstep. Afterwards, relax in the lounge and enjoy views of Red Pike and along to High Stile.

Location: OS 89, GR 178168.

Great for... families and walkers looking for a quieter break.

You need to know... breakfast is included in the price.

Accommodation: 70 beds: 1x2- but mostly 4-6-bed rooms.

Family rooms: Yes. **Rent-a-Hostel:** No.

Classroom: No. **Education packages:** Yes.

Facilities: Lounges, dining room, self-catering kitchen, table licence,

● BORROWDALE ☆☆☆☆

**Longthwaite, Borrowdale, Keswick, Cumbria
CA12 5XE; borrowdale@yha.org.uk
Tel: 0870 770 5706 Fax: 0870 770 5707**

Surrounded by mountains, Borrowdale offers all the comfort and facilities of a large Lakeland hostel while retaining a relaxed, informal atmosphere. Derwentwater is ideal for watersports and Whinlatter Forest Park offers orienteering courses. There are many local walking routes too and the hostel lies on the long-distance Coast-to-Coast path and the Cumbria Way.

Location: OS 90, GR 254142.
Great for... families wanting a varied outdoor holiday.
Accommodation: 88 beds: mostly 2-, 4- and 6- plus 1x8-bed rooms (two rooms converted for disabled access with shower and toilet opposite).
Family rooms: Yes. **Rent-a-Hostel:** No.

Classroom: Yes. **Education packages:** Yes.
Facilities: Lounge, self-catering kitchen (with disabled access), dining room, drying room, showers, laundry, shop, cycle store, bike hire, TV, table tennis, internet access and grounds.
Daytime access: All public areas.
Reception open: 1pm.
Meals: Breakfast, picnic lunch, evening meal.
Getting there: Follow Borrowdale signs and take B5289 from Keswick. Turn second right after Rosthwaite village. Follow YHA signs to lane end.
Public transport: BUS: Stagecoach in Cumbria 79 from Keswick. (For train connections see Keswick).
RAIL: Workington 25 miles, Penrith 26.
Parking: Yes.
Nearest other hostels: Honister 2 miles, Derwentwater 5, Buttermere 7.

Price Band: C   **Opening category:** ❸

Perfect families of all ages looking for an active break: YHA Borrowdale.

showers, drying room and cycle store.
Daytime access: All public areas.
Reception open: Staff available before 10am and after 5pm.
Meals: Breakfast, picnic lunch, evening meal.
Getting there: The hostel is half a mile south of Buttermere village on B5289 road to Honister Pass and Borrowdale.
Public transport: BUS: Stagecoach in Cumbria 77/A from Keswick (Easter-Oct only). (For train connections see Keswick).
RAIL: Workington 18 miles.
Parking: Yes.
Nearest other hostels: Black Sail by mountain path 3.5 miles, Honister 4, Borrowdale 7.

Price Band: D   **Opening category:** ❸

● CARLISLE ☆☆

**Old Brewery Residences, Bridge Lane,
Caldewgate, Carlisle CA2 5SR;
deec@impacthousing.org.uk
Tel: 0870 770 5752 Fax: 0870 770 5752**

Stay in an award-winning conversion of the former Theakston's Brewery. These university halls of residence offer comfortable rooms just a few minutes' walk from Carlisle's city centre and historic castle. Also within easy reach are Hadrian's Wall and the Lake District.
Location: OS 85, GR 394560.
Great for... shopping, exploring Hadrian's Wall and a stop en-route to Scotland.
You need to know... this accommodation is only available during July and August.

Accommodation: 56 beds: single beds in flats for up to 7 people.
Family rooms: No. **FBR:** Yes. **Rent-a-Hostel:** No.
Classroom: No. **Education packages:** No.
Facilities: Self-catering kitchens, bathrooms, cycle store and laundry. **Daytime access:** All public areas.
Reception open: 5pm- although staff available most of the day.
Meals: Self-catering only.
Getting there: Head for Carlisle town centre and take A595 west. The Old Brewery Residences are on the right past the castle.
Public transport: BUS: 61, 63, 67, 68 from Carlisle bus station to Bridge Lane on Caldergate. RAIL: Carlisle 2 miles.
NATIONALEXPRESS Carlisle bus station 1 mile.
Parking: Yes.
Nearest other hostels: Greenhead 18 miles, Cockermouth 24.

> **Price Band:** C

CATBELLS CAMPING BARN
Booking: 017687 72645

Part of a traditional set of farm buildings dating back to the 14th century, this camping barn is on the slopes of Catbells in the tranquil Newlands Valley. The Cumberland Way passes through the farmyard and both Borrowdale and Buttermere are within walking distance.
Great for... exploring the northern fells.
Accommodation: Sleeps 12, mattresses provided.
Facilities: Shower, electric light, electric point, cooking area and toilet in adjacent building, hot water, gas heaters. Breakfast may be booked in advance. Shower and electric point on meters.
Nearest pub: 1 mile. **Nearest shop:** 2 miles.
Location: OS 90, GR 243208.

> **Price Band:** C **Opening category:** ❸

● ● COCKERMOUTH ☆
Double Mills, Cockermouth, Cumbria CA13 0DS;
cockermouth@yha.org.uk
Tel: 0870 770 5768 Fax: 0870 770 5768

This 17th century watermill on the banks of the River Cocker is just a 10-minute walk from the centre of busy Cockermouth where you'll find William Wordsworth's birthplace and Jenning's Brewery. Crummock Water and Loweswater are both within easy reach, as is excellent walking on the quiet western edge of the Lake District. It's also popular with cyclists riding the Coast-to-Coast route and the new Hadrian's Wall cycle route.
Location: OS 89, GR 118298.
Great for... those combining touring with walking.
You need to know... parking is limited.
Accommodation: 26 beds: 1x4-, 1x10- and 1x12-bed rooms.
Family rooms: No. **FBR:** Yes. **Rent-a-Hostel:** Yes.
Classroom: No. **Education packages:** No.
Facilities: Lounge, self-catering kitchen, showers, drying room, large cycle store and grounds. **Daytime access:** To shelter, store and toilet via keypad lock (number available from manager).
Reception open: 5pm.
Meals: Self-catering only.

Getting there: From Main Street follow Station Street, then left into Fern Bank and at the end take the track down to river. From A66, take A5086 to Cockermouth then first right into Park Avenue. At the end turn right down track.
Public transport: BUS: Stagecoach in Cumbria X4/5 Penrith station-Workington (passes close to Workington station).
RAIL: Workington 8 miles.
NATIONALEXPRESS Monument, Main Street 0.5 miles.
Parking: Yes, but limited.
Nearest other hostels: Buttermere 10 miles, Keswick 13, Derwentwater 15.

> **Price Band:** A **Opening category:** ❷

● ● CONISTON COPPERMINES ☆☆
Coniston, Cumbria LA21 8HP;
coppermines@yha.org.uk
Tel: 0870 770 5772 Fax: 0870 770 3267

If you're planning to scale the slopes of the Old Man of Coniston, give yourself a head start by staying at Coniston Coppermines. Almost halfway up a mountain with a view to match, this hostel is surrounded by fells, allowing hillwalkers easy access onto Wetherlam and the Old Man of Coniston itself.
Location: OS 96, GR 289986.
Great for... walkers who want to stay in the hills.
You need to know... the track leading to the hostel is unsurfaced; the hostel is one-and-a-quarter miles from the village.
Accommodation: 26 beds: 3x4-, 1x6- and 1x8-bed rooms.
Family rooms: No. **FBR:** Yes. **Rent-a-Hostel:** Yes.

HOSTEL MANAGERS CHOOSE...
THE BEST WALKS FOR ALL LEVELS

Old Man of Coniston YHA Coniston Coppermines: "No hill-walking visit to the Lakes is complete without climbing this impressive mountain. By staying here at the hostel, you're almost halfway there."

Buttermere circuit YHA Buttermere: "With virtually no ascent on this five-mile circuit, this walk is ideal for anyone wishing to spend some time among the mountains without expending too much energy!"

'Catbells' YHA Derwentwater: "From the top you can enjoy wonderful views of Derwentwater and the surrounding fells."

Pillar YHA Ennerdale: "Take a walk up the eleventh highest mountain in the area."

Scafell Pike YHA Wastwater: "For the quickest route to the summit of England's highest peak, walk from Wastwater. It's just over two miles."

Leighton Moss RSPB reserve YHA Arnside: "This reserve is beautiful. Combine a good walk with varied scenery and a huge range of bird life."

Classroom: No. **Education packages:** No.
Facilities: Common room, self-catering kitchen, dining room, showers, drying room, residential licence and cycle store.
Daytime access: All public areas.
Reception open: Staff available before 10am and after 5pm.
Meals: Breakfast, picnic lunch, evening meal.
Getting there: From Coniston, take road between Black Bull pub and Co-op supermarket, and opposite post office, signposted to hostel, which becomes a mile-long track. Pass several waterfalls on left and, as the track levels, the hostel can be seen at head of valley.
Public transport: BUS: Stagecoach in Cumbria 505/6 from Ambleside (with connections from Windermere station), then 1 mile.
RAIL: Ulverston 14 miles. **Parking:** Yes.
Nearest other hostels: Coniston Holly How 1.25 miles, Elterwater 6, Hawkshead 6.

Price Band: **B**   Opening category: **②**

●● CONISTON HOLLY HOW ☆☆
Far End, Coniston, Cumbria LA21 8DD;
conistonhh@yha.org.uk
Tel: 0870 770 5770 Fax: 0870 770 5771

Leave your car at home and enjoy a wide range of activities from this hostel. All levels of walking routes, including the Old Man of Coniston, lead from the hostel's door, as do some of Britain's finest mountain biking trails. Sail, canoe or cruise on the lake, climb a classic Lake District crag or try pony trekking. John Ruskin's home and museum and lots of Arthur Ransome connections are nearby.
Location: OS 96, GR 302980.
Great for... a family holiday to please all tastes.
Accommodation: 60 beds: 4x4-, 4x8- and 1x12-bed rooms.
Family rooms: Yes. **Rent-a-Hostel:** No.
Classroom: No. **Education packages:** Yes.
Facilities: Lounge, games/TV room, drying room, self-catering kitchen, showers, cycle store, bike hire, laundry facilities and garden.
Daytime access: All public areas.
Reception open: Staff available before 10am and after 5pm.
Meals: Breakfast, picnic lunch, evening meal.
Getting there: From Coniston village take A593 towards Ambleside. After 200 metres look for hostel sign on old-fashioned finger post, pointing the way to hostel up a short lane on left.
Public transport: BUS: Stagecoach in Cumbria 505/6 from Ambleside (with connections from Windermere station).
RAIL: Ulverston 13 miles. **Parking:** Yes.
Nearest other hostels: Coniston Coppermines 1.25 miles, Hawkshead 5, Elterwater 5.

Price Band: **B**   Opening category: **❸**

CRAGG CAMPING BARN
Booking: 017687 72645

This camping barn is among traditional buildings on a typical hill farm with hardy Herdwick sheep. In one of the least developed (and quietest) valleys in the Lake District, between Buttermere and Crummock Water, it provides a good base for walking, climbing and fishing. Book your break here for peace and a plethora of outdoor activities.
Great for... exploring the northwest Lakes.
Accommodation: Sleeps 8 on the first floor.
Facilities: Cooking slab, eating area, electric light, toilet and shower.
Nearest pub: 200 yards. **Nearest shop:** 6 miles.
Location: OS 90, GR 174172.

Price Band: **C**   Opening category: **❸**

Picturesque: YHA Derwentwater.

●● DERWENTWATER ☆☆☆
Barrow House, Borrowdale, Keswick, Cumbria
CA12 5UR; derwentwater@yha.org.uk
Tel: 0870 770 5792 Fax: 0870 770 5793

This 200-year-old mansion is ideally situated for a relaxing family or group break. Boasting extensive grounds with a large play area and woodlands, children will find plenty of space in which to vent excess energy. It's also right on the shore of Derwentwater, which many say is the most picturesque lake in Britain, and has a waterfall in the grounds. The lake itself will keep you occupied for days – children can paddle while the more adventurous can take part in a wide variety of watersports. Or catch the launch nearby and stop off at any of the six jetties to explore the shoreline. There is also a selection of spectacular walks to suit all levels.
Location: OS 89, GR 268200.
Great for... a relaxing family holiday.
Accommodation: 88 beds: mostly 4-8-, 1x10- and 1x22-bed rooms.
Family rooms: Yes. **Rent-a-Hostel:** No.
Classroom: No. **Education packages:** Yes.
Facilities: Common rooms, games room, self-catering kitchen, TV room, cycle store, table licence, drying room, laundry, showers and toilets.
Daytime access: All public areas.

Reception open: All day.

Meals: Breakfast, picnic lunch, evening meal.

Getting there: From Keswick, follow the signs to Borrowdale. The hostel is 2 miles south on the Borrowdale road (B5289), 100 metres on the left past the turn off to Watendlath. Walkers should follow the lakeside path from Keswick.

Public transport: BUS: Stagecoach in Cumbria 79 Keswick-Seatoller. (For train connections see Keswick).

RAIL: Penrith 20 miles, Windermere 24.

NATIONALEXPRESS Keswick 2.25 miles.

Parking: Yes.

Nearest other hostels: Keswick 2 miles, Borrowdale 5.

Price Band: B   Opening category: 3

DINAH HOGGUS CAMPING BARN
Booking: 017687 72645

This traditional Lakeland field barn of Hogg-house is now a camping barn. Near the hamlet of Rosthwaite in the Borrowdale Valley and beside the old packhorse route to Watendlath, it is convenient for the Coast-to-Coast walk.

Great for... exploring the Borrowdale Valley.

You need to know... access to the first-floor sleeping area is via external stone steps.

Accommodation: Sleeps 12 on the first floor.

Facilities: One ring electric cooker, microwave, two radiators and metered electricity. Tumble dryer in washroom. Eating area, electric kettle, washbasin, toilet, radiator available for hire.

Nearest pub: 300 metres. **Nearest shop:** 200 metres.

Location: OS 90, GR 259151.

Price Band: C   Opening category: 3

● ● DUDDON ESTUARY ☆☆☆
Borwick Rails, Millom, Cumbria LA18 4JU;
duddon@yha.org.uk
Tel: 0870 770 6107 Fax: 0870 770 6108

This purpose-built hostel sits on the banks of the Duddon Estuary with a stunning panorama of the Lake District fells. It's the ideal location for walkers, cyclists, birdwatchers and botanists and is on the Cumbria Cycle Way and Cumbria Coastal Way. Hodbarrow RSPB Reserve is a mile away and it's a short walk to a long sandy beach. Available primarily as Rent-a-Hostel, it can be booked by individuals. **Location:** OS 96, GR 186799.

Great for... a holiday with a group of active friends.

You need to know... individuals should check availability less than 14 days ahead of your stay.

Accommodation: 18 beds: 1x2- and 2x8-bed rooms.

Family rooms: No. **FBR:** Yes. **Rent-a-Hostel:** Yes.

Classroom: No. **Education packages:** Yes.

Facilities: Lounge/dining room, kitchen, showers, laundry facilities, grounds and cycle store.

Daytime access: All public areas via numbered lock.

Reception open: 5pm.

Meals: Self-catering only.

Getting there: Turn off A5093 over the railway bridge into Millom town centre. Go through market place and continue on Devonshire Road for 1 mile, passing rugby club and Duddon Pilot Hotel. At end of the road there is a YHA sign and hostel is down lane on left.

Public transport: BUS: Stagecoach 511 from Ulverston, X7 from Barrow, X6 from Whitehaven. RAIL: Millom (Not Sun) 1.25 miles.

NATIONALEXPRESS Whitehaven 36 miles, Kendal 35.

Parking: Yes.

Nearest other hostels: Coniston Holly How 16 miles, Coniston Coppermines 17, Eskdale 20, Arnside 40.

Price Band: A   Opening category: 1

● ● ELTERWATER ☆☆
Elterwater, Ambleside, Cumbria LA22 9HX;
elterwater@yha.org.uk
Tel: 0870 770 5816 Fax: 0870 770 5817

Converted from Elterwater's oldest farm, this hostel is superbly located for the Langdale fells in a popular, but peaceful village. Accommodation is comfortable, warm and friendly, the food is good

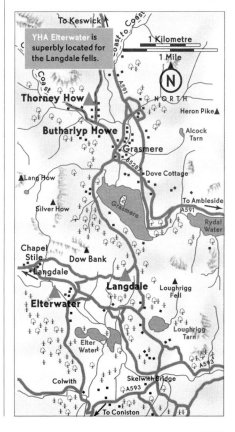

YHA Elterwater is superbly located for the Langdale fells.

and the pub and village shop are close to hand. There are outdoor activities for all levels, with easy access to the Cumbria Way, road and mountain biking trails and crags for rock climbing.

Location: OS 90, GR 327046.

Great for... peace, quiet and walks for all abilities.

You need to know... there's parking at the nearby National Trust pay and display car park in the village.

Accommodation: 43 beds: 6x2-, 1x3-, 1x4- and 4x6-bed rooms.

Family rooms: No. **FBR:** Yes. **Rent-a-Hostel:** No.

Classroom: No. **Education packages:** Yes.

Facilities: Self-catering kitchen, lounge/dining room, showers, drying room, cycle store, garden and internet access.

Daytime access: All public areas.

Reception open: Staff available before 10am and after 5pm.

Meals: Breakfast, picnic lunch, evening meal.

Getting there: Take A593 from Ambleside in direction of Coniston . After 2 miles (Skelwith Bridge) turn right onto B5343, signposted Elterwater. After 2 miles cross a cattle grid and take next left signposted Elterwater 0.25 miles. Go through village and cross bridge. Hostel is 100 metres on right.

Public transport: Bus: Stagecoach in Cumbria 516 from Ambleside (connections from X Windermere) X Windermere 9m.

NATIONALEXPRESS» Ambleside, King Street 3.5 miles.

Parking: Free parking for National Trust Members, otherwise pay and display.

Nearest other hostels: Langdale 1 mile, Ambleside 4, Grasmere 4.

Price Band: B **Opening category:** 3

● ENNERDALE ☆

Cat Crag, Ennerdale, Cleator, Cumbria CA23 3AX; ennerdale@yha.org.uk

Tel: 0870 770 5820 Fax: 0870 770 5821

Two forestry cottages form this hostel in a remote wooded valley surrounded by fells, ridges and many famous peaks. Forest tracks offer sheltered, low-level walks and cycle rides while upland routes will challenge the more adventurous. It's also on the Coast-to-Coast walk, Sculpture Trail and the Ennerdale to Whitehaven cycle path.

Location: OS 89, GR 142141.

Great for... keen walkers who enjoy a remote location.

You need to know... Ennerdale now has electricity.

Accommodation: 24 beds comprised of 3x4- and 2x6-bed rooms.

Family rooms: No. **FBR:** Yes. **Rent-a-Hostel:** Yes.

Classroom: No. **Education packages:** No.

Facilities: Self-catering kitchen, common room, drying room, showers, alcohol licence and grounds. Limited shop.

Daytime access: All public areas.

Reception open: Staff available before 10am and after 5pm.

Meals: Breakfast, picnic lunch, evening meal.

Getting there: The hostel is 2.5 miles from Bowness Knott car park along Forest Road, 5 miles from Ennerdale Bridge.

Public transport: BUS: Stagecoach in Cumbria 77/A from Keswick (Apr-Oct only), alight Buttermere, 3 miles by path; Ennerdale Rambler 263 from Buttermere (Sat, Sun, July/Aug only), alight Bowness Knott, then 2 miles; otherwise Stagecoach in Cumbria 219 from Cockermouth, alight Kirkland, 7 miles or 79 from Keswick, alight Seatoller, 7 miles by path (for train connections see Keswick). RAIL: Whitehaven 15 miles.

Parking: Limited.

Nearest other hostels: Buttermere 3 miles (by path), Black Sail 4, Honister 7.

Price Band: B **Opening category:** 2

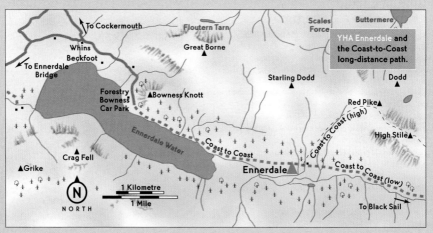

YHA Ennerdale and the Coast-to-Coast long-distance path.

●● ESKDALE ☆☆☆

Boot, Holmrook, Cumbria CA19 1TH;
eskdale@yha.org.uk
Tel: 0870 770 5824 Fax: 0870 770 5825

Nestling among the fells and set in its own extensive grounds, this purpose-built, child-friendly Youth Hostel is a good base for those seeking to explore a quieter corner of the Lake District. There are walking routes suitable for all abilities including an idyllic trail along the River Esk. Visit Upper Eskdale, home to Hardknott Roman Fort and Muncaster Castle. If you want to arrive in style, book a ticket on the Ravenglass & Eskdale Miniature Gauge Steam Railway.
Location: OS 89, GR 195010.
Great for... families whose children enjoy walking.
You need to know... public transport is limited.
Accommodation: 50 beds: 8x2-6- and 2x8-bed rooms.
Family rooms: Yes. **Rent-a-Hostel:** Yes.
Classroom: Yes. **Education packages:** Yes.
Facilities: Classroom/games room, self-catering kitchen, common room, dining room, drying room, laundry, showers, cycle store and grounds. **Daytime access:** All public areas.
Reception open: Staff available before 10am and after 5pm.
Meals: Breakfast, picnic lunch, evening meal.
Getting there: Via the Hardknott Pass, a steep and narrow approach. An alternative is via the A595.
Public transport: X Eskdale (Ravenglass & Eskdale Rly) 1m; Ravenglass (Not Sun) 10m; Drigg (Not Sun) 10m
Parking: Yes.
Nearest other hostels: Wastwater 7 miles, Coniston Coppermines 10, Elterwater 9 (all by mountain path).

Price Band: B	Opening category: ❷

FELL END CAMPING BARN
Booking: 017687 72645

This camping barn, 400 metres from the working farm, overlooks superb scenery in southwest Lakeland and is within easy distance of Coniston, Langdale and the Duddon Valley. The camping barn is an ideal base for exploring the Lake District.
Great for... getting away from it all.
You need to know... there is no electricity so bring a torch.
Accommodation: Sleeps 12 on a platform on the ground floor.
Facilities: Cooking slab, eating area and heaters available for hire.
Nearest pub: 2 miles. **Nearest shop:** 3 miles.
Location: OS 96, GR 239881.

Price Band: C	Opening category: ❸

●● GRASMERE THORNEY HOW ☆

Easedale Road, Grasmere, Cumbria LA22 9QG;
grasmere@yha.org.uk. Bookings handled by
YHA Grasmere Butharlyp Howe.
Tel: 0870 770 5836 Fax: 0870 770 5837

This was the first hostel bought by the YHA in 1931 and, while the original farmhouse retains its character, it has been extended and modernised. It's a 15-minute walk to Grasmere's town centre, making

The first hostel bought by the YHA: YHA Grasmere Thorney How.

this a secluded spot for walkers with virtually no passing traffic. There are routes to suit all levels of abilities – hikers will want to head into the hills but there are nine lakes and tarns within reach for those wanting shorter expeditions. Wainwright's Coast-to-Coast long-distance path also passes the front door.
Location: OS 90, GR 332084.
Great for... walkers, cyclists and activity groups.
Accommodation: 49 beds: 3x4-, 1x5-, 2x2- and 2x6- and 2x9-bed rooms.
Family rooms: No. **FBR:** Yes. **Rent-a-Hostel:** Yes.
Classroom: No. **Education packages:** Yes.
Facilities: Lounge with open fire, dining room and common room, self-catering kitchen, drying room, showers and cycle store.
Daytime access: All public areas.
Reception open: 5pm.
Meals: Breakfast, picnic lunch, evening meal.
Getting there: From Grasmere centre bus stop, follow Easedale Road past the entrance to Grasmere Butharlyp Howe on your right and continue for another half a mile. After crossing the river at the sign turn right. Thorney How is approximately 0.75 miles on your left and is signed. Access for cars and minibuses but not coaches.
Public transport: BUS: Stagecoach in Cumbria 555/6 Lancaster-Keswick, 599 from Windermere; alight Grasmere, 0.5 miles (all pass Windermere station). RAIL: Windermere 9 miles.
NATIONALEXPRESS Thistle Hotel 2 miles.
Parking: Yes.
Nearest other hostels: Grasmere Butharlyp Howe 0.75 miles, Langdale 2.5, Elterwater 4, Ambleside 5, Borrowdale 9 (via footpath), Patterdale 9.

Price Band: B	Opening category: ❷

● GRASMERE BUTHARLYP HOWE ☆☆☆☆

Easedale Road, Grasmere, Cumbria LA22 9QG; grasmere@yha.org.uk
Tel: 0870 770 5836 Fax: 0870 770 5837

Take your children to Butharlyp Howe and test their energy levels. The hostel, a traditional Lakeland Victorian house, has extensive grounds with a safe play area for children and plenty of outdoor games equipment. Staff at the hostel can help you book a wide range of outdoor activities including watersports, climbing, orienteering, cycling and fishing. It goes without saying that there's walking galore, including high-level ridge and fell routes.

Location: OS 90, GR 336077.
Great for... families who enjoy a range of outdoor activities.
Accommodation: 80 beds: 5x2-, 8x4-, 2x5-, 2x6-, 1x8- and 1x10-bed rooms.
Family rooms: Yes. **Rent-a-Hostel:** No.
Classroom: Yes. **Education packages:** Yes.
Facilities: Lounge with open fire, games room and pool table, TV room, self-catering kitchen, dining room, table licence, showers, drying room, laundry, cycle store and grounds.
Daytime access: All public areas.
Reception open: All day.
Meals: Breakfast, picnic lunch, evening meal.
Getting there: From Grasmere centre bus stop (opposite Sam Reeds bookshop) take Easedale Road. In approx 200 metres, drive to YHA Grasmere Butharlyp Howe is on right, well signed. Cars may be driven up to house to unload but must be returned to the car park.
Public transport: BUS: Stagecoach in Cumbria 555/6 Lancaster-Keswick, 599 from Windermere; alight Grasmere, 0.5 miles. All pass Windermere station.
RAIL: Windermere 8.5 miles.
NATIONALEXPRESS» Thistle Hotel 1 mile.
Parking: Yes.
Nearest other hostels: Grasmere Thorney How 0.75 miles, Ambleside 5, Borrowdale 9 (by path), Patterdale 9 (by path).

Price Band: C	Opening category: ❸

Ideal for children: YHA Grasmere Butharlyp Howe.

●● HAWKSHEAD ☆☆☆

Hawkshead, Ambleside, Cumbria LA22 0QD; hawkshead@yha.org.uk
Tel: 0870 770 5856 Fax: 0870 770 5857

Only six miles from the hustle and bustle of Ambleside you can relax on the terrace of this Regency Mansion. Extensive lawned gardens and a Nature Trail provide a safe haven for children of all ages to play and explore. The South Lakes contains some of the best mountain biking in the country. Add to that the Coniston and Langdale Fells, Grizedale Forest Park and Go Ape! and you have all the ingredients for a perfect break.

Location: OS 96, GR 354966.
Great for... an elegant base to explore Beatrix Potter country.
You need to know... there is a separate family annexe.
Accommodation: 109 beds: 14x3-4- and 8x6-8-bed rooms.
Family rooms: Yes. **Rent-a-Hostel:** Yes.
Classroom: Yes. **Education packages:** Yes.
Facilities: Lounge, TV and games room, self-catering kitchen, two drying rooms, laundry, showers, shop, cycle store, cycle hire and grounds. **Daytime access:** All public areas.
Reception open: 1pm.
Meals: Breakfast, picnic lunch, evening meal.
Getting there: From M6 J36 follow A590 toward Barrow in Furness. At Newby Bridge go straight on at the roundabout then take next right following signs to Lakeside and Hawkshead. The hostel is approximately 1 mile before Hawkshead village on left (with Esthwaite Water on right). From Hawkshead village, follow signs to Newby Bridge and then hostel. Hostel is 1 mile along road on right.
Nearest other hostels: Coniston Holly How 5.5 miles, Ambleside 6, Windermere 9 (via ferry).
Public transport: BUS: Stagecoach in Cumbria 505/6 from Ambleside (connections from Windermere station), alight Hawkshead, 1 mile. RAIL: Windermere 7 miles (by vehicle ferry).

Price Band: B	Opening category: ❸

●● HELVELLYN ☆☆

Greenside, Glenridding, Penrith, Cumbria CA11 0QR; helvellyn@yha.org.uk
Tel: 0870 770 6110 Fax: 0870 770 5863

Approached by a three-quarter-mile track from the village of Glenridding, this hostel is in an isolated and peaceful spot, 900 feet above sea level. Enjoy a hike up Helvellyn or the surrounding peaks or, for less strenuous walking, try the scenic lakeshore paths around Ullswater. Steam boat trips on the lake are also popular.

Location: OS 90, GR 366173.
Great for... high level and lakeside walking.
You need to know... the hostel is 1.5 miles from the village.
Accommodation: 60 beds: mostly 2-4- and 2x6-bed rooms.
Family rooms: No. **FBR:** Yes. **Rent-a-Hostel:** No.
Classroom: No. **Education packages:** Yes.
Facilities: Common rooms, self-catering kitchen, dining room, games room, showers, drying room, cycle store and grounds.
Daytime access: All public areas.

Meals: Breakfast, picnic lunch, evening meal.
Reception open: Staff available before 10am and after 5pm.
Getting there: The hostel is signposted from Glenridding village, 1 mile past the Travellers Rest. The lane which leads to the hostel is unsurfaced but suitable for most vehicles.
Public transport: BUS: Stagecoach in Cumbria 108 from Penrith station, alight Glenridding, 1.5 miles. RAIL: Penrith 14 miles, Windermere 15. **Parking:** Yes.
Nearest other hostels: Patterdale 2.5 miles, Grasmere 8 (both by mountain path).

Price Band: **B**   Opening category: **②**

If you want complete relaxation, YHA Helvellyn is perfect.

HIGH GILLERTHWAITE CAMPING BARN (ENNERDALE)
Booking: 017687 72645

This camping barn is in the most remote of the Lakeland valleys with outstanding views of Pillar and the adjacent fells. It's a traditional barn dating back to the 16th century, which makes it an excellent base for fell walking and rock climbing plus cycling along the Coast-to-Coast long-distance route.
Great for... mountain scenery, peace and quiet.
You need to know... mattresses are provided; there are no electrical sockets.
Accommodation: Sleeps 14 in three sleeping areas on first and second floors.
Facilities: Sitting room with wood-burning stove, cooking area with hot water, bathroom, toilet, basin, shower and heaters. Electricity is supplied by generator for lighting only. Evening meals and breakfasts may be booked in advance by arrangement with YHA Ennerdale.
Nearest pub: 5 miles. **Nearest shop:** 5 miles.
Location: OS 89, GR 142141.

Price Band: **C**   Opening category: **③**

● HONISTER HAUSE ☆☆☆
Seatoller, Keswick, Cumbria CA12 5XN;
honister@yha.org.uk
Tel: 0870 770 5870

This former quarry workers' building is in a spectacular setting at the summit of Honister Pass, a high-level route connecting the valleys of Borrowdale and Buttermere, next to the famous Honister Slate Mine. This true mountain hostel provides easy access to the famous high peaks of Central Lakeland – Scafell, Great Gable, Pillar, Red Pike and Dale Head, as well as many other classic walking routes.
Location: OS 89, GR 226135.
Great for... dedicated walkers who are at home on the hills.
You need to know... electricity is provided by an on-site generator, and there are no power points in the bedrooms.
Accommodation: 26 beds: all 2-4-bed rooms.
Family rooms: No. **FBR:** Yes. **Rent-a-Hostel:** No.
Classroom: No. **Education packages:** No.
Facilities: Lounge/dining room, self-catering kitchen, showers, drying room and residential licence. **Daytime access:** Outside porch and toilet.
Reception open: 5pm.
Meals: Breakfast, picnic lunch, evening meal.
Getting there: From Keswick follow the B5289 (signed Borrowdale) for approx 9 miles. The hostel is on left at top of pass.
Public transport: BUS: Stagecoach in Cumbria 77/A from Keswick, Apr-Oct only; otherwise 79 Keswick-Seatoller, then 1.5 miles. (For train connections see Keswick). RAIL: Workington 23 miles.
Parking: Limited. Car park next to hostel. Also pay and display National Trust car park to rear.
Nearest other hostels: Borrowdale 2 miles, Black Sail 3 (by mountain path), Buttermere 4.

Price Band: **B**   Opening category: **②**

HUDSCALES CAMPING BARN
Booking: 017687 72645

This barn is part of a group of traditional farm buildings and lies at 1,000 feet on the northernmost flank of the Lakeland fells. With views over Caldbeck and Hesket Newmarket, it is an ideal base for exploring the northern fells and is on the Cumbria Way. And, with breakfast available, you can start your days in style.
Great for... exploring the quieter fells.
Accommodation: Sleeps 12 on the ground floor.
Facilities: Shower, power points, heaters (all on meter), cooking slab, eating area, toilet, washing facilities and electric light. Breakfast must be booked in advance.
Nearest pub: 2 miles. **Nearest shop:** 2 miles.
Location: OS 90, GR 332375.

Price Band: **C**   Opening category: **③**

●● KESWICK ☆
Station Road, Keswick, Cumbria CA12 5LH;
keswick@yha.org.uk
Tel: 0870 770 5894 Fax: 0870 770 5895

Combine extensive walking with a wealth of evening entertainment at this hostel, which sits on the banks of the River Greta. There's plenty of walking here in the northern Lakes – if you need tempting then Skiddaw, one of the highest mountains in the Lake District, forms an impressive backdrop to the view from the hostel. It's just a

● **KENDAL** ☆☆

118 Highgate, Kendal, Cumbria LA9 4HE;
kendal@yha.org.uk
Tel: 0870 770 5892 Fax: 0870 770 5893

An attractive Georgian townhouse at the centre of a historic market town, this hostel forms part of the Brewery Arts complex. It's a convenient base from which to explore the southern Lakes and the Yorkshire Dales. Kendal itself has many attractions to keep all the family entertained, including the castle ruins. Explore further afield and you'll find the National Trust's Sizergh Castle and Levens Hall with its famous topiary gardens.

Location: OS 97, GR 515924.

Great for... a base for exploring southern Lakeland.

You need to know... cars must be left in a nearby pay and display car park (free between 6pm and 9am); breakfast is included in the overnight price.

Accommodation: 48 beds: 4x2-, 1x3-, 2x4-, 3x6-, 1x11-bed rooms.

Family rooms: Yes. **Rent-a-Hostel:** No.

Classroom: No. **Education packages:** Yes.

Facilities: Lounge, TV, self-catering kitchen, dining rooms, meeting room, showers, drying room and cycle store.

Daytime access: Public areas, via numbered lock.

Reception open: 1pm.

Meals: Evening meals and packed lunches are available when pre-booked.

Picturesque: YHA Kendal is an attractive Georgian townhouse.

Getting there: The hostel is on the main street in Kendal (part of the one-way system).

Public transport: BUS: frequent from surrounding areas. RAIL: Kendal 0.5 miles, Oxenholme 1.5.
NATIONALEXPRESS Bus station 0.25 miles.

Parking: No. Nearby pay and display car park.

Nearest other hostels: Windermere 11 miles, Arnside 12, Ambleside 13.5.

Price Band: D	Opening category: ❷

few minutes' walk into the town centre, where you'll find plenty of pubs, a cinema and a theatre.

Location: OS 89, GR 267235.

Great for... those wanting to combine a host of outdoor activities with nearby attractions.

You need to know... daytime parking is restricted.

Accommodation: 91 beds: mostly 3-4- plus 1x5-, 2x6- and 1x10-bed rooms.

Family rooms: No. **FBR:** Yes. **Rent-a-Hostel:** No.

Classroom: No, but large multi-functional rooms are available.

Education packages: No.

Facilities: Reception, lounge, TV and games room, dining room, self-catering kitchen, showers, drying room, laundry, educational resources, shop, map and towel hire and cycle store.

Daytime access: All public areas.

Reception open: All day.

Meals: Breakfast, picnic lunch, evening meal.

Getting there: Approaching Keswick from Ambleside/Penrith, hostel is signposted on right turn into Station Road. After 50 metres turn left following hostel sign along the walkway by the River Greta.

Public transport: BUS: Stagecoach in Cumbria X4/X5/X50 Penrith-Workington (passes close to Penrith station); 555 Lancaster-Carlisle. RAIL: Penrith 17 miles.
NATIONALEXPRESS Bus terminal, Booth's supermarket 0.5 miles.

Parking: Restricted daytime parking on roadside.

Nearest other hostels: Derwentwater 2 miles, Borrowdale 7.

Price Band: B	Opening category: ❶

●● **LANGDALE** ☆

High Close, Loughrigg, Ambleside, Cumbria LA22 9HJ; langdale@yha.org.uk
Tel: 0870 770 5908 Fax: 0870 770 5909

Bookings are made through YHA Ambleside

This rambling Victorian mansion with open fires is owned by the National Trust and stands in its own grounds between Elterwater and Grasmere. Close to the Langdale Pikes, it's an ideal base for walkers wanting to explore the Langdale valleys.

Location: OS 90, GR 338052.

Great for... getting away from it all.

You need to know... although the facilities are basic, this hostel's charm more than compensates; the hostel is signposted 'High Close'.

Accommodation: 96 beds: 2x2-, 2x3-4-, 7x5- and 4x11-bed rooms.

Family rooms: Yes. **FBR:** Yes. **Rent-a-Hostel:** Yes.

Classroom: Yes. **Education packages:** Yes.

Facilities: Lounges, TV, dining room, games room, self-catering kitchen, showers, cycle store and large grounds.

Daytime access: All public areas.

Reception open: Staff available before 10am and after 5pm.

Meals: Breakfast, picnic lunch, evening meal.

Getting there: From Ambleside take the A593 (Coniston and Langdale). After 1.5 miles, turn right and follow a minor road uphill for 1.75 miles. At the summit of Red Bank, turn left and the hostel is a quarter of a mile on the left.

Public Transport: BUS: Stagecoach in Cumbria 516 from Ambleside (connections from Windermere station), alight 0.5 miles south east of Elterwater, then 0.5 miles; otherwise any of the services to Grasmere Hostels, alight Grasmere, then 1.5 miles. RAIL: Windermere 10 miles. **NATIONALEXPRESS▶** Ambleside, King Street 3.5 miles.

Parking: Yes.

Nearest other hostels: Elterwater 1 mile, Grasmere Butharlyp Howe 2, Ambleside 4.

Price Band: B	Opening category: ❸

MILL HOUSE CAMPING BARN
Booking: 017687 72645

You'll find this camping barn on a large working farm in a secluded valley 1 mile from the thriving village of Gosforth. It makes a good base to explore the western fells close to Wastwater and Scafell Pike.

The vast Langdale valley: within easy reach of YHA Langdale.

Accommodation: Sleeps 12 on the ground floor.

Facilities: Cooking slab, electric light, metered power point, gas heater available for hire, metered electricity. Toilet and hot water are in adjacent building. Breakfast can be booked in advance.

Nearest pub: 0.5 miles. **Nearest shop:** 0.25 miles.

Location: OS 91, GR 800044.

Price Band: G	Opening category: ❸

MURT CAMPING BARN
Booking: 017687 72645
Arrival time: Mr & Mrs Grant, 019467 26044

Murt is a traditional Lakeland farm, dating back to 1728, and is situated in the Wasdale Valley. The camping barn is a converted stone hayloft and byre and enjoys stunning views to the Scafell Massif, Great Gable and the surrounding fells. Situated less than a mile from Wastwater, it's an ideal base for high fell, lake and valley walking with direct access to footpaths and bridleways.

Accommodation: Sleeps 8 on the first floor, mattresses provided.

Facilities: Cooking area, toilet, washing-up facilities, metered electric light, water heater, shower, power point and electric heater. Dogs by prior arrangement only. Car parking next to barn.

Nearest pub: 10-minute walk. **Nearest shop:** 4 miles.

Location: OS 91, GR 131040.

Price Band: G	Opening category: ❸

●● PATTERDALE ☆
Patterdale, Penrith, Cumbria CA11 0NW;
patterdale@yha.org.uk
Tel: 0870 770 5986 Fax: 0870 770 5987

Situated on the Coast-to-Coast route, this Scandinavian-style building was designed to blend in with the glorious scenery just south of Ullswater. It makes the ideal base to explore the ridges and fells around Ullswater. The energetic who stay at this unique hostel will want to climb Helvellyn while those seeking more gentle pursuits can enjoy a cruise on the Ullswater steamer.

Location: OS 90, GR 399156.

HOSTEL MANAGERS CHOOSE...
THE BEST DAYS OUT IN LAKELAND

Jennings Brewers & Tours YHA Cockermouth: "Jennings have been brewing traditional beers in Cumbria for 170 years. Take a brewery tour which gives you an insight into the beers and the brewing methods used."

Go! Ape YHA Hawkshead: "Spend a fun day at Grizedale Forest high wire forest adventure, which was voted Rural Tourist Attraction of the Year 2003."

Castlerigg Stone Circle YHA Keswick: "The stone circle is on the level top of a low hill with views across to Skiddaw, Blencathra and Lonscale Fell."

Lake Windermere YHA Ambleside: "The Windermere Lake cruises leave from the doorstep of the hostel. How could you leave without a trip across England's largest lake?"

Derwentwater YHA Derwentwater: "Cruise on the Derwent Water launch for spectacular views."

Great for... high and low level walks, watersports, mountain biking and birdwatching.

Accommodation: 82 beds: 3x2-, 7x8- and 2x10-bed rooms.

Family rooms: No. **FBR:** Yes. **Rent-a-Hostel:** No.

Classroom: No. **Education packages:** Yes.

Facilities: Reception, lounge, self-catering kitchen, dining room, showers, drying room, cycle store, laundry facilities, internet access and grounds. **Daytime access:** All public areas.

Reception open: Staff available before 10am and after 5pm.

Meals: Breakfast, picnic lunch, evening meal.

Getting there: The hostel is a quarter of a mile south of Patterdale village on the A592 to Kirkstone Pass.

Public transport: BUS: Stagecoach in Cumbria 108 from Penrith station. YHA shuttlebus from YHA Ambleside - summer service. RAIL: Penrith 15 miles.

Parking: Yes. Coaches by arrangement.

Nearest other hostels: Helvellyn 2.5 miles, Grasmere 9 (by path), Ambleside 10.

Price Band: B   Opening category: ❸

Mountain biking heaven: the countryside around YHA Patterdale.

High level walking near YHA Patterdale.

ST JOHN'S-IN-THE-VALE CAMPING BARN

Booking: 017687 72645

Arrival time: Mrs Chaplin-Brice, 01768 779242

This camping barn was once an 18th century stable and hayloft and stands in an idyllic setting overlooking St John's Beck on a peaceful hill farm. With stunning views to Blencathra, Helvellyn and Castle Rock, why not take advantage of sunny afternoons in the farm's tea garden, where generous slices of home-made cake await.

Great for... walking, climbing, peace and quiet.

Accommodation: Sleeps 8.

Facilities: Sitting and dining area, toilet, shower (charge for hot water), cooking areas, wood-burning stove (fuel extra), BBQ and outside seating area. Use of washing machine and dryer available. Breakfasts can be booked in advance (with 24 hours notice).

Nearest pub: 2 miles. **Nearest shop:** 6 miles.

Location: OS 90, GR 316205.

Price Band: C   Opening category: ❸

SWALLOW CAMPING BARN

Booking: 017687 72645

In the picturesque Loweswater Valley, this camping barn is part of a traditional set of farm buildings dating back to 1670. Permits for fishing and boat hire on Loweswater are available at the farm, or spend your days exploring the quiet western fells, nearby Crummock Water and Buttermere.

Accommodation: Sleeps 18 in four separate areas on ground floor.

Facilities: Eating area, cooking slab, electric light, cold water tap, toilets, showers (coin-operated) and hot-water heater.

Nearest pub: 1 mile. **Nearest shop:** 3 miles.

Location: OS 89, GR 116226.

Price Band: C   Opening category: ❸

SWIRRAL CAMPING BARN
Booking: 017687 72645

One of a group of nine buildings, this remote camping barn is situated at 1,000 feet on the flank of the Helvellyn range. Popular routes to Striding Edge and Swirral Edge pass the door and there is quick access to Ullswater and the eastern fells.

Great for... individual families or mixed groups; also walking the Helvellyn range and access to Ullswater lake.

You need to know... the showers take 50p coins.

Accommodation: Sleeps 8 on the first floor.

Facilities: Electric light and toilet in adjacent building.

Nearest pub: 1 mile. **Nearest shop:** 2 miles.

Location: OS 90, GR 364174.

Price Band: G	Opening category: ❸

The Lake District offers walkers a range of routes to choose from.

TARN FLATT CAMPING BARN
Booking: 017687 72645
Arrival time: Janice Telfer, 01946 692162

This camping barn is a traditional sandstone building on St Bees Head overlooking the Scottish coastline and the Isle of Man. It's usually busy with walkers embarking on the Coast-to-Coast long-distance walk at St Bees. There's also easy access to the quieter western Lakeland fells and lakes. The Georgian town of Whitehaven is within easy reach.

Great for... rock climbing (at North Head St Bees), fishing, birdwatching (RSPB nature reserve).

You need to know... long- and short-stay car parking is available.

Accommodation: Sleeps 8 on ground floor.

Facilities: Electric light, cooking slab, open fire (wood available from farm), metered shower and toilets in adjacent building.

Dinner, packed lunches and breakfast bookable in advance.

Nearest pub: 1 mile. **Nearest shop:** 2 miles.

Location: OS 89, GR 947146.

Price Band: G	Opening category: ❸

●● WASTWATER ☆☆☆
Wasdale Hall, Wasdale, Seascale, Cumbria
CA20 1ET; wastwater@yha.org.uk
Tel: 0870 770 6082 Fax: 0870 770 6083

A stunning half-timbered National Trust-owned house, this hostel dates from 1829 and still retains many original features. Enjoy beautiful mountain and lake views from its grounds, which extend to the shores of Wastwater, England's deepest lake. Within easy reach of England's highest mountain, walkers will be busy here.

Location: OS 89, GR 145045.

Great for... getting away from it all.

You need to know... public transport is limited; the nearest shop is 5 miles away.

Accommodation: 50 beds: 2x4-, 1x6-, 1x8- and 2x14-bed rooms.

Family rooms: Yes. **Rent-a-Hostel:** No.

Classroom: Yes. **Education packages:** Yes.

Facilities: Lounge, games room, dining room, showers, drying room, cycle store and shop. **Daytime access:** All public areas.

Reception open: Staff available before 10am and after 5pm.

Meals: Breakfast, picnic lunch, evening meal.

Getting there: From the south, follow A590 to Greenodd, then A595 Broughton-in-Furness to Nether Wasdale. From the north via Cockermouth, take A5086 to Egremont, then A595 to Gosforth and on to Nether Wasdale.

Public transport: BUS: Stagecoach in Cumbria 6, X6 Whitehaven-Ravenglass (passes close to Seascale and Ravenglass stations), alight Gosforth, 5 miles. Taxibus service from Seascale and Gosforth on Thurs, Sat and Sun (book by 6pm previous day on 019467 25308). RAIL: Seascale (Not Sun) 9 miles, Irton Road (Ravenglass & Eskdale Rly) 5.5.

Parking: Yes.

Nearest other hostels: Black Sail 7 miles (by mountain path), Eskdale 10.

Price Band: B	Opening category: ❸

YHA Wastwater offers stunning views of England's deepest lake.

● WINDERMERE ☆☆☆

**Bridge Lane, Troutbeck, Windermere, Cumbria
LA23 1LA; windermere@yha.org.uk
Tel: 0870 770 6094 Fax: 0870 770 6095**

This hostel enjoys a spectacular setting overlooking Lake
Windermere with its own extensive grounds and panoramic views
of the Lakeland mountains. Two miles outside the busy town of
Windermere, it's ideal for a peaceful countryside setting close to
local attractions. The quiet Troutbeck Valley offers a variety of
good low and high level walking routes or, for a more sedate day
out, visit the nearby National Park visitor centre, the Aquarium,
World of Beatrix Potter or join a cruise on Lake Windermere.

Location: OS 90, GR 405013.

Great for... families wanting a range of attractions.

You need to know... the hostel is 2 miles outside Windermere town.

Accommodation: 69 beds: mostly 4-bed rooms, plus 1x2-, 1x3-,
1x5-, 1x6- and 1x8-bed options.

Family rooms: Yes. **Rent-a-Hostel:** No.

Classroom: No. **Education packages:** Yes.

Facilities: Lounge, TV, self-catering kitchen, showers, drying/
laundry room, internet and cycle hire and store.

Daytime access: All public areas.

Reception open: All day except between 12 and 1pm.

Meals: Breakfast, picnic lunch and evening meal.

Getting there: From Windermere take A591 to Troutbeck
Bridge. Turn right after filling station and hostel is 0.75 miles
up Bridge Lane. **Public transport:** BUS: frequent from surrounding
areas, alight Troutbeck Bridge 0.75 miles. RAIL: Windermere 2
miles. **NATIONALEXPRESS** Windermere bus station 2 miles.
From Spring to Autumn YHA Shuttle bus meets most trains arriving
at Windermere station and offers free transfer to the Youth Hostel.

Parking: Yes. **Nearest other hostels:** Ambleside 3 miles,
Hawkshead 9 (by ferry), Kendal 11, Patterdale 11.

Price Band: **B**   Opening category: **3**

Close by the shore of
Lake Windermere:
YHA Ambleside and
YHA Windermere.

Unspoilt: the view from Lake Windermere to Langdale Pikes typifies the natural beauty of the area.

Yorkshire & South Pennines

Enjoy traditional northern hospitality as you explore the hills, moors, beaches and wild coastal cliffs that give Yorkshire its unique appeal.

Great for the outdoors: YHA Boggle Hole.

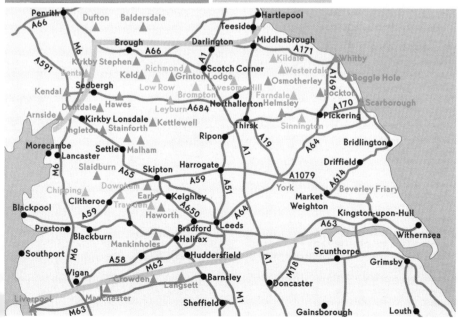

● **BEVERLEY FRIARY** ☆☆☆
Friar's Lane, Beverley, East Yorkshire HU17 0DF;
beverleyfriary@yha.org.uk
Tel: 0870 770 5696 Fax: 0870 770 5697

Beverley is one of northeast England's premier towns, its Minster the superior of many an English cathedral. A beautiful old building in a quiet corner of the town, this hostel is close to the Minster and ideally placed to explore the cobbled lanes and elegant Georgian and Victorian terraces. It also affords easy access to Hull, York and the Yorkshire Wolds, while the coast is just 15 minutes away. Whether you want to go cycling or shopping, birdwatching or relaxing on the beach, this hostel makes a wonderful setting for your break.

Location: OS 107, GR 038393.

Great for... cycling, birdwatching and relaxing.

Accommodation: 34 beds: 1x5-, 1x13- and 1x16-bed rooms.

Family rooms: No. **FBR:** Yes. **Rent-a-Hostel:** No.

Classroom: Yes. **Education packages:** No.

Facilities: Lounge, self-catering kitchen, laundry and drying room, dining room, showers, cycle store and garden. **Daytime access:** Sorry, no access until 5pm.

Reception open: 5pm.

Meals: Breakfast, picnic lunch and evening meal available if booked in advance.

Getting there: From M62 leave at junction for North Cave. Follow signs for Beverley (B1230). In Beverley follow signs to Minster and Friary. The Friary is at the end of Friar's Lane on the left.

Public transport: Bus: frequent from surrounding areas. (Bus Line 01482 222 222). RAIL: Beverley 0.25 miles.

NATIONALEXPRESS》 Beverley bus station 0.5 miles.

Parking: Yes.

Nearest other hostels: York 30 miles, Scarborough 36, Lincoln 50.

Price Band: **B** Opening category: **❸**

● **BOGGLE HOLE** ☆☆☆
Mill Beck, Fylingthorpe, Whitby, North Yorkshire
YO22 4UQ; bogglehole@yha.org.uk
Tel: 0870 770 5704 Fax: 0870 770 5705

The bay in front of Boggle Hole Youth Hostel was once a notorious smugglers' haunt. Nowadays all ages will love beachcombing and searching for fossils and rockpool life on its shore. There's plenty to do nearby – the fishing village of Robin Hood's Bay is just a mile to the north. Walk part of the Cleveland Way to Whitby where you can take a boat ride to catch your own dinner. Or hire a bike to cycle the old Whitby to Scarborough railway line, which is safe, traffic-free and boasts stunning views.

Location: OS 94, GR 954040.

Great for... families looking for a quiet break.

You need to know... parking is quarter of a mile away down a very steep road with access over a narrow footbridge; some rooms are in an annexe accessed via 45 steps.

Accommodation: 80 beds: 4x2-, 14x4-, 1x6-, 1x10-beds.

Family rooms: Yes. **Rent-a-Hostel:** No.

Classroom: Yes. **Education packages:** No.

Facilities: Lounge, TV, self-catering kitchen, dining room (licensed),

Robin Hood's Bay: close to YHA Boggle Hole.

showers, toilets, drying room and cycle store.

Daytime access: All public areas. **Reception open:** 1pm.

Meals: Breakfast, picnic lunch, evening meal.

Getting there: From A171, take road signed to Boggle Hole. After 2.5 miles, the car park is on right. Road to the hostel is unsuitable for vehicles. Park in National Park car park and walk.

Public transport: Whitby station now open Sundays all year.

BUS: Arriva 93 Scarborough-Whitby (passes Whitby and Scarborough stations), alight Robins Hood's Bay, 1 mile.

RAIL: Whitby 7 miles, Scarborough 15.

Parking: Yes, 0.25 miles.

Nearest other hostels: Whitby 7 miles, Scarborough 13.

Price Band: **B** Opening category: **❸**

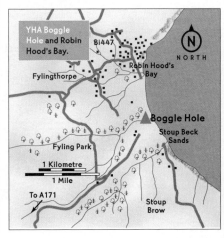

BROMPTON-ON-SWALE CAMPING BARN
campingbarns@yha.org.uk
Booking: 0870 770 8868
Arrival time: Mr & Mrs Wilkin, 01748 818326

This former byre, now a camping barn, is in the farmyard of Village Farm in the village of Brompton-on-Swale. It is an excellent stopping-off point for the Coast-to-Coast walk which is just half a mile away at Catterick Bridge. The historic town of Richmond is three miles away.
Accommodation: Sleeps 12 in three rooms with bunks, duvets and pillows.
Facilities: Washing and drying facilities, toilet, shower, electric light, heater, kitchen area with pans, crockery, cutlery, fridge, cooker and microwave, metered electricity. Dogs welcome.
Nearest pub: 100 metres. **Nearest shop:** 100 metres.
Location: OS 99, GR 216997.

Price Band: G   Opening category: ❸

CHIPPING CAMPING BARN
campingbarns@yha.org.uk
Booking: 0870 770 8868
Arrival time: Mrs Stott, 01995 61209

A former stable and hayloft opposite the farmhouse, this camping barn is just half a mile from the village of Chipping and is an ideal base for group activities. You'll find orienteering, a fell walking area and a wild boar park nearby.
Accommodation: Sleeps 15 on the first floor.
Facilities: Dining area, separate kitchen with two hot plates,

microwave, cutlery and pans, toilets, shower, metered electricity, recreation area, children's play area, BBQ, electric light, fridge, woodburner (wood available to buy). Dogs and tents by arrangement. Breakfast can be booked in advance.
Nearest pub: 0.5 miles. **Nearest shop:** 0.5 miles.
Location: OS 102, GR 616435.

Price Band: G   Opening category: ❸

● ● DENTDALE ☆☆☆
Cowgill, Dent, Sedbergh, Cumbria LA10 5RN;
dentdale@yha.org.uk
Tel: 0870 770 5790 Fax: 0870 770 5791

This recently refurbished hostel is a haven for walkers and cyclists, situated in the upper reaches of Dentdale. The valley offers riverside walks as well as higher-level hikes to Whernside or adjacent dales. The picturesque village of Dent with its cobbled streets and old world atmosphere is just five miles away. And don't worry if it rains – White Scar Cave, the Dales Countryside Museum and Wensleydale Creamery are all within 10 miles of this former shooting lodge.
Location: OS 98, GR 773850.
Great for... walkers and cyclists of all abilities.
You need to know... this hostel has good facilities for those with mobility problems.
Accommodation: 41 beds: 1x4-, 2x4–5- and 3x7–10-bed rooms. 1x4-bed wheelchair accessible room on ground floor with adjacent toilet and shower facilities.
Family rooms: Yes. **Rent-a-Hostel:** Yes.
Classroom: No. **Education packages:** Yes.

Passionate about cycling? You'll find the perfect place to stay at YHA Dentdale.

Better than ever: YHA Dentdale has been recently refurbished.

Facilities: Lounge, self-catering kitchen, dining room (can be used as classroom outside meal times), showers, drying room and cycle store. **Daytime access:** All public areas.

Reception open: Staff available before 10am and after 5pm.

Meals: Breakfast (packed breakfast also available), picnic lunch, evening meal.

Getting there: Hostel is on Dentdale road northeast of Whernside, 2 miles from junction with Hawes–Ingleton road and 5 miles east of Dent.

Public transport: BUS: Stagecoach/Woofs 564A/B to Oxenholme 20 miles from Kendal (passes Oxenholme station) Wed, Sat only. RAIL: Dent 2 miles.

Parking: Nearby, accessible by a short, level track.

Nearest other hostels: Hawes 8 miles, Ingleton 11, Stainforth 15, Kendal 20.

Price Band: B	Opening category: ❸

DOWNHAM CAMPING BARN

(NEW HEY) campingbarns@yha.org.uk
Booking: 0870 770 8868
Arrival time: Mr S Roney 01200 441667 or 07773 245212

This field barn is on the Downham Estate, near the foot of Pendle Hill and the picturesque village of Downham. Close to the Witches Way, Pendle Way, Ribble Way and the Lancashire Cycleway, walkers and cyclists will find plenty to do here.

Great for... stunning views of Pendle Hill.

You need to know... cars should be parked in the former quarry on the opposite side of the road from the barn.

Accommodation: Sleeps 12.

Facilities: Metered gas lighting, cooking rings, shower, hot water and wall-mounted heater. External BBQ. Dogs welcome.

Nearest pub: 0.5 miles. **Nearest shop:** 0.5 miles.

Location: OS 103, GR 795445.

Price Band: C	Opening category: ❸

● ● EARBY ☆☆☆
9-11 Birch Hall Lane, Earby, Lancashire BB18 6JX; earby@yha.org.uk
Tel: 0870 770 5802 Fax: 0870 770 5802

A cottage on the outskirts of Earby village with a large and attractive garden, this hostel is close to the Yorkshire Dales. Visit historic Skipton, the Forest of Bowland and Pendle Hill, home of Lancashire's witches. As well as a rich array of industrial heritage, you'll find plenty of walking and cycle routes with the Pennine Way, Pendle Way and Lancashire Cycleway all nearby.

Location: OS 103, GR 915468.

Great for... those who want busy days and peaceful nights.

You need to know... it's self-catering accommodation only.

Accommodation: 22 beds: 1x2-, 2x6- and 1x8-bed rooms.

Family rooms: Yes. **Rent-a-Hostel:** Yes.

Classroom: No. **Education packages:** No.

Facilities: Two lounges, self-catering kitchen, dining room, showers, drying room and cycle store. **Daytime access:** Conservatory (tea making facilities) lounge, drying room and toilet.

Reception open: 5pm.

Meals: Self-catering only. Evening meal arrangement with adjacent pub (10% discounts for advance bookings). Breakfasts available in the village.

Getting there: The hostel is 300 metres beyond the Red Lion pub.

Public transport: BUS: Various services from Burnley and Skipton (passing close to Colne and Skipton stations), alight Earby 0.5 miles. RAIL: Colne 5miles, Skipton 8.

NATIONALEXPRESS Barnoldswick, Station Road 3.5 miles.

Parking: At rear of hostel.

Nearest other hostels: Haworth 15 miles (via Pennine Way), Malham 13 (via Pennine Way), Slaidburn 19.

Price Band: B	Opening category: ❷

FARNDALE CAMPING BARN
campingbarns@yha.org.uk
Booking: 0870 770 8868
Arrival time: Mr & Mrs Mead, 01751 433053

Located in the farmyard of Oak House in the North York Moors National Park, this camping barn boasts excellent views over High Farndale. It is 1.5 miles from the Coast-to-Coast walk, two miles from the Lyke Wake Walk and three miles from the Cleveland Way.

Great for... getting off the beaten track.

You need to know... parking is limited to four vehicles; no dogs please.

Accommodation: Sleeps 12 on a wooden platform in barn loft.

Facilities: Electric light, wood-burning stove (one bag of logs provided per night), small cooker, toilet and shower in adjacent building. £1 charge per person per night for gas, electricity and logs. Breakfast is available but must be booked in advance.

Nearest pub: 0.75 miles. **Nearest shop:** 8 miles.

Location: OS 94, GR 659986.

Price Band: C	Opening category: ❸

● GRINTON LODGE ☆☆☆☆☆

Grinton, Richmond, North Yorkshire DL11 6HS;
grinton@yha.org.uk
Tel: 0870 770 5844 Fax: 0870 770 5845

This impressive former shooting lodge in the Yorkshire Dales National Park stands high on heather-clad grouse moors and commands spectacular views of Swaledale and Arkengarthdale. Whatever your ability, you'll find excellent walking and cycling which will lead you to splendid natural features such as Kisdon and Wainwath Falls, the Buttertubs, Aysgarth Falls and Hardraw Force in Wensleydale. The hostel is situated on the Herriott Way, close to the coast-to-coast path. The historic town of Richmond, with cobbled alleys and castles, is just 10 miles away.

Location: OS 98, GR 048975.

Great for... walkers and cyclists keen on exploring natural wonders and spectacular countryside.

You need to know... the Salthouse annexe has 12 beds and can be hired under the Rent-a-Hostel scheme.

Accommodation: 69 beds: 2x2-, 1x3-, 7x4-, 3x6- and 2x8-bed rooms.

Family rooms: Yes. **Rent-a-Hostel:** Yes.

Classroom: Yes. **Education packages:** Yes.

Facilities: Self-catering kitchen, TV lounge (licensed), drying room, laundry, games room, showers, quiet room, cycle store, bike hire and grounds. **Daytime access:** All public areas.

Reception open: Staff available before 10am and after 5pm.

Meals: Breakfast, picnic lunch, evening meal.

Getting there: The hostel is 0.75 miles up hill from Grinton, due south on the Reeth to Leyburn road.

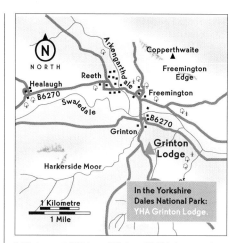

In the Yorkshire
Dales National Park:
YHA Grinton Lodge.

Public transport: BUS: Arriva 30 Richmond-Keld (infrequent with connections from Darlington station), alight Grinton 0.5 miles; also Dales Bus from West Yorkshire.

RAIL: Kirkby Stephen 24 miles, Darlington 25.

Parking: Yes.

Nearest other hostels: Keld 14 miles, Osmotherley 31, Hawes 17.

Price Band: B   **Opening category:** ❸

Wonderful scenery: you can walk to Aysgarth Falls from YHA Grinton Lodge.

●● HAWES ☆☆

**Lancaster Terrace, Hawes, North Yorkshire
DL8 3LQ; hawes@yha.org.uk
Tel: 0870 770 5854 Fax: 0870 770 5855**

This modern hostel makes a great base for families, individuals and groups looking to explore the beautiful Yorkshire Dales. Ideally situated on the edge of the traditional market town of Hawes, home of the famous Wensleydale Cheese Factory, it is within easy distance of a range of tourist attractions and activities and on key walking and cycling routes including the Pennine Way.

Location: OS 98, GR 867897.

Great for... views of Upper Wensleydale.

You need to know... the car park is a short walk away.

Accommodation: 54 beds: 1x6-, 2x7-, and 1x8-bed rooms, some en-suite in autumn/winter.

Family rooms: Yes. **Rent-a-Hostel:** No.

Classroom: No. **Education packages:** Yes.

Facilities: Lounge, games room, self-catering kitchen, showers, drying room, cycle store and laundry facilities.

Daytime access: All public areas.

Reception open: Staff available before 10am and after 5pm.

Meals: Breakfast, picnic lunch, evening meal.

Getting there: The hostel is at the top of the steep rise on the B6255 (signposted to Ingleton), just off the junction with the A684.

Public transport: BUS: Clifford Ellis shared car hire from Garsdale station (book up to 6pm previous day on 01969 667598); Dales & District 156/7 from Bedale, with connections from Northallerton station); Dales Bus from West Yorkshire. RAIL: Garsdale 6 miles.

Parking: Nearby.

Nearest other hostels: Dentdale 8 miles, Keld 9.

Price Band: B **Opening category:** ❸

HOSTEL MANAGERS CHOOSE...

THE BEST SPOTS FOR PEACE AND QUIET

Pennine Way bridleway YHA Dentdale: "Walk, cycle or horseride through Derbyshire to the South Pennines enjoying the panoramic views as you go."

The Tanhill Inn YHA Keld: "Stop and relax in this 17th century inn which is the highest pub in England."

Mount Grace Priory YHA Osmotherley: "A preserved 14th century monastery in a tranquil setting shows visitors what life was like for the Carthusian monks."

Dalby YHA Sinnington: "See for yourself why Dalby is known as the great Yorkshire forest."

Sunset views YHA Whitby: "When the sun sets in the east over the sea, it's simply a sight not to be missed."

Haworth heather YHA Haworth: "To walk in a sea of purple, visit in late July or August when the heather is in full flower."

●● HAWORTH ☆☆☆

**Longlands Drive, Lees Lane, Haworth, Keighley, West Yorkshire BD22 8RT; haworth@yha.org.uk
Tel: 0870 770 5858 Fax: 0870 770 5859**

Revisit the tempestuous world of the Brontë classics, Wuthering Heights and Jane Eyre. This large Victorian mansion is built in a grand style and overlooks the village of Haworth. Brontë fans will enjoy the museum and leisurely walks to spots that inspired the famous books. There's also plenty of entertainment for everyone with the Keighley & Worth Valley stream railway, National Museum of Photography, Film and Television & Eureka. There is also swimming, bowling and ice-skating within a five-mile radius.

Location: OS 104, GR 038378.

Great for... families; combining attractions with a variety of walks.

Discover the home of the Brontë sisters near YHA Haworth.

Accommodation: 92 beds: 1x2-, 1x3-, mostly 4-8- plus 1x10 and 1x12-bed rooms.

Family rooms: Yes. **Rent-a-Hostel:** No.

Classroom: Yes. **Education packages:** No.

Facilities: Lounge, games room, self-catering kitchen (licensed), showers, toilets, drying room, cycle store, laundry facilities and garden. **Daytime access:** All public areas.

Reception open: All day.

Meals: Breakfast, picnic lunch, evening meal.

Getting there: From Haworth centre, take B6142 towards Keighley for 0.75 miles. From Keighley, travel 3 miles south on A629 then take A6033 and B6142. Longlands Drive is almost opposite the Brontë Hotel.

Public transport: BUS: Keighley & District 663-5, 720 from Keighley (passes close to Keighley station).
RAIL: Keighley 4 miles, Haworth (Worth Valley Rly) 0.5.
NATIONALEXPRESS Keighley bus station 3.25 miles.
Parking: Yes.
Nearest other hostels: Mankinholes 12 miles (18 via Pennine Way), Earby 18 (15 via Pennine Way), York 45.

Price Band: [B]   Opening category: ❸

● HELMSLEY ☆☆☆
**Carlton Lane, Helmsley, York, North Yorkshire
YO62 5HB; helmsley@yha.org.uk
Tel: 0870 770 5860 Fax: 0870 770 5860**

This newly refurbished hostel is in one of the prettiest country towns in North Yorkshire. It's a cosy stone-walled building with comfortable facilities on the edge of the National Park just a few minutes' walk from the shops and pubs of Helmsley. A favourite choice for groups, families and outdoor clubs, it's close to a host of attractions including Rievaulx Abbey and is at the start of the Cleveland Way.
Location: OS 100, GR 616840.
Great for... those who want top attractions on their doorstep.
Accommodation: 35 beds: mainly 4- and 6-bed rooms. Plus 1x3-bed en-suite room with disabled facilities.

Family rooms: Yes. **Rent-a-Hostel:** Yes.
Classroom: No. **Education packages:** Yes.
Facilities: Lounge, dining room, self-catering kitchen, showers, conservatory, patio area and grounds. **Daytime access:** Public areas via numbered lock.
Reception open: 5pm.
Meals: Breakfast, picnic lunch, evening meal.
Getting there: The hostel is a few minutes from Helmsley market square at junction of Carlton Road and Carlton Lane (just off A170).
Public transport: BUS: Stevensons 31X from York station; Scarborough & District 128 from Scarborough (passes close to Scarborough station). RAIL: Thirsk 15 miles, Malton 16, York 24.
Parking: At hostel.
Nearest other hostels: Osmotherley 15 miles (20 by Cleveland Way), Lockton 19, York 23.

Price Band: [B]   Opening category: ❸

● KELD ☆☆☆
**Upper Swaledale, Richmond, North Yorkshire
DL11 6LL; keld@yha.org.uk
Tel: 0870 770 5888 Fax: 0870 770 5889**

Amid hills at the head of Swaledale sits the small village of Keld, its cottages clustered around a tiny square. The hostel, formerly a

● INGLETON ☆☆☆☆
**Sammy Lane, Ingleton, Carnforth, Lancashire
LA6 3EG; ingleton@yha.org.uk
Tel: 0870 770 5880 Fax: 0870 770 5881**

This renovated Victorian house is in the village of Ingleton and offers excellent accommodation for individuals and families alike. Within easy access of the M6, it's ideally located for exploring the Dales and just a short distance from the Lakes. Walks range from the gentle Waterfalls Walk to Thornton Force to the demanding Three Peaks Walk. There's also excellent limestone climbing for the adventurous. Children will love White Scar Cave, the largest show cave in Europe, and the open-air swimming pool and park next door.
Location: OS 98, GR 695733.
Great for... a family holiday with easy access.
Accommodation: 66 beds: 2x2-, the rest 4- and 6-bed rooms.
Family rooms: Yes. **Rent-a-Hostel:** No.
Classroom: No. **Education packages:** No.
Facilities: Dining room, lounge (licensed), showers, toilets, drying room, self-catering kitchen, cycle store and grounds.
Daytime access: All public areas.
Reception open: Staff available before 10am and after 5pm.
Meals: Breakfast, picnic lunch, evening meal.
Getting there: From High Street, take the lane between Barclays Bank and the newsagents down to the park.
Public transport: BUS: Stagecoach in Lancashire 80/A from

Enjoy a stroll to Ingleton Waterfalls, near YHA Ingleton.

Lancaster (passes close to Lancaster & Bentham station).
RAIL: Bentham 3 miles, Clapham 4.
Parking: At hostel.
Nearest other hostels: Stainforth 10 miles, Dentdale 11, Kendal 17.

Price Band: [B]   Opening category: ❸

The typical patchwork fields and dry stone walls of the Yorkshire countryside that surrounds YHA Keld.

shooting lodge, stands overlooking the village and is a welcome resting place for walkers and cyclists at the crossover point of the Pennine Way and Coast-to-Coast path. A variety of walking is on offer, ranging from gentle riverside rambles to hikes over the open fells. Birdwatchers should keep a keen eye out for a glimpse of the rare black grouse.

Location: OS 91, GR 892009.
Great for... keen walkers of all abilities.
You need to know... there are no shops or pubs in the village.
Accommodation: 38 beds: 1x2-, 5x4-, 1x6- and 1x10-bed rooms.
Family rooms: Yes. **Rent-a-Hostel:** Yes.
Classroom: No. **Education packages:** Yes.
Facilities: Lounge, self-catering kitchen, licensed dining room,

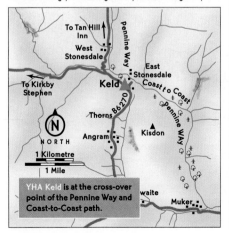

showers, drying room and cycle store. **Daytime access:** Public areas via numbered lock.
Reception open: 5pm.
Meals: Breakfast, picnic lunch, evening meal.
Getting there: The village of Keld lies just off the B6270 Reeth to Kirkby Stephen road. Hostel sits on roadside southwest of village.
Public transport: BUS: Arriva 30 from Richmond (infrequent with connections from Darlington station); Dales Bus from West Yorkshire. RAIL: Kirkby Stephen 11 miles.
Parking: Roadside only.
Nearest other hostels: Hawes 9 miles, Kirkby Stephen 11, Grinton 13, Baldersdale 15.

Price Band: B	Opening category: ❷

●● KETTLEWELL ☆☆☆
Kettlewell, Skipton, North Yorkshire BD23 5QU;
kettlewell@yha.org.uk
Tel: 0870 770 5896 Fax: 0870 770 5897

For a relaxing holiday in the heart of the Dales, choose Kettlewell in the upper reaches of Wharfedale. Local walks take in some of the finest scenery in Yorkshire and are suitable for all abilities and age ranges. There are many local attractions nearby and children and adults alike will enjoy a ride on the Embsay Steam Railway and a visit to Bolton Abbey. If you're planning a visit in August, don't miss the bizarre Scarecrow Festival held in the village.
Location: OS 98, GR 970724.
Great for... an attraction-packed family holiday.
You need to know... parking is limited.
Accommodation: 43 beds: 2x2-, 1x4-, 1x5- and 5x6-bed rooms.
Family rooms: Yes. **Rent-a-Hostel:** No.
Classroom: No. **Education packages:** Yes.

Facilities: Dining room, TV, drying room, lounge (licensed), showers, self-catering kitchen, cycle store, lockers and grounds.
Daytime access: All public areas.
Reception open: Staff available before 10am and after 5pm.
Meals: Breakfast, picnic lunch, evening meal.
Getting there: From Skipton, take B6160 towards Grassington. Follow road for 15 miles to Kettlewell. Go over bridge and turn first right in front of the Bluebell Inn. At the village shop, follow the hostel sign to the left.
Public transport: BUS: Pride of the Dales 72 from Skipton station. RAIL: Skipton 16 miles.
Parking: Limited. Additional parking in village.
Nearest other hostels: Malham 14 miles (10 by path), Hawes 15.

Price Band: ▨   Opening category: ❸

KILDALE CAMPING BARN
campingbarns@yha.org.uk
Booking: 0870 770 8868
Arrival time: Mr & Mrs Cook, 01642 722135

Now a camping barn, this former barn and wheelhouse is a listed building in the farmyard at Park Farm in the North York Moors National Park. The Cleveland Way is on the doorstep as are many good local walks.
Great for... exploring Captain Cook country and the Esk Valley railway line.
You need to know... the toilets are in an adjacent building.
Accommodation: Sleeps 18 in the first floor loft.
Facilities: Electric light, heat and cooking facilities (all on meter), toilets, showers, crockery, cutlery, drying facilities, hot water and fridge. Dogs welcome. Ample parking.
Nearest pub: 2 miles. **Nearest shop:** 1 mile.
Location: OS 94, GR 602085.

Price Band: ▨   Opening category: ❸

● KIRKBY STEPHEN ☆☆☆
Market St, Kirkby Stephen, Cumbria CA17 4QQ;
kirkbystephen@yha.org.uk
Tel: 0870 770 5904 Fax: 0870 770 5905

Kirkby Stephen is a converted methodist chapel with the original pews now in the dining room. Situated on Kirkby Stephen's main street in the upper Eden Valley and on Wainwright's Coast-to-Coast path, it offers easy access to Lady Anne's Walk, the peaceful Eden Valley and the Settle to Carlisle railway.
Location: OS 91, GR 774085.
Great for... walkers keen to explore the area.
Accommodation: 40 beds, 1x2-, 3x4-, 3x6- 1x8-bed rooms.
Family rooms: Yes. **Rent-a-Hostel:** Yes.
Classroom: No. **Education packages:** No.
Facilities: Lounge, self-catering kitchen, dining room, showers, drying room, luggage store and laundry facilities.
Daytime access: Bedrooms locked till 5pm; front door open from 12 noon.
Reception open: Staff available before 10am and after 5pm.

Wainwright's Coast-to-Coast path near YHA Kirkby Stephen.

Meals: Breakfast, picnic lunch, evening meal.
Getting there: From M6 J38 take second exit on left from roundabout, signed Kirkby Stephen. From A66 Penrith direction, follow signs for Brough then turn right for A685 (Kendal direction). From Coast-to-Coast path, pass Spar shop and traffic lights. The hostel is on the west side of the main street.
Public transport: BUS: Various connections from Kirkby Stephen station; also Classic Coaches 352 Newcastle-upon-Tyne-Blackpool. RAIL: Kirkby Stephen 1.5 miles.
Parking: Roadside or free car park 100 metres away.
Nearest other hostels: Keld 11 miles, Hawes 15, Dufton 16.

Price Band: ▨   Opening category: ❷

LEYBURN CAMPING BARN
campingbarns@yha.org.uk
Booking: 0870 770 8868
Arrival time: Mr & Mrs Iveson, 01969 622204

This camping barn at Craken House Farm has featured in the TV series All Creatures Great and Small, and the BBC's Countryfile. Only a mile from the market town of Leyburn, it boasts magnificent views over Wensleydale and the Yorkshire Dales and there are plenty of interesting river and fell walks all around.
Great for... visiting Richmond, Middleham, Hawes and the Dales.
You need to know... bring a pillow case, sleeping bag and £1 coins for the meter. **Accommodation:** Sleeps 12 in partitioned bunk beds.
Facilities: Electric light, heaters, fridge and shower (all metered), wash basins, toilets, gas cooker, cutlery, crockery, pans, multi-fuel stove, TV outlet and extra plugs for own equipment. Dogs by arrangement.
Nearest pub: 1 mile. **Nearest shop:** 1 mile.
Location: OS 99, GR 121895.

Price Band: ▨   Opening category: ❷

LOVESOME HILL CAMPING BARN
campingbarns@yha.org.uk
Booking: 0870 770 8868
Arrival time: Mr & Mrs Pearson, 01609 772311
(fax: 01609 774715)

This former corn store, now a camping barn, is in the farmyard at Lovesome Hill Farm. Centrally placed for exploring the Yorkshire Dales and the North York Moors National Parks, the barn is just 200 metres from the Coast-to-Coast walk. The bustling market town of Northallerton is four miles away. From there, it is north along the A167 on the right-hand side.

Great for... experiencing life on a working farm and exploring the Dales and Moors.

You need to know... small groups can book breakfast by arrangement; you can hire sheets and duvets.

Accommodation: Sleeps 10 in bunks in two rooms on the first floor.

Facilities: Electric light, two heaters, cooker, shower, toilets and metered electricity. Food available at barn (order in advance).

Nearest pub: 2.5 miles. **Nearest shop:** 2.5 miles.

Location: OS 99, GR 361998.

Price Band: G   Opening category: ❸

Purpose-built: YHA Malham was designed by the talented John Dower.

LOW ROW CAMPING BARN
campingbarns@yha.org.uk
Booking: 0870 770 8868
Arrival time: Mrs Clarkson, 01748 884601

This bunk barn is on Low Whita Farm, an outstanding location in Swaledale at the heart of the Yorkshire Dales National Park. It is a mile from the Coast-to-Coast walk and there are many routes close by, including the Corpse Road running between Keld and Reeth.

Great for... exploring the Yorkshire Dales.

You need to know... there is a car park next to the barn.

Accommodation: Sleeps 15 in bunk beds on the first floor; mattresses are provided.

Facilities: Dining area, fully equipped kitchen with electric cooker, cutlery, crockery and pans, electric light, oil central heating and hot water on a meter, showers, toilets, washbasin and drying room. Dogs welcome.

Nearest pub: 1.25 miles. **Nearest shop:** 2 miles.

Location: OS 92, GR 003983.

Price Band: G   Opening category: ❸

●● MALHAM ☆☆☆
Malham, Skipton, North Yorkshire BD23 4DE;
malham@yha.org.uk
Tel: 0870 770 5946 Fax: 0870 770 5947

Designed by John Dower, one of the most influential figures in the initiative to establish National Parks in Britain, this is a purpose-built Youth Hostel. Walking and cycling are the main attractions and the Pennine Way and Yorkshire Dales Cycleway both pass through this village at the heart of the Yorkshire Dales National Park. The hostel has great facilities for educational groups as well as youngsters, with a safe, secure garden, a range of toddler's equipment for hire and a child-friendly menu. The famous Limestone pavements and Malham Tarn are within walking distance.

Location: OS 98, GR 901629.

Great for... walkers and cyclists.

Accommodation: 82 beds: 1x2-, 4x4-, 1x5- and 9x6–8-bed rooms.

Family rooms: Yes. **Rent-a-Hostel:** Yes.

Classroom: Yes. **Education packages:** No.

Facilities: Lounge, self-catering kitchen (licensed), showers, lockers, laundry, cycle store, shop and grounds.

Daytime access: All public areas.

Reception open: Staff available before 10am and after 5pm.

Meals: Breakfast, lunch, evening meal.

Getting there: The hostel is situated in the centre of the village, next to the Listers Arms pub.

Public transport: BUS: Various operators from Skipton (pass close to Skipton station); Dales Bus from West Yorkshire.
RAIL: Skipton 13 miles.

Parking: Yes. Take first left after YHA Malham sign to the car park.

Nearest other hostels: Stainforth 8 miles, Kettlewell 10 (by path).

Price Band: B   Opening category: ❸

● LOCKTON ☆

Old School, Lockton, Pickering, North Yorkshire YO18 7PY
Tel: 0870 770 5938 Fax: 0870 770 5939

An old village school in a rural hamlet, Lockton offers basic facilities for those who want to get away from it all. A few miles away is Levisham Station on the North York Moors Steam Railway, allowing linear walks over uncrowded moorland terrain. We are on the edge of North Yorks Moors. Dalby Forest is great for walking and cycling. If the countryside looks familiar then you'll remember that this is where the popular TV series Heartbeat is filmed.

Location: OS 94, GR 844900.
Great for... a secluded break for keen walkers and cyclists.
You need to know... this hostel has been refurbished and is now YHA's first Eco-hostel.
Accommodation: 21 beds: 1x4-, 1x8- and 1x6- and 1x3-bed rooms.

Family rooms: Yes. **Rent-a-Hostel:** Yes.
Classroom: No. **Education packages:** No.
Facilities: Self-catering kitchen, lounge, showers, drying room, cycle store and car park. **Daytime access:** All public areas.
Reception open: Staff available before 10am and after 5pm.
Meals: Self-catering only.
Getting there: From the A169, turn west at the sign for Lockton and Levisham.
Public transport: BUS: Yorkshire Coastliner 840 Whitby-Malton (passes close to Whitby and Malton Station).
RAIL: Malton 14 miles, Levisham (North York Moors Rly and connecting with line at Grosmont) 2.
Parking: Yes, at hostel.
Nearest other hostels: Boggle Hole 15 miles, Whitby 15, Scarborough 19 (12 by path).

Price Band: ⑤	Opening category: ❸

Famous: TV series Heartbeat is filmed near YHA Lockton.

●● OSMOTHERLEY ☆☆

Cote Ghyll, Osmotherley, Northallerton, North Yorkshire DL6 3AH; osmotherley@yha.org.uk
Tel: 0870 770 5982 Fax: 0870 770 5983

You'll find this hostel, formerly a mill, in a secluded valley on the edge of the North York Moors National Park. It's popular with walkers but also those wishing to tour the coast and the Yorkshire Moors and Dales, which are all within an hour's drive. There are plenty of attractions to suit all tastes nearby, such as Mount Grace Priory, Rievaulx Abbey, World of James Herriot and Lightwater Valley Theme Park.

Location: OS 100, GR 461981.
Great for... families and groups wanting to walk and tour the area.
Accommodation: 72 beds: 1x2-, 2x3-, 1x4- and 5x6-bed rooms, some en-suite.
Family rooms: Yes. **Rent-a-Hostel:** No.
Classroom: Yes. **Education packages:** No.
Facilities: Lounge/reception, TV room, self-catering kitchen, showers, drying room, dining/games room, cycle store, laundry, grounds and residential licence.
Daytime access: All public areas.

On the edge of the North York Moors National Park: YHA Osmotherley.

Reception open: 1pm.
Meals: Breakfast, picnic lunch, evening meal.
Getting there: Go north out of the village and after quarter of a mile turn right down a private drive past a caravan/camping site.
Public transport: BUS: Abbott 80/9 Northallerton station-Stokesley, alight Osmotherley 0.5 miles.
RAIL: Northallerton 8 miles.
Parking: Yes.
Nearest other hostels: Helmsley 15 miles, Grinton 31.

Price Band: B	Opening category: ❸

Scarborough makes an ideal destination for family fun.

RICHMOND CAMPING BARN
campingbarns@yha.org.uk
Booking: 0870 770 8868
Arrival time: Mr & Mrs Atkinson, 01748 822940

These three former byres at East Applegarth Farm have been converted into a camping barn with magnificent views across Swaledale. It is a great base for exploring the Yorkshire Dales National Park with many scenic local trails and the Coast-to-Coast walk passing close by.
Accommodation: Sleeps 12 in two rooms, mattresses provided.
Facilities: Electric light, heat and cooking facilities on meter, cutlery, crockery, pans. Dogs welcome.
Nearest pub: 3 miles.
Nearest shop: 3 miles.
Location: OS 92, GR 135017.

Price Band: C	Opening category: ❸

●● SCARBOROUGH ☆☆☆
Burniston Road, Scarborough, North Yorkshire YO13 0DA; scarborough@yha.org.uk
Tel: 0870 770 6022 Fax: 0870 770 6023

This former water mill – built around 1600 – provides the perfect antidote to a day spent exploring Scarborough's many attractions such as the Sea Life Centre, Kinderland and Atlantis Water Park. Only two miles from the hectic town centre, its wooded riverside location attracts herons, foxes, kingfishers, deer and, occasionally, otters. This hostel has good facilities for children and is just 15 minutes' walk from the sea, making it perfect for a traditional seaside holiday.
Location: OS 101, GR 026907.
Great for... summer fun for seaside-loving families.
Accommodation: 48 beds: 3x4- and 6x6-bed rooms.
Family rooms: Yes. **Rent-a-Hostel:** Yes.
Classroom: No. **Education packages:** No.
Facilities: Lounge, self-catering kitchen, showers, drying room,

laundry and cycle store.

Daytime access: Public access via numbered lock.

Reception open: 5pm.

Meals: Breakfast, picnic lunch, evening meal.

Getting there: From Scarborough, follow signs to North Bay attractions, then the A165 to Whitby. The hostel is 2 miles north of the town centre. There is a very sharp turn immediately after the bridge – you are advised to drive past and turn around in the lay-by (see map on page 173).

Public transport: BUS: Frequent from surrounding areas. RAIL: Scarborough 2 miles.

NATIONAL EXPRESS Westwood coach park 2 miles.

Parking: Yes.

Nearest other hostels: Boggle Hole 13 miles, Lockton 19 (12 by path), Whitby 20.

Price Band: B **Opening category:** ❸

SINNINGTON CAMPING BARN

campingbarns@yha.org.uk

Booking: 0870 770 8868

Arrival time: Mrs Scaling, 01751 473792

This former granary is now a camping barn on the family-run Cliff Farm. Enjoy local walks, visit the steam railway or take a day trip to

---

● MANKINHOLES ☆☆☆☆

Mankinholes, Todmorden, Lancashire OL14 6HR; mankinholes@yha.org.uk

Tel: 0870 770 5952 Fax: 0870 770 5952

Once the local manor house dating back to the 17th century, this refurbished hostel on the edge of moorland is a charming place to stay. The Pennine Way and Calderdale Way are close by and you'll find an abundance of other footpaths, bridleways and pack-horse trails to explore. Despite the quiet, rural location, it's within easy reach of other attractions should the weather prove inclement. Eureka!, the interactive childrens' museum in Halifax, Haworth, The Keighley & Worth Valley Steam Railway and Hollingworth Lake & Activity Centre are all nearby.

Location: OS 103, GR 960235.

Great for... walkers, individuals, families and small groups.

You need to know... it's self-catering accommodation only.

Accommodation: 32 beds: 2x2-, 4x4- and 2x6-bed rooms.

Family rooms: Yes. **Rent-a-Hostel:** Yes.

Classroom: No. **Education packages:** No.

Facilities: Self-catering kitchen, dining room (licensed), lounge, hostel shop, showers, cycle store, laundry facilities and grounds.

Daytime access: All public areas.

Reception open: Staff available before 10am and after 5pm.

Meals: Self-catering only.

Getting there: Follow road to Lumbutts. The hostel is a quarter of a mile east of the Top Brink public house.

Public transport: BUS: First T6/8 from Todmorden (passes close to Todmorden station). RAIL: Todmorden 2 miles.

Parking: Yes.

Nearest other hostels: Haworth 12 miles (18 by Pennine Way), Crowden 24 (by Pennine Way), Earby 25 (by Pennine Way).

Price Band: B **Opening category:** ❷

Charming: YHA Mankinholes is a refurbished 17th century manor house.

Flamingoland, the North York Moors or the coast.

Great for... access to the North York Moors and Ryedale.

You need to know... the shower, washing and toilet facilities are in an adjacent building and shared with a small campsite.

Accommodation: Sleeps 12, mattresses provided.

Facilities: Electric light, heat, shower and cooking facilities on meter, toilets, washing facilities, cutlery, crockery, pans and fridge. Dogs welcome by prior arrangement.

Nearest pub: 1 mile. **Nearest shop:** 2.5 miles.

Location: OS 94, GR 752849.

Price Band: C	Opening category: ❸

● SLAIDBURN ☆☆☆

King's House, Slaidburn, Clitheroe, Lancashire BB7 3ER; slaidburn@yha.org.uk

Tel: 0870 770 6034 For bookings more than 7 days ahead: 0870 770 5802.

Those of you who love the outdoors life will adore Slaidburn's location. In the middle of the Forest of Bowland, there's an excellent network of quiet roads and cycle paths while walking routes will take you across moorland and alongside the river and reservoir. For peace and solitude, head to the relatively undiscovered fells and valleys of the nearby Area of Outstanding Natural Beauty. The hostel is a comfortable retreat – a 17th century village inn, it's a listed building which has recently been refurbished to a high standard.

Location: OS 103, GR 711523.

Great for... adults happy to spend a week walking or cycling.

You need to know... Slaidburn offers self-catering accommodation.

Accommodation: 30 beds: 1x3-, 4x4-, 1x5- and 1x6-bed rooms.

Family rooms: Yes. **Rent-a-Hostel:** Yes.

Classroom: No. **Education packages:** No.

Facilities: Lounge, dining room, self-catering kitchen, showers and cycle store. Limited shop. Credit cards accepted for advance bookings only.

Daytime access: Kitchen, shower, toilet, payphone and drying room.

Reception open: 5pm.

Meals: Self-catering only.

Getting there: From Clitheroe, take B6478 Settle road. The hostel is in the centre of the village opposite the pub.

Public transport: BUS: Bowland Transit B10, B15 from Clitheroe station. RAIL: Clitheroe 8 miles.

Parking: Yes.

Nearest other hostels: Ingleton 15 miles, Stainforth 15, Earby 19, Arnside 32.

Price Band: B	Opening category: ❷

Sinnington Camping Barn offers easy access to great scenery like this in the North York Moors.

A comfortable retreat: YHA Slaidburn.

●● STAINFORTH ☆☆☆

Stainforth, Settle, North Yorkshire BD24 9PA; stainforth@yha.org.uk

Tel: 0870 770 6046 Fax: 0870 770 6047

This refurbished Georgian country house nestles in wooded grounds on the edge of the Yorkshire Dales National Park, just minutes from the village. It makes an ideal base for families and groups with easy walks to waterfalls, caves and limestone scenery and within easy reach of the River Ribble and Three Peaks walk. The Falconry and Conservation Centre and the market town of Settle are close by, while Skipton and its castle are 20 minutes away.

Location: OS 98, GR 821668.

Great for... families used to the outdoors life.

You need to know... this hostel has good facilities for those with mobility problems.

Accommodation: 47 beds: 1x2-, 2x4-, 2x6-, 1x7-, 1x8- and 1x10-bed rooms, some en-suite.

Family rooms: Yes. **Rent-a-Hostel:** No.

Classroom: Yes. **Education packages:** No.

Facilities: Lounge, dining room, self-catering kitchen (licensed), showers, drying room and cycle store.

Daytime access: All public areas.

Reception open: 3pm. **Meals:** Breakfast, picnic lunch, evening meal.

Getting there: The hostel is 2 miles north of Settle in the Yorkshire Dales National Park, a quarter of a mile south of the village on main B6479 Settle–Horton-in-Ribblesdale road. It is 3.5 miles south of the Pennine Way at Dale Head and 4 miles south of the Pennine Way at Horton.

Public transport: BUS: Kirkby Lonsdale Coaches Settle-Horton (passes Settle station). RAIL: Settle 2.5 miles, Giggleswick 3.

Parking: Yes.

Nearest other hostels: Malham 8 miles, Ingleton 10, Kettlewell 15.

Price Band: ⬛	Opening category: ❸

TRAWDEN CAMPING BARN (MIDDLE BEARDSHAW FARM)

campingbarns@yha.org.uk

Booking: 0870 770 8868

Arrival time: Mr & Mrs Mann, 01282 865257

This recently restored camping barn is in an idyllic setting surrounded by meadows, one mile from Trawden village. There are plenty of opportunities for walking in the Forest of Trawden and on the expansive South Pennine moors. Skipton and its castle are 20 minutes away, as is Haworth House.

Great for... walking on Pendle Hill and Boulsworth.

You need to know... you must make sure you come to Middle Beardshaw Farm; there is also a Lower Beardshaw Farm and a Higher!

Accommodation: Sleeps 15 to 20 in a sleeping gallery; camp-beds are provided.

Facilities: Sitting area with wood-burning stove (fuel can be purchased), bathrooms with hot showers, fully equipped kitchen with gas rings and microwave, toilets, electric light, heater, fridge, metered electricity. Pool room with darts and table tennis. Meals can be enjoyed in attached conservatory in summer.

Nearest pub: 1 mile. **Nearest shop:** 1 mile.

Location: OS 103, GR 903381.

Price Band: ⬛	Opening category: ❸

WESTERDALE CAMPING BARN

campingbarns@yha.org.uk

Booking: 0870 770 8868

Arrival time: Mr & Mrs Alderson, 01287 660259

This former byre, now a camping barn, has lovely views of Westerdale Moor and Castleton Rigg. In the farmyard at Broadgate Farm in the North York Moors National Park, it is within three miles of the Coast-to-Coast and Lyke Wake walks. There are also

On the edge of the Yorkshire Dales National Park: YHA Stainforth.

Enthusiastic walkers will find plenty to choose from at Westerdale Camping Barn.

numerous local trails including the Rosedale Circuit.

Great for... enthusiastic walkers.

Accommodation: Sleeps 12 in bunkbeds in two rooms on the ground floor.

Facilities: Electric lights, heaters, hot water, shower and gas cooker. Dogs welcome.

Nearest pub: 3 miles. **Nearest shop:** 3 miles.

Location: OS 94, GR 671049.

Price Band: G   Opening category: ❸

●● WHITBY ☆

East Cliff, Whitby, North Yorkshire YO22 4JT; whitby@yha.org.uk

Tel: 0870 770 6088 Fax: 0870 770 6089

Perched dramatically on the headland, YHA Whitby has panoramic views of the harbour, coastline and imposing abbey ruins. Watch the brightly coloured fishing boats bringing in their catch or spend a day on the sandy beaches within walking distance of the hostel. Explore the nearby moors and dales and cycle along the disused railway line to Robin Hood's Bay. All in all, it's the perfect seaside holiday for outdoor-minded families.

Location: OS 94, GR 902111.

Great for... active families seeking a seaside break.

You need to know... the car park is half a mile away.

Accommodation: 58 beds: 1x2-, 3x4-, 2x6-, 1x10- and 1x22-bed rooms.

Family rooms: Yes. **Rent-a-Hostel:** No.

Classroom: No. **Education packages:** Yes.

Facilities: Lounge, self-catering kitchen, dining room, showers,

drying room, lockers and garden.

Daytime access: public areas via numbered lock.

Reception open: 5pm.

Meals: Breakfast, picnic lunch, evening meal.

Getting there: By road, follow signs to Abbey up Green Lane, turn left and continue beyond the Abbey to the car park. The hostel is nearby. On foot, climb the 199 steps from town.

Public transport: Whitby station now open Sundays all year. BUS: frequent from surrounding areas. RAIL: Whitby 0.5 miles. **NATIONALEXPRESS** Langborne Road 0.5 miles.

Parking: Drop-off point near to hostel – park in Abbey car park (0.5 miles away and free 7pm–9am).

Nearest other hostels: Boggle Hole 7 miles, Scarborough 20.

Price Band: B   Opening category: ❸

●● YORK ☆☆☆

Water End, Clifton, York, North Yorkshire YO30 6LP; york@yha.org.uk

Tel: 0870 770 6102 Fax: 0870 770 6103

The ancient and beautiful walled city of York has attracted visitors for centuries, some more welcome than others. The Romans, Anglo-Saxons, Vikings and Normans have all left their mark on the city, giving tourists of the 21st century plenty to see and do. This hostel, an attractive Victorian building, allows easy access to the city centre via a soothing stroll along the River Ouse. For extra comfort, premium rooms are available.

Location: OS 105, GR 589528.

Great for... a friendly and efficient base to explore York.

Perfect location: YHA York is a riverside stroll from the city centre.

You need to know... with 150 beds, this hostel can get very busy; breakfast is included in the price.

Accommodation: 150 beds: mostly 4-bed rooms, plus 4x6- and 3x8-bed options. Premium 1-, 2-, 3- and 4-bed rooms.

Family rooms: Yes. **Rent-a-Hostel:** No.

Classroom: Yes. **Education packages:** Yes.

Facilities: Restaurant with full menu and resident's bar, lounge, TV, games room, self-catering kitchen, showers, cycle and luggage stores, laundry facilities, internet access, garden and patio. Conference facilities and night security. **Daytime access:** All public areas (except bedrooms between 10am and 1pm).

Reception open: 7am to 11pm (access 24hrs, only pre-booked arrivals can check in after 11pm).

Meals: Breakfast, picnic lunch, evening meal.

Getting there: From the minster, take A19 to Clifton Green, turning left at Old Grey Mare pub into Water End. Hostel is 300 metres on the right. From A1237 ring road, take A19 towards the city, turning right into Water End at the third set of traffic lights. From the station, turn left and approach the river, turn left and walk up the river bank for half a mile until you reach Water End bridge (see map on page 173).

Public transport: BUS: frequent from surrounding areas.
RAIL: York 1 mile.

NATIONALEXPRESS» McMillans Bar, York station 1 mile.

Parking: Yes, cars and coaches.

Nearest other hostels: Helmsley 24 miles, Beverley Friary 30, Haworth 45, Scarborough 45.

Price Band: **D**   Opening category: **❶**

HOSTEL MANAGERS CHOOSE...

THE BEST FAMILY DAYS OUT IN THE REGION

The Deep YHA Beverly Friary: "Visit the world's only submarium where you will have the chance to ride in the unique underwater lift and experience Europe's deepest viewing tunnel!"

Jurassic Coast YHA Boggle Hole: "This coast is amazing. Step out of the hostel gate on to beach and you can begin looking for fossils immediately."

Wensleydale YHA Howe: "Visit the world famous cheese factory in the heart of the Yorkshire Dales and taste Wallace & Gromit's favourite snack."

Keighley & Worth Valley steam railway YHA Haworth: "Take a trip on a steam train on this delightfully restored five-mile branch line which runs from Keighley through Worth Valley and Haworth and finally to Oxenhope."

Forbidden Corner YHA Leyburn: "Spend a day exploring this labyrinth of tunnels, chambers, follies and surprises created in a four-acre garden in the heart of the Yorkshire Dales."

North Yorkshire Railways YHA Lockton: "A great experience for all the family. These 18 miles of preserved steam railway run through beautiful scenery."

Scarborough Sealife & Marine Sanctuary YHA Scarborough:
"A fun family day out. Otters, turtles and seahorses are just a few of the fascinating creatures you'll see here."

A region where lovers of the outdoors are spoilt for choice while visitors looking for a city break can only be impressed by the excitement on offer.

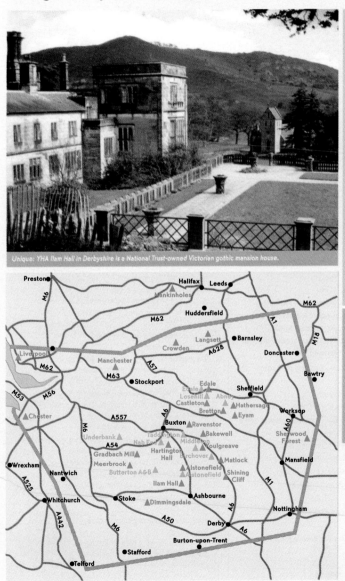

Unique: YHA Ilam Hall in Derbyshire is a National Trust-owned Victorian gothic mansion house.

Cyclists exploring Manifold Valley near YHA Alstonefield.

ABNEY CAMPING BARN

campingbarns@yha.org.uk
Booking: 0870 770 8868
Arrival time: Mr & Mrs Chadwick, 01433 650481

You'll find this camping barn in the small village of Abney, 1,000 feet up on the gritstone hills at the head of Abney Clough. The moors hereabouts are noted for their fine viewpoints.

Accommodation: Sleeps 8 in two separate areas.
Facilities: Electric light, heaters, cooking area with two rings, fridge and microwave, BBQ, outdoor seating and adjacent toilet. Electricity on a meter.
Nearest pub: 2.5 miles. **Nearest shop:** 3 miles.
Location: OS 110, GR 198798.

Price Band: G	Opening category: ❸

●● ALSTONEFIELD ☆☆☆

Gypsy Lane, Alstonefield, nr Ashbourne,
Derbyshire DE6 2FZ; reservations@yha.org.uk
Tel: 0870 770 5670 Fax: 0870 770 5670
Bookings more than 7 days ahead: 0870 770 8868

Overlooking Dovedale, this is a comfortable base from which to explore the Manifold Valley and Beresford and Wolfscote Dales on foot or by bike, with Chatsworth House and Alton Towers both nearby. The hostel consists of two barns, each with its own lounge, dining area and self-catering kitchen. All five bedrooms are en-suite and there is a large patio and garden area.

Location: OS 119, GR 133556.
Great for... a modern base with a range of activities nearby.
You need to know... it's self-catering accommodation only.
Accommodation: 20 beds: 5x4-bed rooms, all en-suite.
Family rooms: Yes. **Rent-a-Hostel:** Yes.
Classroom: No. **Education packages:** No.
Facilities: Lounge, dining room, self-catering kitchen, drying room, showers, bike shed, bedrooms and grounds.
Daytime access: All public areas.
Reception open: Staff available before 10am and after 5pm.
Meals: Self-catering only.
Getting there: From A515 to Alstonefield, go past Overdale B&B into Gypsy Lane. Hostel is on the left.
Public transport: BUS: Postbus from Leek (with connections from Stoke-on-Trent); Warrington 441 from Ashbourne, Thurs, Sat only (connections from Derby and Manchester).
RAIL: Cromford 13 miles, Buxton 14.
Parking: Yes.
Nearest other hostels: Ilam Hall 3.5 miles, Hartington Hall 4.5, Meerbrook 12.

Price Band: B	Opening category: ❶

The Peak District offers tracks and trails for all ages and abilities.

ALSTONEFIELD CAMPING BARN

campingbarns@yha.org.uk
Booking: 0870 770 8868
Arrival time: Mr & Mrs Flower, 01335 310349

This camping barn is near the attractive village of Alstonefield, in the heart of the Peak District between Dovedale and the Manifold Valley. It enjoys fine views of the surrounding limestone hills and is an ideal base for walkers and cyclists. It's also convenient for Alton Towers and visiting historic houses.

Great for... discovering the delights of both Derbyshire and Staffordshire.

You need to know... parking is limited.

Accommodation: Sleeps 12 in a separate upstairs area.

Facilities: Communal cooking area with picnic bench seating, toilet and basin.

Nearest pub: 1 mile. **Nearest shop:** 1 mile.

Location: OS 119, GR 125569.

Price Band: C   Opening category: ❸

●● BAKEWELL ☆

Fly Hill, Bakewell, Derbyshire DE45 1DN;
bakewell@yha.org.uk
Tel: 0870 770 5682 Fax: 0870 770 5682

With fine views over the historic market town of Bakewell and the Wye Valley, this relaxed hostel is the ideal base from which to explore the many delights of the Peak District. Chatsworth House and Haddon Hall, Lathkill Dale and Monsal Dale are all within easy walking distance and there are great public transport links. Bakewell itself is a hive of activity. Famous for its puddings and tarts with a market tradition stretching back over 700 years old, this wonderful town is full of hidden surprises.

Location: OS 119, GR 215685.

Great for... active people exploring the Peak District.

You need to know... parking is limited. No coach access.

Accommodation: 28 beds: 2x2- and 4x6-bed rooms.

Family rooms: No. **FBR:** Yes. **Rent-a-Hostel:** Yes.

Classroom: No. **Education packages:** No.

Facilities: Lounge, drying room, self-catering kitchen, showers and small shop. **Daytime access:** All public areas.

Reception open: Staff available before 10am and after 5pm.

Meals: Breakfast, picnic lunch, evening meal.

Getting there: From the A6 Buxton–Matlock road at Bakewell follow YHA sign up North Church Street near the roundabout and the Rutland Hotel. Follow road up the hill, past the church on the left and take the second right on to Fly Hill (hostel is signposted).

Public transport: BUS: frequent from surrounding areas. RAIL: Matlock 8 miles.

 If travelling towards Nottingham, stop is 100 metres from Rutland Arms on A6 towards Matlock. If travelling to Manchester, stop is adjacent to Rutland Arms on A6 to Buxton.

Parking: Small car park.

Nearest other hostels: Youlgreave 3.5 miles, Matlock 8.

Price Band: B   Opening category: ❷

BIRCHOVER CAMPING BARN

campingbarns@yha.org.uk
Booking: 0870 770 8868
Arrival time: Mr Heathcote, 01629 650245

This camping barn is on a beef farm and campsite at the edge of Birchover, between Bakewell and Matlock. Nearby is Stanton Moor with its Nine Ladies stone circle.

You need to know... it's a minimum booking of five.

Accommodation: Sleeps 10.

Facilities: Communal area with tables, adjacent cooking shelter with stone bench, toilets and showers in farmyard, hot water and shower.

Nearest pub: 0.5 miles. **Nearest shop:** 0.5 miles.

Location: OS 119, GR 241622.

Price Band: C   Opening category: ❸

Perfect for discovering the delights of the Peak District: YHA Bakewell.

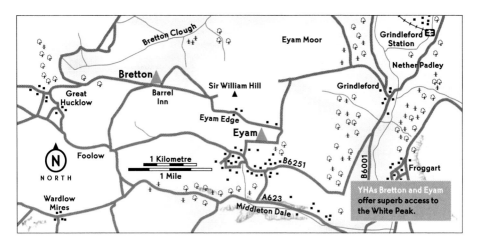

Bretton Clough
Eyam Moor
Grindleford Station
Nether Padley
Bretton
Sir William Hill ▲
Grindleford
Great Hucklow
Barrel Inn
Eyam Edge
Eyam
Foolow
1 Kilometre
1 Mile
B6251
B6001
Froggart
NORTH
Wardlow Mires
A623
Middleton Dale

YHAs Bretton and Eyam offer superb access to the White Peak.

●● BRETTON ☆

**Bretton, nr Eyam, Hope Valley, Sheffield,
Yorkshire S32 5QD; bretton@yha.org.uk
Tel: 0870 770 5720 Fax: 0870 770 5720
Rent-a-Hostel bookings : 0870 770 6113**

The smallest and highest hostel in the Peaks, Bretton is situated above the historic plague village of Eyam with stunning views of the surrounding countryside. An open fire provides a homely welcome and add to the traditional character and friendly atmosphere. Walkers will be in their element here, with clear paths and trails over the White Peak within easy reach.

Location: OS 119, GR 200780.
Great for... active people looking for a small, cosy base.
You need to know... it's self-catering accommodation only. The Barrel Inn is 200 yards away. Credit cards are only accepted for advance bookings.
Accommodation: 18 beds: 1x4-, 1x6-, and 1x8-bed rooms.
Family rooms: No. **FBR:** Yes. **Rent-a-Hostel:** Yes.
Classroom: No. **Education packages:** No.
Facilities: Lounge/dining room, self-catering kitchen, shower, drying room, cycle store and grounds. Limited shop.
Daytime access: All public areas, via numbered lock.
Reception open: 5pm. **Meals:** Self-catering only.
Getting there: Off the A623 Chapel-le-Frith to Baslow Road, follow sign to Foolow. Take first right after the Bulls Head pub (signposted Bretton) and follow road up steep hill. The track to the hostel is on the left, 20 metres before the Barrel Inn.
Public transport: BUS: various services from Sheffield, Buxton and Chesterfield (passing close to Sheffield, Buxton and Chesterfield stations), alight Foolow, 1 mile.
RAIL: Grindleford 4 miles, Hathersage 4.
Parking: Yes.
Nearest other hostels: Eyam 1.5 miles, Hathersage 5, Ravenstor 6.

| Price Band: A | Opening category: ❷ |

The beautiful views of the Peak District near YHA Bretton.

BUTTERTON A CAMPING BARN

campingbarns@yha.org.uk
Booking: 0870 770 8868
Perched high above the Manifold Valley, Waterslacks Barn is a secluded base from which to enjoy the limestone valleys and attractive villages of the southern Peak District.

Great for... walking in the White Peak, rock climbing, caving and cycling on the Manifold track.
You need to know... campfire wood can be pre-booked at a small charge from Mr Renshaw on the telephone number above.
Accommodation: Sleeps 15.
Facilities: Communal area with table and benches, cooking area, toilet, shower, heating, electric light and metered electricity. Campfire allowed.
Nearest pub: 1 mile. **Nearest shop:** 1 mile.
Location: OS 118/119, GR 087561.

| Price Band: C | Opening category: ❸ |

BUTTERTON B CAMPING BARN
campingbarns@yha.org.uk
Booking: 0870 770 8868

Wills Barn is a short walk out of Butterton village and lies beside the minor road to Wetton Mill. It's convenient for exploring the Manifold and Dove Valleys.

Great for... walking in the White Peak, rock climbing, caving and cycling on the Manifold track.

You need to know... campfire wood can be pre-booked at a small charge from Mr Renshaw.

Accommodation: Sleeps 6.

Facilities: Living area with tables and benches, cooking area, toilet and washbasin, shower, lighting and metered electricity. Campfire allowed.

Nearest pub: 0.75 miles. **Nearest shop:** 1 mile.

Location: OS 118/119, GR 083564.

Price Band: G   Opening category: ❸

●● CASTLETON ☆☆☆
Castleton, Hope Valley, Derbyshire S33 8WG;
castleton@yha.org.uk
Tel: 0870 770 5758 Fax: 0870 770 5759

Originally Castleton Hall, this building dates back to the 13th century and, together with the former vicarage, stands at the heart of the village square. Walkers staying at this hostel on two separate sites will be spoilt for choice. There are many fine routes around the valley which is overlooked by the spectacular Winnats Pass and Mam Tor, known as the shivering mountain. Peveril Castle and a choice of underground caves are all within walking distance.

Location: OS 110, GR 150828.

Great for... walkers of all levels and active families.

You need to know... the vicarage is available for exclusive use, as is the self-contained stable and hayloft.

YHA Castleton is in a great location for active walkers.

Accommodation: 134 beds: all 2-, 4-, 6- and 8-bed rooms, half of which are en-suite.

Family rooms: Yes. **Rent-a-Hostel:** Yes.

Classroom: Yes. **Education packages:** Yes.

Facilities: Lounges, TV room, games rooms, self-catering kitchen, showers, drying room, cycle store, luggage store, children's activities and bar.

Daytime access: All public areas.

Reception open: All day.

Meals: Breakfast, picnic lunch, evening meal.

Getting there: Follow A625 from Sheffield. Once in village, turn left into Market Place. Or follow A625 from Manchester and turn into Winnats Pass.

Public transport: BUS: First/Stagecoach East Midland 272-4 from Sheffield (passes Hope station). RAIL: Hope 3 miles.

Parking: Nearby.

Nearest other hostels: Edale 4 miles, Hathersage 6, Eyam 7.

Price Band: B   Opening category: ❸

●● CHESTER ☆☆
40 Hough Green, Chester, Cheshire CH4 8JD;
chester@yha.org.uk
Tel: 0870 770 5762 Fax: 0870 770 5763

This is an ideal location for a historical break in Britain's only completely walled city. The hostel, a large, comfortable Victorian house built in 1856, offers easy access to the city centre and its cathedral just a mile away. Explore the Roman remains and wander through the historic medieval shopping galleries that line the streets. Go boating on the River Dee or visit the world famous zoo. Further afield, visit the Boat Museum and Blue Planet Aquarium at Ellesmere Port, the many historic houses of Cheshire, Jodrell Bank Science Centre, and the castles, coast and mountains of north Wales.

Location: OS 117, GR 397651.

Great for... a civilised city break with historical interest.

HOSTEL MANAGERS CHOOSE...
THE REGION'S BEST OUTDOOR SPOTS

The Roaches YHA Meerbrook : "A popular location for climbing, The Roaches are a gritstone escarpment worn into some fascinating shapes by the elements."

'Go Ape' YHA Sherwood: "Come and enjoy an exhilarating day swinging through the trees at Sherwood Pines Forest."

Kinder Scout YHA Edale: "Walkers can explore Kinder Scout itself or its many side valleys."

Mam Tor YHA Castleton: "I'd recommend all our guests try this. Stand in the mystic ruins of the hill fort and watch the sun rise over its slopes before returning to the hostel for breakfast."

Langsett Reservoir YHA Langsett: "Superb heather moorland."

A stone's throw from YHA Chester: the historic city centre of Britain's only completely walled city.

You need to know... breakfast is included in the price.
Accommodation: 117 beds: all 2-10-bed rooms.
Family rooms: Yes. **Rent-a-Hostel:** No.
Classroom: Yes. **Education packages:** Yes.
Facilities: Lounge, TV lounge, self-catering kitchen, showers, drying room, cycle store, lockers, laundry facilities and internet access. **Daytime access:** All public areas.
Reception open: All day.
Meals: Breakfast, picnic lunch, evening meal (5.30-7pm).
Getting there: The hostel is southwest of the city centre on A5104 (signposted to Saltney), 350 metres from traffic lights on right (see map on page 172).
Public transport: Bus: frequent from surrounding areas.
NATIONAL EXPRESS Opposite Chester Visitor Centre on Little St John Street. RAIL: Chester 1.5 miles.
Parking: Yes.
Nearest other hostels: Liverpool 20, Llangollen 22, Manchester 39, Conwy 43.

Price Band: D **Opening category:** ❸

Large and comfortable: YHA Chester.

●● CROWDEN ☆☆☆

Crowden-in-Longdendale, Glossop, Derbyshire SK13 1HZ
Tel: 0870 770 5784 Fax: 0870 770 5784

Situated in the Peak District, Crowden is a popular overnight stop on the Pennine Way. Groups, families and individuals are all welcome at this comfortably refurbished row of former quarrymen's cottages. There's plenty to do here besides exploring the rugged countryside on foot. With Manchester, Liverpool and Sheffield all less than an hour's drive away, it's within reach of the north's most vibrant cities.
Location: OS 110, GR 073993.
Great for... mixing days out in the city with varied walking.
Accommodation: 38 beds: 2x2-, 4x4- and 3x6-bed rooms.
Family rooms: Yes. **Rent-a-Hostel:** Yes.
Classroom: No. **Education packages:** No.
Facilities: Lounge, self-catering kitchen, showers, drying room, shop and cycle store. **Daytime access:** New arrivals access to kitchen,

dining area and toilet. people staying over: all public areas and rooms.

Reception open: 5pm.

Meals: Breakfast, picnic lunch, evening meal.

Getting there: Situated on A628, Manchester to Barnsley Road. From end of M67, follow Barnsley (A628) signs; Crowden is 3.5 miles after Tintwistle. Take signposted left turn up to hostel. From Barnsley (M1) direction, follow Manchester (A628). Hostel well signed on right. From Glossop, follow B6105 (signposted Barnsley). At junction with A628, carefully turn left; hostel signposted on right.

Public transport: `NATIONAL EXPRESS»` National Express 350 Sheffield-Manchester (passes close to Sheffield station). RAIL: Hadfield (Not Sun) 5 miles.

Parking: Yes.

Nearest other hostels: Langsett 10 miles, Edale 15 (via Pennine Way), Manchester 20, Mankinholes 24 (via Pennine Way).

Price Band: B	Opening category: ❷

● ● DIMMINGSDALE ☆☆
Oakamoor, Stoke-on-Trent, Staffordshire ST10 3AS; dimmingsdale@yha.org.uk Tel: 0870 770 5876 Fax: 0870 770 5877

You take your pick of activities when you stay at Dimmingsdale. With Alton Towers just two miles away, the lure of a fun-filled day is ever-present. The Pottery Museums at Stoke-on-Trent, the Cauldon Canal and several nature reserves offer more sedate entertainment, while an extensive network of rights of way will keep walkers and cyclists busy. Whatever you choose to do, this traditional, purpose-built hostel in secluded woodland offers a quiet base.

Location: OS 119, GR 052436.

Great for... a varied break for small groups.

You need to know... only self-catering accommodation available; the hostel, which now has full central heating, is in an isolated location some two miles from Oakamoor village and the shop is limited.

Accommodation: 20 beds: 2x6- and 1x8-bed rooms.

Family rooms: Yes. **Rent-a-Hostel:** Yes.

Classroom: No. **Education packages:** No.

Facilities: Common room, self-catering kitchen, showers, drying room, cycle store, BBQ and limited shop.

Daytime access: All public areas, via a numbered lock.

Reception open: Staff available before 10am and after 5pm.

Meals: Self-catering only.

Getting there: From Oakamoor off B5417, take road at south end of bridge past Admiral's House B&B. Take road to top of hill, turn left up farm track to hostel.

Public transport: BUS: First 32A from Uttoxeter (passes close to Uttoxeter station), alight Oakamoor, 0.5 miles. RAIL: Blythe Bridge 6 miles.

Parking: Yes.

Nearest other hostels: Ilam 12 miles, Alstonefield 15, Meerbrook 16, Gradbach 17.

Price Band: B	Opening category: ❷

● ● EDALE ☆
Rowland Cote, Nether Booth, Edale, Hope Valley, Derbyshire S33 7ZH; edale@yha.org.uk Tel: 0870 770 5808 Fax: 0870 770 5809

Take a deep breath before you book a bed here because Edale is a dedicated Activity Centre. On the slopes of Kinder Scout in the Peak District National Park, the Edale Valley is one the best known walking and adventure locations in the country. It's the perfect place to try some of the activities on offer at this hostel, such as caving, climbing, kayaking, canoeing, abseiling, orienteering and archery. Whether travelling alone or as part of a group, this is the hostel for you if you want to have fun and improve your outdoor skills.

Location: OS 110, GR 139865.

Great for... active people fuelled by adrenalin.

You need to know... it's advisable to book in advance.

Accommodation: 157 beds: mostly 2- 8- plus 2x12-bed rooms; 8 en-suite and 4 with disabled access.

Family rooms: Yes. **Rent-a-Hostel:** No.

Classroom: Yes. **Education packages:** Yes.

Facilities: Lounge, games room with TV, self-catering kitchen, showers, drying room, cycle store, laundry and grounds. Outdoor activities (book in advance). **Daytime access:** All public areas.

Reception open: All day.

Meals: Breakfast, picnic or buffet lunch, evening meal. Alcohol licence.

Getting there: 1 mile east of Edale village marked 'Rowland Cote' on Ordnance Survey map.

Public transport: RAIL: Edale 2 miles.

Parking: Yes.

Nearest other hostels: Castleton 4 miles, Hathersage 8, Crowden 15 (by Pennine Way).

Price Band: B	Opening category: ❸

Choose from a range of activities at YHA Edale.

EDALE CAMPING BARN
campingbarns@yha.org.uk
Booking: 0870 770 8868
Arrival time: Mr & Mrs Gee, 01433 670273

This camping barn at Cotefield Farm overlooks the famous Mam Tor, at the heart of a popular walking area and at the start of the Pennine Way. The high moorland of Kinder and the wooded Derwent Valley are readily accessible.

You need to know... you have to leave your car at the farm and walk along the footpath across two fields to the barn.

Accommodation: Sleeps 8.

Facilities: Small communal living area with table and benches, cooking area with external access and separate toilet.

Nearest pub: 1 mile. **Nearest shop:** 1 mile.

Location: OS 110, GR 132869.

Price Band: G   Opening category: ❸

YHA Eyam: your chance to explore the Peaks from a Victorian folly.

◐ ● EYAM ☆☆☆
Hawkhill Road, Eyam, Hope Valley, Derbyshire
S32 5QP; eyam@yha.org.uk
Tel: 0870 770 5830 Fax: 0870 770 5831

This Victorian folly resembles a tiny, turreted castle and perches on the hillside overlooking the historic village of Eyam, famous for its tragic past. Two thirds of the village population was wiped out during the Great Plague of the 17th century, and you can trace the tale with a wander through the village to see the Plague Cottages and parish church. As the hostel sits on the boundary of the contrasting landscapes of the White Peak and Dark Peak, there's also a varied array of excellent walking.

Location: OS 119, GR 219769.

Great for... walkers interested in history.

You need to know... there are limited self-catering facilities.

Accommodation: 60 beds: 4x2-, 6x4-, 2x6- and 1x10-bed rooms and 1x6-bed en-suite.

Family rooms: Yes. **Rent-a-Hostel:** No.

Classroom: Yes. **Education packages:** Yes.

Facilities: Lounge, games room, self-catering kitchen, drying room and cycle store. **Daytime access:** All public areas.

Reception open: Staff available before 10am and after 5pm.

Close to the Roaches: YHA Gradbach Mill.

● GRADBACH MILL ☆☆☆
Gradbach, Quarnford, Buxton, Derbyshire
SK17 0SU; gradbachmill@yha.org.uk
Tel: 0870 770 5834 Fax: 0870 770 5835

A former mill in its own secluded grounds on the banks of the River Dane, this hostel is close to the Staffordshire moorlands and gritstone Roaches. If you're a National Trust member then there's plenty to do as National Trust properties Quarry Bank Mill at Styal, Little Morton Hall, Tatton Park, Dunham Massey and Biddulph Grange are all nearby. Or, for a dose of fun, Alton Towers is 15 miles away.

Location: OS 118, GR 993661.

Great for... outdoor enthusiasts looking for a varied break.

You need to know... the hostel is in two separate buildings, with one available separately through the Rent-a-Hostel scheme.

Accommodation: 91 beds: 5x2-, 1x3-, 9x4- and 7x6-bed rooms.

Family rooms: Yes. **Rent-a-Hostel:** Yes.

Classroom: No. **Education packages:** Yes.

Facilities: Lounge, self-catering kitchen, showers, drying room, cycle store, luggage store, laundry facilities and grounds.

Daytime access: All public areas.

Reception open: All day.

Meals: Breakfast, picnic lunch, evening meal.

Getting there: Hostel is clearly signposted from Flash village, just off the A53 Buxton–Keele road.

Public transport: BUS: First X18 Sheffield-Hanley (passes Sheffield, Stoke-on-Trent and Buxton stations), alight Flash Bar Stores, 2.5 miles. RAIL: Buxton 7 miles, Macclesfield 9.

Parking: Yes.

Nearest other hostels: Hartington and Ravenstor 12 miles.

Price Band: B   Opening category: ❸

Meals: Breakfast, picnic lunch, evening meal.
Getting there: Follow hostel signs from village. Go past the museum and car park, continue up the hill and hostel is around 600 metres on left.
Public transport: BUS: As for Bretton, but alight Eyam.
RAIL: Grindleford 3.5 miles, Hathersage 4.
Parking: Yes.
Nearest other hostels: Bretton 1.5 miles, Hathersage 6, Bakewell 7, Ravenstor 7.

Price Band: B	Opening category: ❷

●● HARTINGTON HALL ☆☆☆☆
**Hartington, Buxton, Derbyshire SK17 0AT;
hartington@yha.org.uk
Tel: 0870 770 5848 Fax: 0870 770 5849**

This magnificent 17th century manor house features log fires, oak panelling and a room where Bonnie Prince Charlie stayed. Refurbished with the help of a members' appeal and a grant from the National Heritage Lottery Fund, the hostel offers accommodation and facilities of a high standard and is an ideal base for walkers and cyclists. There is a stream of stately homes to visit, as well as 11th century Pilsbury Castle and tranquil Dovedale. Children are very welcome with a pets area and adventure playground on site.
Location: OS 119, GR 131603.
Great for... families who appreciate history in beautiful surroundings.
You need to know... we hold a wedding licence for that special day!

THE REGION'S BEST CYCLE TRAILS

Monsal Trail YHA Bakewell: "You have to stop and enjoy the views when you get to Monsal Head. It's a great railway viaduct overlooking Monsal Dale."

High Peak Trail YHA Matlock: "Some 17 miles of traffic-free riding. On an old railway track, it runs past abandoned engine houses, sidings and signals, as well as hundreds of wildflowers in the summer."

Manifold Trail YHA Hartington Hall: "Safe, secure and mostly off-road, this follows a disused railway track through a dramatic landscape."

The Silent Valley YHA Castleton: "Undoubtedly the most atmospheric cycle ride in the region. Pedal around two lakes that harbour a ghostly secret. Two villages were flooded to form the reservoirs, and if you listen to the wind you may just hear the lost villagers. Fascinating by day, stunning by moonlight."

Tissington Trail YHA Ilam Hall: "Especially suitable for families with young children as it doesn't cover any roads at all. Hire bikes at Ashbourne and Parsley Hay."

Accommodation: 131 beds: 5x1-, 6x2-, 4x3-, 9x4-, 3x5-, 2x6-, 1x7-, and 4x8- bed rooms. (18 fully en-suite).
Family rooms: Yes (x21) **Rent-a-Hostel:** No.
Classroom: Yes (x2) **Education packages:** Yes.
Facilities: Eliza's Restaurant & Bar, lounges, TV, games room, internet access, shop, laundry, drying room, luggage store, cycle racking, information point, wildlife garden. Facilities for people with disabilities.
Daytime access: All public areas.
Reception open: All day.
Meals: Breakfast, picnic lunch, evening meal. Bar and bar menu during school holidays and over weekends.
Getting there: From Hartington village centre, turn up the lane between the corner shop and the war memorial. The Hall is 200 metres up the lane on the left.
Public Transport: BUS: Bowers 442 from Buxton station; also from other areas on Sun & Bank Holidays only.
RAIL: Buxton 12 miles, Matlock 13.
Parking: Car park and roadside parking. Also village parking.
Nearest other hostels: Alstonefield 5 miles, Youlgreave 6, Ilam 9.

Price Band: C	Opening category: ❶

●● HATHERSAGE ☆☆
**Castleton Road, Hathersage, Hope Valley,
Derbyshire S32 1EH; hathersage@yha.org.uk
Tel: 0870 770 5852 Fax: 0870 770 5852**

This Victorian house is on the edge of a village which is associated with both Little John and Charlotte Brontë's Jane Eyre. It's on the

Cyclists who enjoy a challenge should stay at YHA Hartington Hall.

A Youth Hostel to remember: YHA Ilam Hall is an imposing gothic manor set in 84 acres of parkland.

White Peak Way circular walk and is overlooked by Stanage Edge which attracts climbers of all abilities. As well as countryside pursuits, shoppers will be happy as Sheffield is just 10 miles away.

Location: OS 110, GR 226814.

Great for... walkers and cyclists, those using public transport and rock-climbers.

You need to know... there are plenty of shops in the village.

Accommodation: 40 beds: 1x2-, 2x4- and 5x6-bed rooms.

Family rooms: No. **FBR:** Yes. **Rent-a-Hostel:** Yes.

Classroom: No. **Education packages:** Yes.

Facilities: Lounge, self-catering kitchen, showers, dining room, cycle store and grounds. **Daytime access:** All public areas.

Reception open: Staff available before 10am and after 5pm.

Meals: Breakfast, picnic lunch, evening meal.

Getting there: Hostel is 100 metres on right past the George Hotel on the road from Sheffield to Castleton.

Public transport: BUS: First 272 from Sheffield, Hulleys 175 from Bakewell. RAIL: Hathersage 0.5 miles.

Parking: Limited to six cars.

Nearest other hostels: Bretton 5 miles, Castleton 6, Eyam 6, Edale 12.

Price Band: 🔳	Opening category: ❷

●● ILAM HALL ☆☆☆

Ilam Hall, Ilam, Ashbourne, Derbyshire DE6 2AZ; ilam@yha.org.uk

Tel: 0870 770 5876 Fax: 0870 770 5877

This is a Youth Hostel to remember! A Victorian gothic manor house owned by the National Trust, it makes for a civilised break. Its grounds stretch to 84 acres of country park on the banks of the River Manifold, making outdoor games, woodland wanders and riverside walks an appealing possibility. Walk in the gently undulating White Peak area of the Peak District National Park, visit Dovedale or cycle along the Tissington and Manifold Trails.

Location: OS 119, GR 131506.

Great for... a country house break with gentle pursuits.

You need to know... there's a charge for parking (unless you are an NT member); there is separate accommodation for people with mobility problems.

Accommodation: 139 beds: 1x2-, 1x3-, mostly 4-8-, 1x11- and 1x14-bed rooms, some en-suite.

Family rooms: Yes. **Rent-a-Hostel:** No.

Classroom: Yes. **Education packages:** Yes.

Facilities: Lounge, TV in games room, self-catering kitchen, showers, drying room, cycle store, laundry facilities, full licence and grounds. **Daytime access:** All public areas.

Reception open: All day.
Meals: Breakfast, picnic lunch, evening meal.
Getting there: From Ilam village centre enter National Trust Country Park and follow drive.
Public transport: BUS: Glovers 443 Thurs & Sat only, TM Travel 202 Sun only, Trent 107, Arriva 109 from Ashbourne, Glovers 443 Thurs-Sat only. TM Travel 202 is Sunday only; otherwise from Derby, Manchester (passing close to Derby and Macclesfield stations), alight Ilam Cross Roads, 2.5 miles.
RAIL: Matlock 14 miles, Uttoxeter 15, Derby 18.
NATIONALEXPRESS Ashbourne bus station, 5 miles.
Parking: NT car park (NT charge – tickets from reception).
Nearest other hostels: Alstonefield 3 miles, Hartington 9, Dimmingsdale 12, Matlock 20.

Price Band: B   **Opening category:** ④

Outdoor pursuits are aplenty at YHA Ilam Hall.

◐● LANGSETT ☆

**Langsett, Stocksbridge, Sheffield S36 4GY;
reservations@yha.org.uk
Tel: 0870 770 5912 Fax: 0870 770 5912
Bookings more than 7 days ahead: 0870 770 8868**

Langsett offers open fires and comfortable facilities in a rural location with extensive views, yet is close to good transport links. The hostel is surrounded by superb heather moorland with Margery Hill, the Derwent Valley and Holmfirth, the setting for Last of the Summer Wine, all within easy reach.
Location: OS 110, GR 211005.
Great for... a rural retreat for walkers.
You need to know... there are basic facilities only; credit cards are accepted for advance bookings only; there's a basic shop stocking non-perishable foodstuffs.
Accommodation: 27 beds: 4x4-, 1x5- and 1x6-bed rooms.
Family rooms: No. **FBR:** Yes. **Rent-a-Hostel:** Yes.

Classroom: No. **Education packages:** No.
Facilities: Lounge/dining room, self-catering kitchen, showers, drying room, cycle store and garden. **Daytime access:** Public areas, via numbered lock.
Reception open: 5pm (7pm on Fridays).
Meals: Self-catering only.
Getting there: Hostel is 1 mile southeast of Flouch roundabout, on north side of A616, 100 metres up track between café and Gilbert Hill, on opposite side of road to Waggon & Horses pub. Slow down on approaching Langsett as road is fast. Also 1 mile from Trans-Pennine trail.
Public transport: BUS: Yorkshire Traction 23/4 from Barnsley station (pass close to Penistone station).
RAIL: Penistone 3 miles.
NATIONALEXPRESS Stops in Langsett.
Parking: Yes.
Nearest other hostels: Crowden 10 miles, Hathersage 18, Edale 20.

Price Band: A   **Opening category:** ③

●● LIVERPOOL ☆☆☆☆
**25 Tabley Street, off Wapping, Liverpool,
Merseyside L1 8EE; liverpool@yha.org.uk
Tel: 0870 770 5924 Fax 0870 770 5925**

This is a modern, purpose-built hostel with excellent facilities. Adjacent to the Albert Dock and just a 10-minute walk from the heart of the city, it's a great location for visiting Liverpool's main attractions. On the dock, you'll find the Beatles Story, Tate Gallery and Merseyside Maritime Museum. Take a tour of the famous football ground or visit the Museum of Life. Premium rooms are available.
Location: OS 108, GR 344895.
Great for... a comfortable base to tour Liverpool's attractions.
You need to know... breakfast is included in the overnight price.
Accommodation: 100 beds: all 3-, 4- and 6-bed en-suite rooms.
Family rooms: Yes. **Rent-a-Hostel:** No.
Classroom: Yes. **Education packages:** Yes.
Facilities: Lounge with TV, games rooms, self-catering kitchen, showers, cycle store, luggage store, lockers, laundry facilities and grounds. **Daytime access:** All public areas.
Reception open: 24hrs.
Meals: Breakfast, picnic lunch, evening meal.
Getting there: From Lime Street station follow signs for Albert Dock. Turn left onto main dock road (called Wapping). Hostel is on left after Baltic Fleet pub. From James Street station turn right then left onto Wapping, past the Albert Dock on your right – hostel is on the left after Baltic Fleet pub (see map on page 172).
Public transport: BUS: frequent from surrounding areas.
RAIL: James Street 0.5 miles, Liverpool Lime Street 1.5.
NATIONALEXPRESS Liverpool coach station, Norton St 1 mile.
AIRPORT: From John Lennon airport catch the Airportxpress 500 to Paradise Street bus station.
Parking: Yes.
Nearest other hostels: Chester 20 miles, Manchester 32.

Price Band: E   **Opening category:** ①

LOSEHILL CAMPING BARN

campingbarns@yha.org.uk
Booking: 0870 770 8868
Arrival time: 01433 620373 during office hours

Owned by the Peak District National Park, this camping barn is in the Hope Valley below the steep slopes of Back Tor and Lose Hill, near the village of Castleton.

Accommodation: Sleeps 8. No dogs.
Facilities: Communal area with table and bench, cooking area and separate toilet in adjoining lean-to.
Nearest pub: 1 mile. **Nearest shop:** 1 mile.
Location: OS 110, GR 153838.

| Price Band: G | Opening category: ❸ |

Walking in the Peaks near Losehill Camping Barn.

● MEERBROOK ☆

Old School, Meerbrook, Leek, Staffordshire ST13 8SJ; dimmingsdale@yha.org.uk
Tel: 0870 770 5966 Fax: 0870 770 5966
Bookings more than 7 days ahead: 0870 770 5876

At the centre of Meerbrook in a quiet corner of the Staffordshire moorlands, this hostel offers basic facilities in an old village school complete with original beamed ceiling. The nearby Roaches are a popular location for climbing and the moorland provides excellent walking. Staffordshire's museums, factory shops and potteries are within easy reach should the weather turn inclement.

Location: OS 118, GR 989608.
Great for... outdoor folk who like small, cosy hostels.
You need to know... it's self-catering accommodation only.
Accommodation: 22 beds: 2x2-, 1x8- and 1x10-bed rooms.
Family rooms: No. **FBR:** Yes. **Rent-a-Hostel:** Yes.

Classroom: No. **Education packages:** No.
Facilities: Lounge, self-catering kitchen, shower, drying room, cycle store, BBQ, grounds and basic hostel shop. Credit cards accepted. **Daytime access:** Public areas, via numbered lock.
Reception open: 5pm.
Meals: Self-catering only.
Getting there: From A53 Buxton–Leek road, take turning by Three Horseshoes pub, signposted Meerbrook. Hostel is in village centre on right-hand side, past pub.
Public transport: BUS: First X18 Sheffield-Hanley (passes Sheffield, Stoke-on-Trent and Buxton stations), alight Blackshaw Moor, 2 miles. RAIL: Stoke-on-Trent 15 miles.
NATIONAL EXPRESS» Leek bus station 4.25 miles.
Parking: Yes.
Nearest other hostels: Gradbach 5 miles, Hartington 12, Dimmingsdale 16.

| Price Band: B | Opening category: ❷ |

Atmospheric and peaceful: YHA Meerbrook was once a village school and still retains its original beamed ceiling.

●● MANCHESTER ☆☆☆

Potato Wharf, Castlefield, Manchester, M3 4NB;
manchester@yha.org.uk
Tel: 0870 770 5950 Fax: 0870 770 5951

Purpose-built in 1995, this hostel enjoys a canal-side location close to the heart of the rejuvenated city centre. Ideally situated for a city break, it's within easy reach of some of the best shopping, restaurants, cinemas, concert halls, museums and theatres in northern England. It's hard to narrow down just what to do but don't miss the Manchester United museum and stadium tour and the Trafford Centre.

Location: OS 109, GR 831976.
Great for... a stylish city break.
You need to know... breakfast is included in the overnight charge and premium rooms are available.
Accommodation: 136 beds: 30x4-, 2x5- and 3x2-bed rooms, all en-suite.
Family rooms: Yes. **Rent-a-Hostel:** No.
Classroom: Yes. **Education packages:** Yes.
Facilities: Lounge, TV room, games room, self-catering kitchen, showers, toilets, cycle store, luggage store, lockers, laundry facilities and conference rooms. **Daytime access:** All public areas.
Reception open: 24hrs.
Meals: Breakfast, picnic lunch, evening meal.
Getting there: From bus station and Piccadilly train station, follow signs for Castlefield/Museum of Science and Industry (MSI), or take the Metrolink to the G-Mex station. By road, follow signs for Castlefield/MSI. Hostel is opposite MSI and behind Castlefield Hotel (see map on page 172).
Public transport: GM Metrolink: G-Mex, few minutes' walk (connections from Manchester Piccadilly station). RAIL: Deansgate, few minutes' walk, Manchester Victoria 1 mile.
NATIONALEXPRESS Manchester coach station 0.75 miles.
Parking: Yes.
Nearest other hostels: Crowden 20 miles, Liverpool 32, Chester 39.

Price Band: E	Opening category: ❶

In the heart of the city: the purpose-built YHA Manchester.

YHA Matlock was once Smedley's Memorial Hydropathic Hospital!

●● MATLOCK ☆

40 Bank Road, Matlock, Derbyshire DE4 3NF;
matlock@yha.org.uk
Tel: 0870 770 5960 Fax: 0870 770 5961

This hostel started life as Smedley's Memorial Hydropathic Hospital, serving as a place of rest and rehabilitation for the needy. It still offers a welcome retreat though nowadays it's mainly from the many activities on offer close by. The Heights of Abraham, the Lead Mining Museum, Alton Towers and the American Adventure Theme Park are all nearby, as is excellent walking in the Peak District National Park. Children will be made very welcome, with toddler-friendly facilities and a menu for under-10s.

Location: OS 119, GR 300603.
Great for... a busy family holiday.
Accommodation: 52 beds: 3x1-, 4x2-, 2x3-, 5x4-, 1x6- and 1x9-bed rooms.
Family rooms: Yes. **Rent-a-Hostel:** No.
Classroom: Yes. **Education packages:** No.
Facilities: Lounge, TV room, games room, self-catering kitchen, showers, drying room, cycle store, laundry facilities, grounds, training and conference rooms. **Daytime access:** All public areas.
Reception open: 1pm.
Meals: Breakfast, picnic lunch, evening meal.
Getting there: YHA Matlock is 200 metres up Bank Road on right, clearly signposted from Crown Square roundabout in town centre.
Public transport: BUS: frequent from surrounding areas. RAIL: Matlock 0.5 miles.
NATIONALEXPRESS Matlock bus station 300 metres.
Parking: Yes.
Nearest other hostels: Bakewell 8 miles, Youlgreave 10, Hartington 13.

Price Band: B	Opening category: ❸

MIDDLETON-BY-YOULGREAVE CAMPING BARN

campingbarns@yha.org.uk
Booking: 0870 770 8868
Arrival time: Mr Butterworth, 01629 636746

This camping barn is part of a working farm on the edge of the small village of Middleton-by-Youlgreave. It is a good base for walking in Bradford Dale and Lathkill Dale, an area full of wildlife interest.

Great for... discovering the Peak District National Park.
You need to know... well-behaved dogs on leads are accepted (this is a working farm).
Accommodation: Sleeps 12 on the first floor; access by external stone steps.
Facilities: Communal living area, separate cooking area, toilet in adjacent building, electric light, metered electricity.
Nearest pub: 1 mile. **Nearest shop:** 1 mile.
Location: OS 119, GR 196634.

Price Band: 🄶	Opening category: ❸

NAB END CAMPING BARN

campingbarns@yha.org.uk
Booking: 0870 770 8868
Arrival time: Mr & Mrs Cox, 01298 83225

In one of the quieter parts of the National Park, Nab End camping barn lies between Hollinsclough and Longnor. The upper valley of the River

Dove, marking the boundary between limestone and gritstone, is nearby and the river's source, high up on Axe Edge, lies to the northwest.
Accommodation: Sleeps 16 on the first floor.
Facilities: Living area on first floor, kitchen, toilets and washroom on ground floor, metered electricity, electric light, fridge and shower.
Nearest pub: 1.5 miles. **Nearest shop:** 1.5 miles.
Location: OS 119, GR 077662.

Price Band: 🄶	Opening category: ❸

◗ ● RAVENSTOR ☆☆☆

Millers Dale, Buxton, Derbyshire SK17 8SS;
ravenstor@yha.org.uk
Tel: 0870 770 6008 Fax: 0870 770 6009

This National Trust property stands high above the dales of the River Wye in 60 acres of grounds. Surrounded by the fascinating limestone scenery of the White Peak, the hostel is on the White Peak Way and there is excellent walking for all abilities nearby. It is also within easy visiting distance of Litton Mill.

Location: OS 119, GR 152732.
Great for... walkers looking for a tranquil base from which to explore the Peaks.
Accommodation: 85 beds: 2x2-, 1x3-, 1x4-, 1x5-, 1x6-, 1x7-, 1x8-, 1x12-, 1x16,- and 1x20-bed rooms.
Family rooms: Yes. **Rent-a-Hostel:** No.
Classroom: Yes. **Education packages:** Yes.
Facilities: Lounge, dining room, TV room/study, self-catering

Excellent walking for all abilities can be found near YHA Ravenstor.

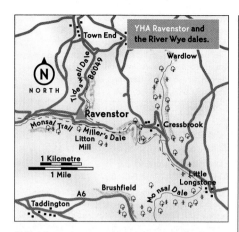

YHA Ravenstor and the River Wye dales.

kitchen, showers, games room, internet access and cycle store.
Daytime access: All public areas.
Reception open: 1pm. **Meals:** Breakfast, picnic lunch, evening meal.
Getting there: From A6 between Bakewell and Buxton take the B6049 to Tideswell. The hostel is 1 mile past Millers Dale.
Public transport: Bus: Stagecoach 65 Sheffield-Buxton, 66 Chesterfield-Buxton (both pass close to Buxton station).
RAIL: Buxton 8 miles.
Parking: Yes.
Nearest other hostels: Bretton 6 miles, Bakewell 7, Eyam 7, Castleton 5.

Price Band: B	Opening category: 4

● SHINING CLIFF ☆

**Jackass Lane, nr Ambergate, Derbyshire
DE56 2RE; reservations@yha.org.uk
Tel: 0870 770 6028 Fax: 0870 770 6029
Bookings more than 7 days ahead: 0870 770 8868**

In the heart of an ancient woodland, Shining Cliff Youth Hostel is ideal for groups of friends and families with a sense of adventure. Close to Derwent Valley World Heritage Site and within easy reach of the Peak District National Park, you can still escape back to tranquility after a fun packed day out.
Location: OS 119, GR 335522.
Great for... a hostelling experience that's off the beaten track.
You need to know... there's no access by car. Bring a torch. Credit cards accepted for advance bookings only.
Accommodation: 22 beds: 1x2-, 2x4- and 2x6-bed rooms.
Family rooms: No. **FBR:** Yes. **Rent-a-Hostel:** Yes.
Classroom: No. **Education packages:** No.
Facilities: Common room, self-catering kitchen, cycle store and grounds. **Daytime access:** Public areas via numbered lock.
Reception open: 5pm.
Meals: Self-catering only. No hostel shop.
Getting there: From Ambergate, cross river by church. Cars/cycles

up hill, turn right into woods by third farm (Netherpark). Walkers turn right by river. At fork take lower path, through works yard then left up path through woods, following signs.
Public transport: BUS: TP from Derby, Stagecoach 142 from Alfreton, Doyles 143/4 from Ripley. On all alight Ambergate.
RAIL: Ambergate 1.5 miles (path) 2 (road).
Parking: Yes, then 10-minute walk to hostel.
Nearest other hostels: Matlock 8 miles, Youlgreave 12.5.

Price Band: A	Opening category: 3

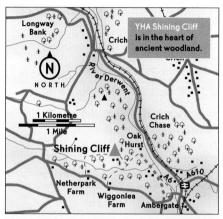

YHA Shining Cliff is in the heart of ancient woodland.

In the heart of an ancient woodland: YHA Shining Cliff.

On the edge of Robin Hood's lair: YHA Sherwood Forest.

● SHERWOOD FOREST ☆☆☆☆

Forest Corner, Edwinstowe, Nottinghamshire NG21 9RN; sherwood@yha.org.uk
Tel: 0870 770 6026 Fax: 0870 770 6027

This modern, purpose-built Youth Hostel is set on the edge of Sherwood Forest and offers a high standard of en-suite family accommodation. Follow in Robin Hood's footsteps through ancient woodland to the Major Oak, visit the excellent visitor centre just 10 minutes' walk from the hostel and enjoy cycling on the network of trails. Nottinghamshire also has many other attractions from magnificent stately homes, country parks and castles to the historic towns of Newark and Southwell.

Location: OS 120, GR 625673.
Great for... a fun-filled family holiday.
Accommodation: 39 beds: all 2-5-bed rooms, mostly en-suite.
Family rooms: Yes. **Rent-a-Hostel option:** No.
Classroom: No. **Education packages:** No.
Facilities: Lounge, dining room, toilets, showers, drying room, self-catering kitchen and cycle store. Facilities for people with disabilities. **Daytime access:** All public areas.
Reception open: All day.
Meals: Breakfast, picnic lunch, evening meal.
Getting there: From M1 northbound, exit motorway at J28 and follow A38 to Mansfield town centre. Follow signs for A60 to Worksop until junction with A6075 to Edwinstowe. Once in Edwinstowe turn left at traffic lights at Royal Oak pub crossroads. Turn left onto Forest Corner 400 metres up this road. From M1 southbound, exit motorway at J31 and follow A57 to Worksop. Stay on this road until signs for Sherwood Forest, Clumber Park and Edwinstowe B6034. On reaching a double roundabout follow signs for A616 Ollerton and Newark. After approx 2 miles turn right onto B6034, signed Edwinstowe and YHA. On entering Edwinstowe, turn right into Forest Corner, signed YHA and Craft Centre.
Nearest other hostels: Lincoln 30 miles and Matlock 30.
Public transport: BUS: Stagecoach 13 and 15 from Mansfield (passes close to Mansfield station); 33 Nottingham-Worksop (passes close to Nottingham and Worksop stations). RAIL: Mansfield Woodhouse 8 miles.
Parking: Yes.

Price Band: C **Opening category:** ❸

TADDINGTON CAMPING BARN

campingbarns@yha.org.uk
Booking: 0870 770 8868
Arrival time: Mr & Mrs Gillott, 01298 85730

This camping barn is in the centre of Taddington village, midway between Buxton and Bakewell at 1,000 feet. Surrounded by hills and dales, there are fine walks and views in all directions.

Accommodation: Sleeps 10.
Facilities: Communal area with tables and benches, cooking area, fridge, toilets, shower, heater, electric light and metered electricity. No dogs.
Nearest pub: 50 metres. **Nearest shop:** 5 miles.
Location: OS 119, GR 145710.

Price Band: C **Opening category:** ❸

HOSTEL MANAGERS CHOOSE...

THE BEST ACTIVITIES & VENUES FOR FAMILIES

Castleton garland ceremony YHA Losehill Barn: "Held on Oak Apple Day (29th May every year except when it falls on a Sunday), this colourful ceremony marks the day that King Charles hid in an oak tree to escape capture by his enemies."

The Arndale Centre YHA Manchester: "Home to one of Europe's largest shopping malls, the Arndale Centre has something for everyone. You can be sure to find whatever you are looking for in one of its many retail parks or markets."

Heights of Abraham YHA Matlock: "Fun and activites for all, from the spectacular cable car ride above Matlock Bath to exploring the two amazing show caverns."

Carnival Week YHA Eyam: "Held over August Bank Holiday week, events include fancy dress, a children's disco and a procession through the village."

Chester Zoo YHA Chester: "A fun and educational day among the 500 different animal species."

Alton Towers YHA Dimmingsdale: "Fun for all the family. From thrillseekers to young children, this theme park is a must no matter who you are."

National Tramway Museum, Crich YHA Shining Cliff: "Ride vintage trams from all over the world using genuine old pennies and ha'pennies given on arrival."

Bass Museum of Brewing YHA Hartington Hall: "It's got shire horses, a children's play area and plenty of tasting opportunities for Dad."

Jodrell Bank Science Centre YHA Chester: "Come see the world famous telescope. The centre also includes hands-on exhibits and a planetarium."

UNDERBANK CAMPING BARN

campingbarns@yha.org.uk
Booking: 0870 770 8868
Arrival time: Mr & Mrs Waller, 01260 227229

This camping barn is part of Blaze Farm, a dairy farm near the western edge of the National Park. It overlooks the Wildboarclough Valley and is close to the well-known viewpoint of Shuttlingsloe. A tea room selling homemade dairy ice-cream is open daily.

Great for... walking, climbing at the Roaches, fishing.
Accommodation: Sleeps 10 on the first floor.
Facilities: Living area, kitchen, toilet, shower, electric light, metered electricity. Dogs accepted, please check first.
Nearest pub: 0.5 miles.
Nearest shop: 1 mile.
Location: OS 118, GR 973677.

Price Band: G	Opening category: ❸

YHA Youlgreave is ideal for adventurous outdoor types.

● YOULGREAVE ☆☆☆

Fountain Square, Youlgreave, near Bakewell, Derbyshire DE45 1UR; youlgreave@yha.org.uk
Tel: 0870 770 6104 Fax: 0870 770 6104

Above the River Bradford and Lathkill Dale, Youlgreave was once the old Co-op village store and it still retains some of the original characteristics – look for the stone beehive (symbol of the Co-op) and the windows inscribed with the shop's services. Rooms are named after the store departments and there are interesting displays to give you a flavour of the period. Many adventures await outside in the White Peak, where walkers, cyclists and mountain bikers will be in their element.
Location: OS 119, GR 210641.
Great for... active people who want to step into yesteryear.
You need to know... you must park in the village.
Accommodation: 42 beds: 1x2-, 5x4-, 2x6- and 1x8-bed rooms.

Family rooms: Yes. **Rent-a-Hostel:** No.
Classroom: No. **Education packages:** No.
Facilities: Lounge/dining room, self-catering kitchen, drying room, cycle store and showers. **Daytime access:** Public areas, via a numbered lock.
Reception open: Staff available before 10am and after 5pm.
Meals: Breakfast, picnic lunch, evening meal.
Getting there: The hostel is in village centre on main street opposite Fountain Well. **Parking:** No.
Public transport: BUS: Hulleys 171/2, First 181 from Bakewell (with connections from Chesterfield and Matlock stations).
RAIL: Matlock 11 miles.
NATIONALEXPRESS» Bakewell, Rutland Arms 3.5 miles.
Nearest other hostels: Bakewell 3.5, Matlock 10.

Price Band: B	Opening category: ❸

Wales

Once the land of legends, Wales has so much more to offer, from the stunning mountains of Snowdonia to the modern attractions of Cardiff.

Picturesque: like so many Welsh Youth Hostels, YHA Llangollen benefits from a stunning setting.

●● BANGOR ☆☆

Tan-y-Bryn, Bangor, Gwynedd LL57 1PZ;
bangor@yha.org.uk
Tel: 0870 770 5686 Fax: 0870 770 5687

For a holiday jam-packed with a diverse range of activities, YHA Bangor, a large, Victorian house just minutes from the town centre, makes a great base. The mountains of Snowdonia are just a 15-minute drive away, offering a range of gentle wanders in the foothills and energetic all-day hikes. There's an awesome array of beaches close by on the Isle of Anglesey and the historic castles at Penrhyn and Caernarfon are within easy visiting distance. To help you explore to the full, mountain bikes, tandems and trailer bikes can be hired by arrangement.
Location: OS 115, GR 590722.
Great for... families with plenty of energy.
You need to know... you should book early as this hostel is popular during term time with school parties.
Accommodation: 70 beds: 1x2-, 3x4-, 6x6- and 2x10-bed rooms.
Family rooms: Yes. **Rent-a-Hostel:** No.
Classroom: Yes. **Education packages:** Yes.
Facilities: Reception, lounge, games room, self-catering kitchen, alcohol licence, internet, showers, drying room, cycle store, laundry facilities, shop, dining room, internet access and grounds.
Daytime access: All public areas.
Reception open: All day.
Meals: Breakfast, picnic lunch, evening meal and alcohol licence.
Getting there: From A55, take the A5 into Bangor. The hostel is on the left by the speed limit sign. From the station, go straight over the traffic lights. Bear left at the first roundabout and straight over the second. Keep on the same road and the hostel is at the top of the hill after Nelson's pub.
Public transport: BUS: frequent from surrounding areas. Bangor 1.5 miles. **NATIONALEXPRESS»** Garth Road bus station 0.75 miles.
Parking: Yes.
Nearest other hostels: Idwal Cottage 9 miles, Llanberis 11, Conwy 15.

Price Band: B	Opening category: ❷

● BETWS-Y-COED ☆☆☆☆

Swallow Falls, Betws-y-Coed, Gwynedd,
LL24 0DW; betwsycoed@yha.org.uk
Tel: 01690 710796 Fax: 01690 710191

This hostel's picturesque location, two miles from the village that shares its name, is part of a very lively and busy hotel and bar complex. The hostel is ideal for school groups and individuals alike, and is a very popular location for walkers and cyclists.
Location: OS 17, GR 764576.
Great for... outdoor types who love walking, cycling and canoeing.
Accommodation: 48 beds: 2 double rooms, 6x6- and 2x4-bed rooms.
Family rooms: Yes. **Rent-a-Hostel:** No.
Classroom: No. **Education packages:** Yes.
Facilities: Small lounge area, self-catering kitchen, showers, toilets, drying room, cycle racks, hotel's bars, large cafeteria, laundry, free parking and children's play area.
Daytime access: All public areas.

Reception open: 8am-10.30pm.
Meals: Self-catering at hostel or comprehensive choice of affordable bar meals at hotel complex.
Getting there: Take the A5 to Betws-y-Coed; the hostel is 2 miles outside the village adjacent to the Swallow Falls Hotel.
Public transport: BUS: Snowdon Sherpa 97A Porthmadog- Betws-y-Coed; also S2 from Betws-y-Coed. RAIL: Betws-y-Coed 2 miles.
Parking: Large car park and coach park.
Nearest other hostels: Capel Curig 3 miles, Idwal 5.

Price Band: B	Opening category: ❶

Picturesque location: YHA Betws-y-Coed.

● BLAENCARON BUNKHOUSE

Blaencaron, Tregaron, Ceredigion SY25 6HL;
reservations@yha.org.uk
Tel: 0870 770 5700
Bookings more than 7 days ahead: 0870 770 8868

Walkers who yearn to lose themselves in unspoilt countryside will be happy here. This former village school is in the quiet Arfon Groes Valley with plenty of activities that will appeal to outdoor folk. Birdwatching is particularly good and there are plenty of mountain bike trails and walking tracks. Cors Caron National Nature Reserve, Strata Florida Abbey and the Devil's Bridge Railway and Waterfall are all within easy reach.
Location: OS 146, GR 713608.
Great for... a quiet break in the country and birdwatching.
You need to know... this hostel only has basic amenities; credit cards are not accepted. There is no hostel shop.
Accommodation: 16 beds: 2x4- and 1x8-bed rooms.

FBR: Yes.
Facilities: Self-catering kitchen/dining/common room, drying room, shower and toilet.
Daytime access: All public areas.
Reception open: 5pm.
Meals: Self-catering only.
Getting there: From Red Lion Inn, Tregaron, take B4343 north. Take first right for 2 miles to phone box and turn right again for 1 mile to reach the hostel.
Public transport: BUS: James 585/9 Aberystwyth-Tregaron then 3 miles. RAIL: Aberystwyth 20 miles, Devil's Bridge (Vale of Rheidol Rly - seasonal) 17.
Parking: Opposite, limited.
Nearest other hostels: Dolgoch 12 miles (9 by mountain path), Tyncornel 14 (8 by mountain path).

Price Band: A   **Opening category:** ❸

●● BORTH ☆☆

Morlais, Borth, Ceredigion SY24 5JS;
borth@yha.org.uk
Tel: 0870 770 5708 Fax: 0870 770 5709

The name of this Edwardian house is Morlais, which translates as 'the voice of the sea'. You'll understand why once you see its position overlooking Cardigan Bay just 20 metres from the beach. Enjoy striking sunsets from the headland or play on the dunes and four miles of sandy beach. The Ynyslas and Ynys Hir nature reserves, Nant Yr Arian Forestry Centre and the world renowned Centre for Alternative Technology are all within reach by bicycle, public transport or car.
Location: OS 135, GR 608907.
Great for... those who love the sea.
Accommodation: 60 beds: 4-, 6- and 8-bed rooms.
Family rooms: Yes. **Rent-a-Hostel:** Yes.

Walking at Cardigan Bay near YHA Borth.

Classroom: Yes.
Education packages: Yes (Book via hostel).
Facilities: TV, showers, cycle store, shop, dining room, self-catering kitchen, conference room, internet access. Lockers in all bedrooms, wildlife garden, birdfeeding station, games room, under-5s playroom, green hostel, BBQ.
Daytime access: Public areas, via numbered lock.
Reception open: Staff available before midday and after 5pm.
Meals: Breakfast, picnic lunch, evening meal.
Getting there: The hostel is on the B4353 between Borth village and the Ynyslas golf links.
Public transport: BUS: Arriva Cymru 511/2 from Aberystwyth. RAIL: Borth 0.5 miles.
⟦NATIONALEXPRESS⟧≫ Birmingham to Aberystwyth.
Parking: Yes, opposite hostel, next to sea wall.
Nearest other hostels: Corris 19 miles, Kings (Dolgellau) 34.

Price Band: B   **Opening category:** ❸

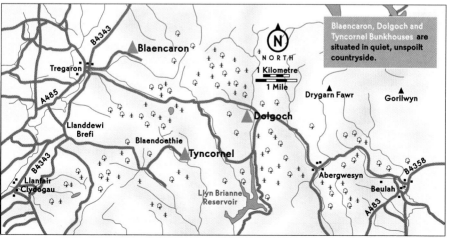

Blaencaron, Dolgoch and Tyncornel Bunkhouses are situated in quiet, unspoilt countryside.

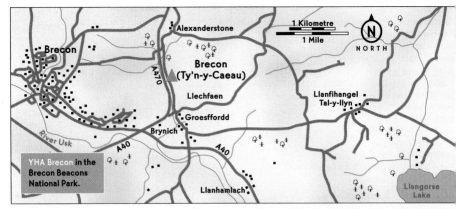

YHA Brecon in the Brecon Beacons National Park.

●● **BRECON** (TY'N-Y-CAEAU) ☆☆☆
Groesffordd, Brecon, Powys LD3 7SW;
brecon@yha.org.uk
Tel: 0870 770 5718 Fax: 0870 770 5719

This Victorian country house is a couple of miles from the historic market town of Brecon, which boasts a wealth of listed properties, narrow streets and a cathedral. A warm and friendly welcome awaits you here, with the hostel making a comfortable, convenient base to explore the area. The Brecon Beacons National Park offers great walking from gentle strolls to spectacular ascents, or save your legs and see the countryside from the saddle on a pony trek. Boating, sailing and canoeing are possible on Llangorse Lake four miles away.

Location: OS 160, GR 074288.

Great for... active families wanting a mix of town and country.

You need to know... special family packages are available, which include free admission to many local attractions. There is no public transport from Brecon to the hostel.

Accommodation: 54 beds: all 2–10-bed rooms, some en-suite.

Family rooms: Yes. **Rent-a-Hostel:** No.

Classroom: No. **Education packages:** Yes.

Facilities: Self-catering kitchen, dining room, drinks licence, TV, showers, drying room, laundry facilities, cycle store, shop, grounds, picnic area and BBQ. **Daytime access:** All public areas.

Reception open: Staff available before 10am and after 5pm.

Meals: Breakfast, picnic lunch, evening meal.

Getting there: From the A40 (Abergavenny–Brecon road) take the Llanfrynach exit. Then follow signs to Groesffordd. Continue through the village following the hostel signs. The hostel is on the right.

Public transport: BUS: Stagecoach in South Wales 21 Abergavenny-Brecon (passes close to Abergavenny station), alight Llanfrynach turn, 1 mile, Stagecoach in South Wales 39 and Yeomans Canyon 40 from Hereford (passes close to Hereford station) and Roy Brown Coaches from Llandrindod Wells, alight Llanddew turn, 0.5 miles.
RAIL: Merthyr Tydfil 20 miles, Abergavenny 19.

Parking: Yes.

Nearest other hostels: Llwyn-y-Celyn 9 miles, Capel-y-Ffin 23.

| Price Band: ⬛ | Opening category: ❸ |

Perfect base: lots of exciting activities await you at YHA Broad Haven.

●● **BROAD HAVEN** ☆☆☆
Broad Haven, Haverfordwest, Pembrokeshire
SA62 3JH; broadhaven@yha.org.uk
Tel: 0870 770 5728 Fax: 0870 770 5729

You'd better be good at making decisions if you stay here. Should you spend the day learning to ride a horse, or climbing and abseiling on spectacular cliffs? Or would sea kayaking, surfing, canoeing, wind-surfing or scuba diving be more fun? All these activities can be arranged at this modern, purpose-built single-storey hostel. There are safe beaches just 100 metres away, the Pembrokeshire Coastal Footpath running past the hostel and boat trips to nearby islands. But whatever you decide to do, toast the day with a glass of wine at the hostel while you watch the sun set over St Brides Bay.

Location: OS 157, GR 863141.

Great for... action men (and women!) keen to try a new skill.

You need to know... the hostel has disabled facilities.

Accommodation: 77 beds: mostly 5- and 7-bed rooms, plus 1x2-bed room, most en-suite.

Family rooms: Yes. **Rent-a-Hostel:** Yes.

Classroom: Yes. **Education packages:** Yes.

Facilities: Self-catering kitchen, dining room, lounge, games area, drying room, showers, suitable for people with disabilities.

Daytime access: Public areas, via numbered keypad.

Reception open: 3pm.

Meals: Breakfast, picnic lunch, evening meal.

Getting there: From the M40 west, take A40 to Haverfordwest. Then follow signs for Broad Haven (7 miles). On approaching village, turn immediately right into Main Beach car park and hostel is on right.

Public transport: BUS: Taf Valley 311 from Haverfordwest (passes close to Haverfordwest station). RAIL: Haverfordwest 7 miles.

Parking: Yes.

Nearest other hostels: Penycwm 8 miles, Marloes 10 (13 by path), St David's 17 (25 by path), Manorbier 28.

Price Band: B	Opening category: ❷

● BRYN GWYNANT ☆☆

**Nantgwynant, Caernarfon, Gwynedd
LL55 4NP; bryngwynant@yha.org.uk
Tel: 0870 770 5732 Fax: 0870 770 5733**

Experience Snowdonia at its most serene in this early Victorian mansion in the heart of the National Park. Set in 40 acres of wooded grounds with stunning views over Llyn Gwynant and Snowdon, this is the perfect escape from the rat race. Walkers will be at home here, with plenty of low and high level routes all around. Don't miss the classic Watkin path up Snowdon, which begins less than a mile from the hostel and leads you into incredible mountain scenery – just don't forget your camera.

Location: OS 115, GR 641513.

Great for... walkers and families who want a quiet escape.

You need to know... Thermos flasks can be hired from the hostel.

Accommodation: 73 beds: mainly 2-, 3-, 4-, 5- and 6-bed rooms, with 1x8-, 1x9- and 1x10-bed option.

Family rooms: Yes. **Rent-a-Hostel:** Yes.

Classroom: Yes.

Facilities: Lounge, self-catering kitchen, bar service, drying room, shop, showers, cycle store and camping.

Daytime access: All public areas.

Reception open: Staff are available before 10am and after 5pm.

Meals: Breakfast, picnic lunch, evening meal.

Getting there: The hostel is on the A498, 8 miles west of Capel Curig and 4 miles east of Beddgelert.

Public transport: BUS: Snowdon Sherpa 97A Porthmadog-Betws-y-Coed. RAIL: Betws-y-Coed 13 miles, Bangor 25 miles.

Parking: Yes.

Nearest other hostels: Pen-y-Pass 4 miles, Capel Curig 8, Snowdon Ranger 9.

Price Band: B	Opening category: ❸

YHA Bryn Gwynant is surrounded by breathtaking views. You will be particularly impressed with the mountain scenery of Snowdon, less than a mile away.

●● CAPEL CURIG ☆☆

**Plas Curig, Capel Curig, Betws-y-Coed, Conwy
LL24 0EL; capelcurig@yha.org.uk
Tel: 0870 770 5746 Fax: 0870 770 5747**

The views of Moel Siabod and the Snowdon Horseshoe from this hostel will have you itching to put on your walking boots and explore Snowdonia. Scale the mountains or enjoy easy wanders through the forest or alongside the River Llugwy. For the more adventurous, Plas-y-Brenin Outdoor Activity Centre is close by, which offers a smorgasbord of adrenalin-filled skills to master.

Location: OS 115, GR 726579.

Great for... active people who want an overdose of fresh air.

You need to know... breakfast is included in the price.

Accommodation: 52 beds: mostly 2-, 4- and 5-bed rooms, plus 1x6- and 1x8-bed option.

Family rooms: Yes. **Rent-a-Hostel:** No.

Classroom: No. **Education packages:** No.

Facilities: Self-catering kitchen, dining room, two lounges, showers, toilets, drying room, cycle store and shop.

Daytime access: Public areas, via numbered lock.

Reception open: 5pm.

Meals: Evening meals for groups only, picnic lunches.

Getting there: Access is difficult from Betws-y-Coed direction. Continue to junction with A4086, turn around and return to hostel up steep driveway. By bus, ask driver to stop at hostel.

Public transport: BUS: Snowdon Sherpa 97A X Porthmadog-Betws-y-Coed; also S2 from Betws-y-Coed, S3 from Bethesda (with connections from Bangor). RAIL: Betws-y-Coed 5 miles.

Parking: Limited.

Nearest other hostels: Pen-y-Pass 5 miles, Idwal Cottage 6, Conwy 18.

Price Band: D   **Opening category:** ❸

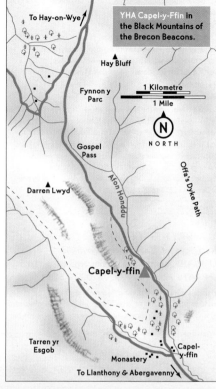

YHA Capel-y-Ffin in the Black Mountains of the Brecon Beacons.

Located in Snowdonia, guests at YHA Capel Curig can choose to climb the many mountains nearby.

⬤⬤ CAPEL-Y-FFIN ☆☆

Capel-y-Ffin, Llanthony, nr Abergavenny, Monmouthshire NP7 7NP

Tel: 0870 770 5748

Nestled in the Llanthony Valley in the stunning Black Mountains of the Brecon Beacons, this small hostel was once a hill farm. It's now an excellent base for walkers and cyclists with routes leading through unspoilt countryside in all directions, including the Cambrian Way, Offa's Dyke trails and Sustrans Route 42. Those with literary interests will want to visit Hay-on-Wye eight miles away, while there are more than enough monastery ruins, stone circles and castles nearby to satisfy history buffs. Horseriders are welcome with stalls for grazing available for horses. Trekking can be arranged locally. The hostel has a nature reserve and bird hide.

Location: OS 161, GR 250328.

Great for... couples and small groups, cyclists and walkers.

You need to know... parking is limited.

Accommodation: 38 beds: 1x3-, 1x4-, 1x6-, 1x8- and 1x18/20-bed rooms.

Family rooms: Yes. **Rent-a-Hostel:** Yes.

Classroom: No. **Education packages:** No.

Facilities: Lounge/dining room, self-catering kitchen, showers, tumble dryer, cycle store, shop and camping. Licenced premises and accredited member of Taste of Wales quality food scheme and Green Dragon environment award.

Daytime access: Dry shelter and toilets.

Reception open: 5pm.

Meals: Breakfast, picnic lunch, evening meal.

Getting there: From A449, A4042 take A465 towards Hereford from Abergavenny. Turn off at Llanfihangel Crucorney, follow signs to Llanthony then to Capel-y-Ffin. Hostel is 1 mile on other side of Capel-y-Ffin village on left. From Hay-on-Wye, turn left opposite Swan Hotel (road signed Capel-y-Ffin). Follow road and signs. Go over mountain road and two cattle grids. Hostel is down road on right-hand side.

Public transport: BUS: Stagecoach in South Wales 39, Yeomans Canyon 40 Hereford-Brecon (passes close to Hereford station), alight Hay-on-Wye 8 miles. RAIL: Abergavenny 16 miles.

NATIONALEXPRESS➤ Abergavenny 14 miles.

Parking: In lay-by. Restricted at hostel.

Nearest other hostels: Brecon 23 miles (16 by mountain path), Welsh Bicknor 33.

Price Band: 🄰 Opening category: ❷

⬤ CARDIFF ☆☆☆

2 Wedal Road, Roath Park, Cardiff CF14 3QX; cardiff@yha.org.uk

Tel: 0870 770 5750 Fax: 0870 770 5751

As the capital city of Wales, Cardiff is a stylish, cosmopolitan city with a rich heritage and a reputation for hosting national and international sporting events. Expect history-filled days (Cardiff Castle and the Museum of Welsh Life at St Fagans are both close by) and excellent nightlife. Located in the student area, the hostel makes a convenient base to explore all the city has to offer.

Location: OS 171, GR 185788.

Great for... experiencing Cardiff's vibrant atmosphere.

You need to know... breakfast is included in the price.

Accommodation: 68 beds: 3x4-, 1x6-, 1x8- and 3x14-bed rooms.

Family rooms: No. **FBR:**Yes. **Rent-a-Hostel:** No.

Classroom: No. **Education packages:** Yes.

Facilities: Two lounges, TV, dining room, self-catering kitchen, showers, shop, laundry, cycle store and luggage store.

Daytime access: All public areas.

A former hill farm: YHA Capel-y-Ffin nestles in the Llanthony Valley in the stunning Black Mountains.

Harmonious: YHA Corris's philosophies reflect its peaceful setting.

Reception open: All day.
Meals: breakfast only. Evening meals for pre-booked groups.
Getting there: From M4, take J29 and follow the A48M to the exit for A470. Take first left off roundabout. Follow Whitchurch Road to traffic lights and turn left into Fairoak Road. Follow road to the roundabout then turn left into Wedal Road and the hostel is on the right.
Public transport: BUS: Cardiff Bus 28 from Cardiff Central station. RAIL: Heath High or Low Level, both 0.5 miles, Cardiff Central 2.5. **NATIONALEXPRESS** Cardiff bus station 2 miles.
Parking: Yes.
Nearest other hostels: Llwyn-y-Celyn 42 miles, Port Eynon 56.

Price Band: D   **Opening category:** 1

●● CONWY ☆☆☆☆
Larkhill, Sychnant Pass Road, Conwy LL32 8AJ; conwy@yha.org.uk
Tel: 0870 770 5774 Fax: 0870 770 5775

This is a modern hostel. Expect high quality accommodation in spacious communal areas with panoramic views. All rooms have en-suite showers and children are well catered for with baby changing facilities, cots and a special menu. It's an ideal base for visiting the North Wales coast and Snowdonia National Park, with the medieval castle and town centre of Conwy a 10-minute walk away.
Location: OS 115, GR 775773.
Great for... families and youth organisations.
You need to know... advance booking is essential.
Accommodation: 80 beds: 2- and 4-bed rooms, en-suite showers.
Family rooms: Yes. **Rent-a-Hostel:** No.
Classroom: Yes (35 to 60 people). **Education packages:** Yes.
Facilities: Lounges, TV room, games room, self-catering kitchen, drying room, shop, cycle store, lockers, laundry facilities, residential licence, internet access, large grounds with summer house, roof terrace, picnic and BBQ area. Disabled facilities.
Daytime access: Public areas, via numbered lock.

Reception open: 2pm.
Meals: Cafeteria/restaurant, alcohol licence.
Getting there: From A55, take J17 second exit for Conwy, A547. Head to Conwy centre and at town walls turn right into Mount Pleasant then right again at T-junction. The hostel is on the left after 150 metres.
Public transport: BUS: frequent from surrounding areas. RAIL: Conwy 0.5 miles, Llandudno Junction 1.5. **NATIONALEXPRESS** Llandudno Junction 0.5 miles.
Parking: Yes.
Nearest other hostels: Bangor 15 miles, Capel Curig 18, Chester 44.

Price Band: C   **Opening category:** 3

●● CORRIS ☆☆☆
Canolfan Corris, Old School, Corris, Machynlleth, Powys SY20 9TQ; corrishostel@canolfancorris.com
Tel: 0870 770 5778 Fax: 0870 770 5778

Do you know your essential oils and understand the greenhouse effect? If so, you'll find a welcoming smile at this award-winning hostel that's run on environmental and Celtic themes and focuses on conservation and inner harmony. This hostel, once a school, has won Green Tourism and WTB Dragon environmental standard award. You'll find it in the Dyfi Eco Valley, close to the Centre for Alternative Technology, Dyfi Biosphere and King Arthur's Labyrinth. Cader Idris mountain, ancient sites and Sustrans National Cycle Route 8 are all within easy reach.

HOSTEL MANAGERS CHOOSE...
THE BEST LOCATIONS FOR NATURE LOVERS

Tyncornel YHA Tyncornel Bunkhouse: "This is a wonderful area for birdwatching. You will see red kites, ravens and buzzards."
Skomer YHA Broadhaven: "Take a trip to the offshore islands of Skomer, Skokholm and Grassholm in search of seal, dolphin, porpoise and whale."
The Black Mountain red kite feeding station: YHA Llanddeusant: "Feeding times for these magnificent birds is 2pm in the winter and 3pm in the spring and summer."
Seals YHA Pwll Deri: "See the seals with their pups in the cave below the hostel."
Newborough beach and nature reserve YHA Bangor: "On Anglesey this long, sandy beach backed by dunes has spectacular views of Snowdonia National Park, Caernarfon and the Lleyn Peninsula. Newborough Warren National Nature Reserve is just behind the beach and covers 1,565 acres."
Conwy RSPB reserve YHA Conwy: "Visit in spring and autumn to see migrants, including ospreys."
Marloes Sands Beach YHA Marloes Sands: "Spectacular views well away from the crowds, plus seals and birds galore."

Location: OS 124, GR 753080.

Great for... folk looking for a caring, holistic atmosphere.

You need to know... credit cards are not accepted (make cheques payable to Canolfan Corris).

Accommodation: 48 beds: 1x2-, 1x10-, 1x22- and few 4-6-bed rooms.

Family rooms: Yes. **Rent-a-Hostel:** No.

Classroom: No. **Education packages:** Yes.

Facilities: Lounge/dining room, self-catering kitchen, showers, drying room, lockers, laundry room, cycle store and grounds.

Daytime access: All public areas.

Reception open: Staff available before 10am and after 5pm.

Meals: Breakfast, picnic lunch, evening meal.

Getting there: From A487 at Briach Goch Hotel turn off downhill (signposted) into village. After 400 metres at Slaters Arms pub and crossroads (signposted), turn left uphill. A small car park is 150 metres on right and the hostel is a further 30 metres uphill on right.

Public transport: BUS: Arriva Cymru 32/4/5, X32 Aberystwyth-Dolgellau (passes Machynlleth station). RAIL: Machynlleth 6 miles.

Parking: Yes.

Nearest other hostels: Kings (Dolgellau) 15 miles, Borth 19, Llanbedr 28.

Price Band: B	Opening category: ❸

● DANYWENALLT

Talybont-on-Usk, Brecon, Powys LD3 7YS

Tel: 0870 770 6136 Fax: 0870 770 6137

Danywenallt Centre is a charmingly converted Welsh farmhouse. Nestling below the Talybont Reservoir, the centre is surrounded by wooded slopes, high peaks, waterfalls and trails. It's secluded location with great access makes it a perfect destination for groups and families. A full catering service is provided; local produce and regional flavours are a speciality. The cosy lounge with its wood-burning stove gives a relaxing end to fun-filled days.

Location: OS 12/13 GR 108205

Great for... groups and National Park education packages, special events, hiking and trekking.

You need to know... Danywenallt has room prices only. There is no self-catering kitchen. Breakfast is included in the price.

Accommodation: 38 beds: 1x2-, 2x3-, 4x6- and 1x5-bed rooms. Most rooms have private facilities.

Family rooms: Yes. **Rent-a-Hostel:** No.

Classroom: No. **Education packages:** Yes.

Facilities: Common room, cycle store, luggage store, wheelchair facilities and laundry facilities.

Daytime access: All public areas.

Reception open: 8am-12noon and 5pm- 10.30pm.

Meals: Breakfast inclusive, cafe/restaurant, packed lunches.

Getting there: From Brecon or Abergavenny on the A40, take the turn signed Talybont. In the village turn right at the T-Junction then opposite the post office turn left across the drawbridge. Follow signs to Talybont reservoir (1.5 miles), at the reservoir turn left across the dam wall and take the track signposted to the hostel. The reservoir can be approached by the mountain road from Merthyr Tydfil and the Pontsticill Reservoir.

Public transport: Bus: From Brecon or Abergavenny 21 (Mon-Sat only). Drop off at Talybont 1.5 miles.

NATIONALEXPRESS≫ Abergavenny bus station 13 miles.

Parking: Car and minibus parking available at the hostel.

Nearest other hostels: Brecon 8 miles , Llwyn-Celyn 12 (by mountain footpath) or 16 by road.

Price Band: D	Opening category: ❸

Charming and secluded: YHA Danywenallt is a converted farmhouse nestling among hills and wooded slopes.

●● CYNWYD ☆☆

The Old Mill, Cynwyd, Corwen, Denbighshire LL21 0LW

Tel: 0870 770 5786 Fax: 0870 770 5786

This small hostel, which offers basic amenities, provides access to unlimited walking and cycling. Follow a mountain path to Pistyll Rhaeadr, the highest waterfall in Wales, or head further afield to Bala Lake, where a plethora of watersports is on offer. Llangollen, Chirk Castle and Lake Vyrnwy RSPB Reserve are also close by. After an action-packed day, this former woollen mill offers a riverside retreat to rest your weary bones.

Location: OS 125, GR 057409.

Great for... walkers and cyclists wanting a rural retreat.

You need to know... it's self-catering accommodation only.

Accommodation: 30 beds: 1x2-, 1x4-, 1x6-, 1x8- and 1x10-bed room.

Family rooms: No. **FBR:** Yes. **Rent-a-Hostel:** Yes.

Classroom: No. **Education packages:** No.

Facilities: Lounge/dining room, self-catering kitchen, showers, toilets, drying room, cycle store, shop, grounds and camping.

Daytime access: Public areas, via numbred lock.

Reception open: 5pm.

Meals: Self-catering only.

Getting there: The hostel is on B4401 from Corwen. In Cynwyd, bear left before bridge and follow road for 100 metres. From Bala, turn right immediately before bridge on B4401, then first left. Go over second bridge and turn immediately right.

Public transport: BUS: Arriva Cymru/GHA 94 Wrexham-Barmouth (passes close to Ruabon and Barmouth stations).

RAIL: Ruabon 18 miles. **Parking:** Yes.

Nearest other hostels: Llangollen 14 miles.

Price Band: **A**	Opening category: **❷**

Small but perfectly formed: YHA Cynwyd.

Birdwatching near the remote YHA Dolgoch Bunkhouse.

● DOLGOCH BUNKHOUSE ☆

Dolgoch, Tregaron, Ceredigion SY25 6NR; reservations@yha.org.uk

Tel: 0870 770 5796

Bookings more than 7 days ahead: 0870 770 8868

Head into the wilds to this remote, gas-lit farmhouse in the lovely Tywi Valley for an experience to remember. There is no electricity and the only heating is an open fire. You'll have to make your own entertainment, but with excellent birdwatching and walking country all around, you won't have trouble keeping yourself busy. The Welsh National Cycle Route runs nearby.

Location: OS 147, GR 806561.

Great for... an escape into the wilds of Wales.

You need to know... the track to the hostel is unsurfaced.

Accommodation: 19 beds: 1x4-, 1x5- and 1x10-bed rooms.

FBR: Yes.

Facilities: Self-catering kitchen/dining room and shower.

Daytime access: All public areas. **Reception open:** 5pm.

Meals: Self-catering only. No shop.

Getting there: From Tregaron take Abergwesyn mountain road for 9 miles. From Beulah on A483, take road to Abergwesyn and then Tregaron mountain road for 6 miles. Hostel is 0.75 miles south of Bridge in Tywi Valley.

Public transport: BUS: James 585/9 Aberystwyth-Tregaron, alight Tregaron, 9 miles. RAIL: Llanwrtyd Wells 10 miles.

Parking: In hostel grounds only.

Nearest other hostels: Blaencaron 12 miles (9 by mountains), Tyncornel 19 (5 by mountains).

Price Band: **A**	Opening category: **❸**

●●● IDWAL COTTAGE ☆☆☆☆

**Nant Ffrancon, Bethesda, Bangor, Gwynedd
LL57 3LZ; idwal@yha.org.uk
Tel: 0870 770 5874 Fax: 0870 770 5875**

Stay below the impressive Glyder mountains with views of the Nant Ffrancon Valley at this former quarry manager's cottage. Recently refurbished, you can be sure of a warm welcome at this environmentally-conscious hostel. All levels of walks can be found in the immediate area, and you won't need to travel far for world-class mountain bike trails. It's perfectly placed for strolls to see Rhaeadr Ogwen Waterfalls or Cwm Idwal nature reserve (with its dramatic lake) and Devil's Kitchen.

Location: OS 115, GR 648603.
Great for... a relaxing stay in the mountains of Snowdonia.
You need to know... it's self-catering accommodation only.
Accommodation: 38 beds: mostly small and medium-sized rooms.
Family rooms: Yes. **Rent-a-Hostel:** No.
Classroom: No. **Education packages:** No.
Facilities: Excellent self-catering kitchen, gathering room, table licence, showers, drying room, cycle store, grounds and camping. Shop with extensive store including frozen meals.
Daytime access: All public areas.
Reception open: Staff available before 10am and after 5pm.
Meals: Self-catering only.
Getting there: The hostel is off the A5 at the west end of Llyn Ogwen, 5 miles south of Bethesda.
Public transport: BUS: Snowdon Sherpa S3 from Bethesda, with connections from Bangor. RAIL: Bangor 12 miles, Betws-y-Coed 11.
Parking: Yes, private car park opposite hostel.
Nearest other hostels: Capel Curig 6 miles, Pen-y-Pass 10 (5 by mountain path), Bangor 10, Llanberis 12 (7 by mountain path).

Price Band: B	Opening category: ❸

●● LAWRENNY ☆☆☆

**Lawrenny, Pembrokeshire SA68 0PN
Tel: 0870 770 5914 Fax: 0870 770 5915**

Pembrokeshire National Park is a rich habitat for waders, wildfowl... and summer tourists. Escape the crowds at this former village school in a quiet corner of the park close to several waterways and footpaths. There are dozens of on- and off-road cycle routes, while Oakwood Pleasure Park, Folly Farm and Carew Castle are all nearby.
Location: OS 158, GR 018070.
Great for... exploring the quieter parts of Pembrokeshire, but only nine miles from Tenby.
You need to know... it's self-catering accommodation without a hostel shop. There is a village shop and post office close by.
Accommodation: 23 beds: 1x3-, 3x4- and 1x8-bed rooms.
Family rooms: No. **FBR:** Yes. **Rent-a-Hostel:** Yes.
Classroom: Yes. **Education packages:** No.
Facilities: Lounge, self-catering kitchen, showers and drying room.
Daytime access: Pre-booked guest access on request otherwise none before 5pm.
Reception open: 5pm.

● KINGS (DOLGELLAU) ☆☆

**Kings, Penmaenpool, Dolgellau, Gwynedd
LL40 1TB; kings@yha.org.uk
Tel: 0870 770 5900 Fax: 0870 770 5901**

Combine a beach holiday with countryside pursuits at YHA Kings, at the southern end of the Snowdonia National Park. Large sandy beaches are close by in Barmouth. Try mountain biking at Coed-y-Brenin, or pony trekking, watersports and fishing in Dolgellau. Walkers will be busy at this country house and can choose between a high-level hike up Cader Idris or gentle trails leading to the Mawddach Estuary, whose low tide sands and woodlands are a haven for wildlife and migrant waders.
Location: OS 124, GR 683161.
Great for... individuals and groups combining quiet days on the beach with energetic walking.
You need to know... it's open to organised groups all year.
Accommodation: 42 beds: all 6-bed rooms. (4 en-suite)
Family rooms: Yes. **Rent-a-Hostel:** Yes.
Classroom: No. **Education packages:** No.
Facilities: Lounge, dining room, licence, showers, drying room, shop, cycle store, camping and grounds.
Daytime access: Public areas, via numbered keypad.
Reception open: 5pm.
Meals: Breakfast. Full catering for pre-booked groups from April to September, otherwise self-catering.
Getting there: The hostel is off the A493 Dolgellau–Tywyn road. 1 mile west of Penmaenpool, turn uphill opposite Abergwynant Trekking Centre. Then drive along the lane for 1 mile.
Public transport: BUS: Arriva Cymru 28, 35 Dolgellau-Aberystwyth, alight Abergwynant then 1 mile to hostel. RAIL: Fairbourne 8 miles then bus 28/35 stops at station or Mawddach 5 miles.
Parking: Yes.
Nearest other hostels: Corris 15 miles, Llanbedr 17.

Price Band: B	Opening category: ❷

Country house: the peaceful YHA Kings.

Great for families: one of the many beaches near child-friendly YHA Llanbedr.

Meals: Self-catering only.
Getting there: Follow A40 west from Carmarthen to Canaston Bridge. Take A4075 Tenby Road past Oakwood Leisure Park to CC2000/ Canaston Bowl. Turn right, follow signs to Lawrenny (6 miles).
Public transport: BUS: DialaBus Tue/Thu only. Minibus available for self drive hire. RAIL: Narberth 10 miles. **Parking:** Yes.
Nearest other hostels: Manorbier 9 miles, Marloes Sands 23.

Price Band: A	Opening category: ❶

◉◉ **LLANBEDR** (HARLECH) ☆☆
Plas Newydd, Llanbedr, Barmouth LL45 2LE;
llanbedr@yha.org.uk
Tel: 0870 770 5926 Fax: 0870 770 5927

Bring the kids to this Youth Hostel and feel like the best parents in the world. If you can drag them away from the swing park and football pitch next to the hostel, there are beaches and mountains aplenty to explore. Cycle the Mawddach Trail, walk the Rhinog mountains and mountain bike on world-class tracks in Coed-y-Brenin Forest. Shell Island, Harlech Castle and Llanfair Slate Caverns are all within three

miles of the hostel.
Location: OS 124, GR 585267.
Great for... families who like beaches, hills and a relaxed atmosphere.
Accommodation: 42 beds: all 3-, 4- and 6-bed rooms.
Family rooms: Yes. **Rent-a-Hostel:** Yes.
Classroom: No. **Education packages:** No.
Facilities: Lounge, self-catering kitchen, dining room, shop, showers, drying room, cycle store and garden.
Daytime access: All public areas.
Reception open: 5pm.
Meals: Breakfast, picnic lunch, evening meal. Local specialities.
Getting there: The hostel is on A496 in centre of village beside stone bridge over river. Tight turn into hostel drive.
Public transport: BUS: Arriva Cymru 38 Barmouth-Blaenau Ffestiniog. RAIL: Llanbedr 0.5 miles.
Parking: Yes, narrow entrance.
Nearest other hostels: Kings 17 miles, Bryn Gwynant 31, Snowdon Ranger 33, Borth 48.

Price Band: B	Opening category: ❷

● LLANBERIS ☆☆☆

**Llwyn Celyn, Llanberis, Caernarfon, Gwynedd
LL55 4SR; llanberis@yha.org.uk
Tel: 0870 770 5928 Fax: 0870 770 5929**

Mountain bikers, climbers and walkers will find plenty to do at this mountainside hostel. The quickest route up Snowdon, whose summit is visible from the hostel, starts close by, or choose less strenuous valley walks to waterfalls. Llyn Padarn, where you can be instructed in the arts of fishing, canoeing, windsurfing and sailing, is less than a mile from the hostel, or take to the saddle with a day's pony trekking. Castles and craft workshops also abound for the less energetic.

Location: OS 115, GR 574596.

Great for... active, adventurous people.

Accommodation: 56 beds: 3x2-, 1x3-, 4x4-, 1x5-, 2x6- and 1x8-bed rooms, 3 fully en-suite with double beds.

Family rooms: Yes. **Rent-a-Hostel:** No.

Classroom: Yes. **Education packages:** No.

Facilities: Lounge, TV room, self-catering kitchen, dining room, showers, drying room, cycle store and shop.

Daytime access: Public areas, via numbered lock for people staying over. New arrival: no access until after 5pm.

Reception open: 5pm.

Meals: Breakfast, picnic lunch, evening meal.

Getting there: From High Street, take Capel Coch Road (Spar is on the corner) and keep left at the fork in the road halfway up the hill. The hostel is on the left through a farm gate. Please contact hostel for coach access.

Public transport: BUS: KMP/Padarn 85/6 from Bangor (pass close to Bangor station), 88 from Caernarfon. On both alight 0.5 miles north west of Llanberis, then 0.5 miles. RAIL: Bangor 11 miles.

Parking: Cars and minibuses only.

Nearest other hostels: Pen-y-Pass 6 miles, Snowdon Ranger 11 (4 by mountain), Bangor 11, Bryn Gwynant 11.

Price Band: B	Opening category: ❸

● LLANDDEUSANT ☆☆☆

**The Old Red Lion, Llanddeusant,
Carmarthenshire SA19 9UL;
llanddeusant@yha.org.uk
Tel: 0870 770 5930 Fax: 0870 770 5930**

A break in this rural retreat will restore your spirits. Set in the least developed area of the Brecon Beacons, the hostel overlooks the magical Sawdde Valley. Trails lead up to the legendary Llyn y Fan glacial lake and the heights of the Carmarthen Fans. Circular walks will take you to an Iron Age fort, Roman camps and standing stones. The hostel, a former inn built in 1789, retains many of its original features and offers a warm welcome with an open fire in the lounge. The Black Mountain Red Kite feeding station is a mile away.

Location: OS 160, GR 776245.

Great for... getting away from it all.

You need to know... the hostel has no shop.

Accommodation: 26 beds: 3x4-, 1x6- and 1x8-bed rooms.

Family rooms: Yes. **Rent-a-Hostel:** Yes.

Classroom: No. **Education packages:** No.

Facilities: Self-catering kitchen, common room, showers, cycle store, drying room and camping. **Daytime access:** Public areas, via numbered lock.

Reception open: 5pm.

Meals: Self-catering only.

Getting there: From M4 either J29 (A449 to A40) or J32 (A470 to A40). From A40 Brecon–Llandovery road, turn left in Trecastle at Castle Coaching Inn. After 9 miles on Llanddeusant Road turn left opposite Cross Inn, then 1 mile to hostel on right. From Carmarthen, take A40 via Llandeilo then right for A4069 (Llangadog to Brynamman Road). Turn left opposite Three Horseshoes pub. Follow road round to right in Twynllannan, turn right and immediately left. Look for hostel signs on the left by the church.

Public transport: RAIL: Llangadog 7 miles.

Parking: Cars/minibuses only.

Nearest other hostels: Ystradfellte 23 miles, Llwyn-y-Celyn 25, Brecon 29.

Price Band: A	Opening category: ❸

HOSTEL MANAGERS CHOOSE...

THE BEST LOCATIONS FOR WELSH HISTORY

Museum of Welsh Life YHA Cardiff: "In the grounds of St Fagans Castle, this open air museum shows visitors how the people of Wales have lived and worked for the past 500 years."

St David's Cathedral YHA St David's: "Built upon the site of St David's 6th century monastery, St David's Cathedral is a majestic building set in a magnificent setting."

Beaumaris Castle YHA Bryn Gwynant: "Although never completed, this is Britain's most technically advanced moated castle. Enjoy a picnic in the grounds and see the ducks and swans on the castle moat."

Llanfair Slate Caverns YHA Llanbedr: "A different era of history, but one which has helped shape Wales nonetheless. For those interested in going further back in time, Harlech Castle is also within three miles of the hostel."

Caernarfon Castle YHA Snowdon Ranger: "Just eight miles from the hostel, Caernarfon Castle and the walled town is a World Heritage site. It's one of the six 13th century castles built by Edward I and makes an impressive contrast to the smaller castles of the Welsh princes."

The Iron Age YHA Trefdraeth: "Visit Castell Henllys Iron Age fort just a short distance from the hostel."

Conwy Castle YHA Conwy: "The views from the battlements are amazing. Looking over to the coast, you'll see Llandudno and the Ormes, with the mountains of Snowdonia in the opposite direction."

●● LLANGOLLEN ☆☆☆

**Tyndwr Road, Llangollen, Denbighshire
LL20 8AR; llangollen@yha.org.uk
Tel: 0870 770 5932 Fax: 0870 770 5933**

Tyn Dwr Hall is a large Victorian manor and coach house set in over seven acres of private grounds which specialises in group visits. The surrounding area is ideal for a huge range of adventure activities including hill walking, gorge walking, canoeing and climbing. Educational visits, especially in geography and history, are also very popular, making Llangollen ideal for schools, youth groups, clubs, community groups and larger family groups.

Location: OS 117, GR 232413.

Great for... group activities, social and learning skills.

You need to know... the centre must be booked in advance.

Accommodation: 134 beds: 2-, 4- and 6-bed rooms, with several 10–20-bed options.

Family rooms: Yes. **Rent-a-Hostel:** Yes.

Classroom: Yes. **Education packages:** Yes.

Facilities: Self-catering kitchen, lounge, dining room, drying room, cycle store, showers, games room, table licence, residential licence, and dance floor. **Daytime access:** All public areas.

Reception open: 3pm.

Meals: Breakfast, picnic lunch, evening meal.

Getting there: From A5 east of Llangollen, turn left after golf club and follow hostel signs. From town, follow A5 towards Shrewsbury and, after fire station, bear right up Birch Hill. Turn right at Y-junction, then 0.5 miles to hostel.

Public transport: BUS: Arriva Cymru/GHA 94, Bryn Melyn X5, GHA 555 Wrexham-Llangollen (passes Ruabon station), alight Llangollen, then 1.5 miles. RAIL: Chirk 5 miles, Ruabon 5.

NATIONALEXPRESS» Market St, Memorial Hall 2 miles.

Parking: Yes.

Nearest other hostels: Cynwyd 14 miles, Chester 23, Capel Curig 38.

Price Band: B	Opening category: ❸

●● LLWYN-Y-CELYN ☆☆☆

**Libanus, Brecon, Powys LD3 8NH;
llwynycelyn@yha.org.uk
Tel: 0870 770 5936 Fax: 0870 770 5937**

This hostel offers access to some of the best walking in Wales. Choose gentle strolls alongside the Brecon and Monmouth Canal or ascend across the spectacular ridges and peaks of Pen-y-Fan (2,907 feet) and Corn Du (2,863 feet). Guided walks are organised by the National Park between April and October. Cosy accommodation greets your return to the hostel, an 18th century Welsh farmhouse set in 15 acres of ancient woodland.

Location: OS 160, GR 973225.

Great for... walkers of all abilities.

Accommodation: 41 beds: 5x2-, 3x4-, 1x5-, 1x6- and 1x8-bed rooms.

Family rooms: Yes. **Rent-a-Hostel:** No.

Classroom: Yes. **Education packages:** No.

Facilities: Self-catering kitchen, full meals service, dining room, lounge with open fire, showers, drying room, shop, cycle store, small seminar rooms, grounds with nature trail and camping.

Daytime access: All areas.

Reception open: Staff available before 10am and after 5pm.

Meals: Breakfast, picnic lunch, evening meal.

Getting there: From M4 take J32 north to A470. Hostel is 13 miles north of Merthyr Tydfil, signed on road. From Brecon take A470 towards Merthyr Tydfil. Hostel is on left, 2 miles beyond Libanus village. Access on foot from Taff Trail 1 mile north of Storey Arms.

Public transport: BUS: Sixty Sixty Coaches 43 Merthyr Tydfil-Brecon RAIL: Merthyr Tydfil 11 miles, Abergavenny 28.

Parking: Yes.

Nearest other hostels: Brecon 9 miles, Ystradfellte 12, Llanddeusant 25, Capel-y-Ffin 33, Cardiff 35.

Price Band: B	Opening category: ❸

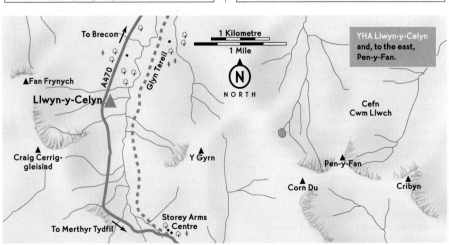

To Brecon

1 Kilometre
1 Mile

N
NORTH

YHA Llwyn-y-Celyn and, to the east, Pen-y-Fan.

▲Fan Frynych

A470

Glyn Tarell

Llwyn-y-Celyn

Cefn Cwm Llwch

▲Craig Cerrig-gleisiad

Y Gyrn

Pen-y-Fan

Corn Du

Cribyn

To Merthyr Tydfil

Storey Arms Centre

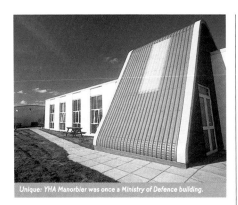

Unique: YHA Manorbier was once a Ministry of Defence building.

● MANORBIER ☆☆☆

Manorbier, nr Tenby, Pembrokeshire
SA70 7TT; manorbier@yha.org.uk
Tel: 0870 770 5954 Fax: 0870 770 5955

An action-packed break awaits at YHA Manorbier in the Pembrokeshire Coast National Park. From the clifftops overlooking Caldey Island, the coastal path and Church Doors beach will no doubt beckon. But it's the children who will be in their element here. Visit Oakwood, Wales's largest theme park. Or, for open spaces and a dose of Welsh history, try Heatherton Country Park, Wedlock Dinosaur Park, or Pembroke and Carew Castles. Even staying in this hostel, a futuristic former Ministry of Defence building is an adventure!

Location: OS 158, GR 081975.
Great for... families with energetic kids.
You need to know... self-catering apartments are also available.
Accommodation: 69 beds: 1x2-, 1x3-, 5x4-, 6x6 and 1x8-bed rooms, plus 2 separate apartments sleeping 4–6.
Family rooms: Yes. **Rent-a-Hostel:** Yes.
Classroom: Yes. **Education packages:** Yes.
Facilities: Lounge/TV room, games room, self-catering kitchen, dining room, shop, showers, cycle store, laundry facilities, grounds and camping. **Daytime access:** To reception area with seating, toilet, drinks machine and laundry room.
Reception open: 5pm.
Meals: Breakfast, picnic lunch, evening meal.
Getting there: From Tenby follow A4139 towards Pembroke. Turn left at junction of B4585 to Manorbier. This is also signposted to the Royal Artillery Range (RAR Station). Turn left at signpost to hostel and Shrinkle Haven. Go straight over roundabout by children's playground and up hill. At the top, turn left in front of RAR gates. Hostel is on left 0.5 miles along this road on clifftops.
Public transport: BUS: First 349, Silcox 358 Tenby-Haverfordwest, alight Skrinkle 1 mile. RAIL: Manorbier 2.5 miles.
NATIONAL EXPRESS Tenby, Upper Park Road 4.25 miles.
Parking: Yes.
Nearest other hostels: Lawrenny 9 miles, Broad Haven 28.

Price Band: **B**	Opening category: **❷**

●● MARLOES SANDS ☆☆

Runwayskiln, Marloes, Haverfordwest,
Pembrokeshire SA62 3BH;
reservations@yha.org.uk
Tel: 0870 770 5958 Fax: 0870 770 5959
Bookings more than 7 days ahead: 0870 770 8868

Wake up to the sounds of the sea. A cluster of National Trust farm buildings with exceptional sea views, YHA Marloes Sands is on the Pembrokeshire Coastal Path. Famous bird sanctuary and marine reserve Skomer Island can be reached by ferry from nearby Martin's Haven or try your hand at watersports at Dale.
Location: OS 157, GR 778080.
Great for... walkers and outdoor folk looking for a seaside haven.
You need to know... parking is limited to six cars.
Accommodation: 26 beds: 1x2-, 2x4-, 1x6- and 1x10-bed rooms.
Family rooms: No. **FBR:** Yes. **Rent-a-Hostel:** Yes.
Classroom: No. **Education packages:** No.
Facilities: Combined lounge/dining room/self-catering kitchen, showers, drying room, cycle store and small shop.
Daytime access: All public areas.
Reception open: 5pm.
Meals: Self-catering only.
Getting there: Follow B4327 from Haverfordwest for 11 miles and turn right to Marloes. At village church, turn left to car park. The hostel is down a private track on left approx 200 metres (coaches not allowed, speed limit 5mph).
Public transport: BUS: Puffin Shuttle 400 Milford Haven-St Davids (May-Sep only); otherwise Edwards 316 from Haverfordwest and Milford Haven to Marloes, then 1 mile.
RAIL: Milford Haven 11 miles, Haverfordwest 14.
Parking: Limited to 12 cars. Minibuses in National Trust car park.
Nearest other hostels: Broad Haven 13 miles (path), St David's 22.

Price Band: **A**	Opening category: **❷**

●● PENYCWM ☆☆☆☆☆

Whitehouse, Penycwm, Haverfordwest,
Pembrokeshire SA62 6LA; penycwm@yha.org.uk
Tel: 0870 770 5988 Fax: 0870 770 5989

This is the very first hostel in Britain to be awarded a five-star grade so expect a warm welcome, wholesome food, en-suite rooms (some with double beds) with TV and an exceptional level of comfort. It makes a great base to explore Pembrokeshire. The award-winning hostel is close to a number of Blue Flag beaches including the extensive beach at Newgale and the attractive harbour village of Solva. There are walks to suit all and watersports, boat rides and horseriding are easy to arrange.
Location: OS 157, GR 857250.
Great for... a comfortable family holiday.
You need to know... you must book evening meals 24 hours ahead.
Accommodation: 26 beds: 2x2-, 4x4- and 1x6-bed rooms, all en-suite.
Family rooms: Yes. **Rent-a-Hostel:** No.
Classroom: Yes. **Education packages:** Yes.
Facilities: Lounge, TV room, self-catering kitchens, showers, cycle

store, luggage store, indoor recreation area and lawned grounds. No hostel shop. **Daytime access:** All public areas and rooms for people staying. New arrivals access; to games room and toilet.
Reception open: 5pm.
Meals: Breakfast, picnic lunch, evening meal.
Getting there: Access via A487 Newgale to Solva road. At Penycwm take minor road north towards Letterston/Mathry and follow signs to the hostel.
Public transport: BUS: Richards 411 Haverfordwest-Fishguard (passes close to Fishguard Harbour), alight Penycwm, then 1.5 miles. RAIL: Haverfordwest 10 miles.
Parking: Yes.
Nearest other hostels: Broad Haven 8 miles, Trefin 8, St David's 9 (17 by path).

| Price Band: C | Opening category: ❸ |

●● PORT EYNON ☆☆☆
**Old Lifeboat House, Port Eynon, Swansea
SA3 1NN; porteynon@yha.org.uk
Tel: 0870 770 5998 Fax: 0870 770 5999**

Once a lifeboat station, YHA Port Eynon is in a beautiful position on the Gower with an award-winning beach on its doorstep. The beach has enough sand and rock pools to keep the children entertained for hours. The bay is also extremely popular for all watersports and there is storage for surfboards, canoes and other bulky equipment at the hostel. With the Gower Coastal Path and cycle trails crossing this Area of Outstanding Natural Beauty and its 34 miles of heritage coast, YHA

Port Eynon is an outdoor enthusiast's dream.
Location: OS 159, GR 468848.
Great for... outdoor activities in a quiet setting.
You need to know... parking is 400 metres away so you'll have to carry that surfboard.
Accommodation: 28 beds: 3x2-, 2x4-, 1x6- and 1x8-bed rooms.
Family rooms: Yes. **Rent-a-Hostel:** Yes.
Classroom: No. **Education packages:** No.
Facilities: Lounge/dining room, self-catering kitchen, showers, drying room, shop and cycle store. **Daytime access:** Public areas, via numbered lock.
Reception open: 5pm.
Meals: Self-catering only.
Getting there: If approaching from Severn Bridge, exit from M4 at J42 in Swansea. Follow the brown and white tourist signs for Gower then the A4118 for Port Eynon. If you are approaching from Carmarthen, exit the M4 at J47 following signs for Gower then South Gower. In Port Eynon follow the road down to the car park at the beach. From the car park walk down the track signed 'parking for permit holders only' to hostel.
Public transport: BUS: Pullman Coaches 118 from Swansea Quadrant bus station (Sun & Bank Holidays: Pullman Coaches 114/119). RAIL: Swansea 16 miles.
NATIONALEXPRESS» Swansea 16 miles.
Parking: Use seafront car park, 400 metres away.
Nearest other hostels: Llanddeusant 44 miles, Cardiff 56.

| Price Band: B | Opening category: ❸ |

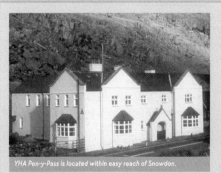
YHA Pen-y-Pass is located within easy reach of Snowdon.

● PEN-Y-PASS ☆☆
**Pen-y-Pass, Nantgwynant, Caernarfon,
Gwynedd LL55 4NY; penypass@yha.org.uk
Tel: 0870 770 5990 Fax: 0870 770 5991**

This hostel was once the haunt of Victorian climbers – George Mallory of Everest fame once stayed here on his early climbing trips to Wales. With such a prestigious history, it now makes the ideal base to ascend Snowdon and explore the surrounding mountains.

Location: OS 115, GR 647556.
Great for... walkers wanting easy access to Snowdon.
You need to know... parking is limited.
Accommodation: 79 beds: a few 2-, mostly 4–6-bed rooms, plus 1x12-bed option. Some ensuite.
Family rooms: Yes. **Rent-a-Hostel:** No.
Classroom: Yes. **Education packages:** No.
Facilities: Two lounges, residents' bar and lounge, games room, self-catering kitchen, dining room, shop, showers, drying room, cycle store and lockers. **Daytime access:** All public areas.
Reception open: All day.
Meals: Breakfast, picnic lunch, evening meal.
Getting there: From A55 coast road follow signs for Llanberis then A4086 to hostel. From A5 turn onto A4086 at Capel Curig. Turn right at Pen-y-Gwryd Hotel. The hostel is on the right.
Public transport: BUS: Snowdon Sherpa S1 from Llanberis (connections from Bangor station), S2 from Betws-y-Coed, S3 from Bethesda, S4 from Caernarfon, 97A Porthmadog-Betws-y-Coed. RAIL: Bangor 18 miles, Betws-y-Coed 12.
Parking: Public car park opposite – limited permits available. **Nearest other hostels:** Bryn Gwynant 4 miles, Capel Curig 5, Idwal Cottage 5 (by path), Llanberis 6.

| Price Band: B | Opening category: ❷ |

●● PWLL DERI ☆☆
**Castell Mawr, Trefasser, Goodwick,
Pembrokeshire SA64 0LR**
Tel: 0870 770 6004 Fax: 0870 770 6004

Perched in an idyllic clifftop setting, this hostel boasts spectacular views and glorious sunsets. Watch the seals and birds as you follow the coastal path that passes alongside the hostel or visit Llangloffan Farmhouse Cheese Centre and Melin Tregwynt Woollen Mill.
Location: OS 157, GR 891387.
Great for... a relaxed break by the sea.
You need to know... it's self-catering accommodation only.
Accommodation: 31 beds: 2x2-, 1x4- and 2x8-bed rooms.
Family rooms: No. **FBR:** Yes. **Rent-a-Hostel:** No.
Classroom: No. **Education packages:** No.
Facilities: Lounge/dining room, self-catering kitchen, shower, drying room, shop and cycle store. **Daytime access:** Entrance hall and toilets.
Reception open: 5pm.
Meals: Self-catering only.
Getting there: Take Pwll Deri road out of Goodwick, keep following signs for Pwll Deri. From St David's–Fishguard road, approach via St Nicholas.
Public transport: BUS: Richard 404 Strumble Shuttle Fishguard-St David's, May-Sep only, alight Trefasser Cross, then 0.75 miles; otherwise Richards 410 Fishguard-Goodwick (connections from Haverfordwest stations), alight Goodwick, then 4 miles.
RAIL: Fishguard Harbour 4.5 miles.
Parking: Nearby.
Nearest other hostels: Trefin 9 miles (by path), Trefdraeth 13 (22 by path), St David's 21, Poppit Sands 37 (by path).

Price Band: A **Opening category:** ❷

● ROWEN ☆☆☆
Rhiw Farm, Rowen, Conwy LL32 8YW
Tel: 0870 770 6012
Bookings more than 7 days ahead: 0870 770 8868

This traditional Welsh hill farmhouse retains much of its rustic charm and original character. Situated at the top of a very steep, narrow lane, it offers breathtaking views over the Conwy Valley and across to Snowdonia. A friendly welcome awaits walkers with open fires in the lounge and dining room to warm you after a day on the hills.
Location: OS 115, GR 747721.
Great for... keen walkers wanting a rural haven.
You need to know... access to the hostel is up a very steep hill (1:3 gradient) on a narrow, rough road and shouldn't be attempted in cars in poor weather.
Accommodation: 24 beds: 1x2-, 1x4-, 1x8- and 1x10-bed rooms.
Family rooms: No. **FBR:** Yes. **Rent-a-Hostel:** Yes.
Classroom: No. **Education packages:** No.
Facilities: Lounge, dining room, self-catering kitchen, shower, small shop and cycle store. No credit cards accepted.
Daytime access: Basic shelter and toilet.
Reception open: 5pm.
Meals: Self-catering only.

Fishing is just one of the activities on offer at YHA Poppit Sands.

●● POPPIT SANDS ☆☆☆
**Sea View, Poppit, Cardigan, Pembrokeshire
SA43 3LP; poppit@yha.org.uk**
Tel: 0870 770 5996 Fax: 0870 770 5996

YHA Poppit Sands is set in five acres of grounds that reach to the sea. It overlooks a fantastic Blue Flag sandy beach and bay where, if you keep your eyes peeled, you may spot dolphins and seals. The hostel has been extensively refurbished and is now run using sustainable technologies. Horseriding, cycling, birdwatching, fishing and boat trips are all available in the area.
Location: OS 145, GR 144487.
Great for... anyone who loves the outdoors.
You need to know... it's self-catering accommodation only.
Accommodation: 36 beds: 2-, 3-, 4-, 5 and 6-bed rooms.
Family rooms: Yes. **Rent-a-Hostel:** Yes.
Classroom: No. **Education packages:** No.
Facilities: Lounge, self-catering kitchen/dining room, showers, drying room, shop and camping.
Daytime access: All public areas.
Reception open: Staff available before 10am and after 5pm.
Meals: Self-catering only.
Getting there: From Carmarthen take the A484 to Cardigan. Follow the signs to St Dogmaels (B4546) and then to Poppit Sands. From Aberystwyth take the A487 to Cardigan then the B4546 to St Dogmaels and Poppit Sands. The hostel is signposted from the lifeboat station (you will find the hostel down a flight of concrete steps).
Public transport: BUS: Richards 405/7/9 and Poppit Rocket from Cardigan to within 0.5 miles.
RAIL: Fishguard Harbour 20 miles, Carmarthen 26.
Parking: Yes.
Nearest other hostels: Trefdraeth 11 miles, Pwll Deri 25, Llanddeusant 43, Borth 48.

Price Band: B **Opening category:** ❷

Getting there: From B5106 follow signs for Rowen to post office. Continue along main street for 500 metres and turn right at hostel sign. Continue straight uphill. Hostel is 0.75 miles further on left. Access is unsuitable for some vehicles.

Public transport: Bus now goes to hostel. Arriva Cymru 19A Llandudno-Llanrwst (passes close to Llandudno Junction and Betws-y-Coed stations). RAIL: Tal-y-Cafn 3 miles.

NATIONALEXPRESS Llandudno Junction 5.5 miles.

Parking: Yes.

Nearest other hostels: Conwy 5 miles, Bangor 12 (by mountain path), Capel Curig 12, Idwal Cottage 17 (by mountain path).

> **Price Band:** A   **Opening category:** ❷

●● SNOWDON RANGER ☆☆☆

Rhyd Ddu, Caernarfon, Gwynedd LL54 7YS; snowdon@yha.org.uk

Tel: 0870 770 6038 Fax: 0870 770 6039

This former inn nestles at the foot of Snowdon and offers lake swimming from its own beach. In an area steeped in Welsh culture, you won't be short of places to visit. The village of Beddgelert, Sygun Copper Mine, Caernarfon Castle and the Maritime Museum are all nearby. The Snowdon Ranger Path up Snowdon also begins here.

Location: OS 115, GR 565550.

Great for... exploring the mountains, lakes and valleys of Snowdonia National Park.

You need to know... the hostel is in a roadside location.

Accommodation: 59 beds: mostly 2- and 4-bed rooms.

Family rooms: No. **FBR:** Yes. **Rent-a-Hostel:** No.

Classroom: No. **Education packages:** No.

Facilities: Lounge, games room, dining room, self-catering kitchen, showers, drying room, cycle store, shop and grounds.

Daytime access: Public areas, via numbered lock.

Reception open: 5pm.

Meals: Breakfast, picnic lunch, evening meal.

Getting there: The hostel is on the A4085, 8 miles south of Caernarfon, 5 miles north of Beddgelert and 12 miles from A55 coastal expressway.

Public transport: BUS: Snowdon Sherpa S4 from Caernarfon (connections from Bangor station).

RAIL: Porthmadog 13 miles, Bangor 16.

Parking: Yes.

Nearest other hostels: Bryn Gwynant 9 miles (7 by path), Llanberis 11 (4 by path), Pen-y-Pass 14 (10 by path), Bangor 17.

> **Price Band:** B   **Opening category:** ❸

●● ST DAVID'S ☆

Llaethdy, Whitesands, St David's, Pembrokeshire SA62 6PR stdavids@yha.org.uk

Tel: 0870 770 6042 Fax: 0870 770 6043

There's plenty of entertainment to be had around St David's, Britain's smallest city. It offers a cathedral, Bishop's Palace, Oceanarium and watersports centre plus Ramsey Island RSPB reserve across the bay.

Explore Britain's smallest city with a stay at YHA St David's.

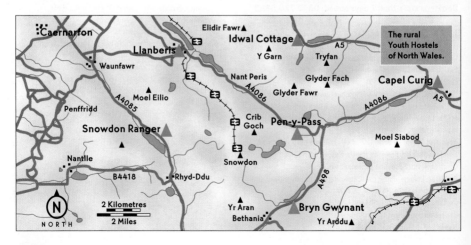

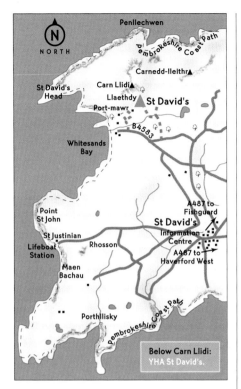

**Below Carn Llidi:
YHA St David's.**

Whitesands Bay, one of the best beaches and seaside resorts in Wales, is a 15-minute walk. After a hectic day, escape the hurly-burly of life in this Youth Hostel, which has simple accommodation in an old farmhouse and outbuildings set below Carn Llidi.

Location: OS 157, GR 739276.

Great for... busy days and quiet evenings.

You need to know... the hostel is on an unmade road.

Accommodation: 40 beds: 1x8-, 1x12- and 1x16-bed rooms, plus 1x4-bed self-contained flat in separate building.

Family rooms: Yes. **Rent-a-Hostel:** No.

Classroom: No. **Education packages:** No.

Facilities: Lounge, self-catering kitchen/dining room, showers, drying room and shop. **Daytime access:** To day room and toilets.

Reception open: 5pm. **Meals:** Self-catering only.

Getting there: Leave A487 Fishguard road just outside St David's on B4583 and follow signs to Whitesands Bay. The hostel is signed from golf club. **Public transport:** BUS: Richards 411 Haverfordwest-Fishguard (passes close to Fishguard Harbour), alight St David's, then 2 miles. RAIL: Fishguard Harbour 15 miles, Haverfordwest 18.

Parking: Yes.

Nearest other hostels: Penycwm 9 miles (by road), 17 (by path) Trefin 11 (by path), Pwll Deri 21 (by path).

Price Band: A	Opening category: ❷

●● TREFDRAETH ☆☆☆

Lower St Mary Street, Newport, Pembrokeshire SA42 0TS; reservations@yha.org.uk
Tel: 0870 770 6072 Fax: 0870 770 6072
Bookings more than 7 days ahead: 0870 770 8868

Families will find themselves busy here. A short walk from the shops, pubs, beach, coastal path and bird sanctuary of Newport, the hostel also offers easy access to the Preseli Hills where wild ponies still roam freely. Those interested in the past will enjoy exploring hut circles and burial chambers, as well as Castell Henllys Iron Age fort. Fishing and pony trekking are also nearby.

Location: OS 145, GR 058393.

Great for... a family holiday packed with activities.

You need to know... parking is limited at this self-catering hostel, and there's no day access.

Accommodation: 28 beds: 2x2-, 3x4- and 2x6-bed rooms.

Family rooms: Yes. **Rent-a-Hostel:** Yes.

Classroom: No. **Education packages:** No.

Facilities: Lounge, self-catering kitchen/dining room, showers and cycle store. No hostel shop. **Daytime access:** None at hostel, shelter and toilets in Newport, within walking distance.

Meals: Self-catering only.

Reception open: Before 10am after 5pm.

Getting there: From Fishguard take A487 to Cardigan road. At Newport turn left down St Mary's Street just before Golden Lion pub. From Aberystwyth take A487 to Cardigan road and continue to Newport. Follow signs to hostel after Golden Lion pub. Hostel is behind the Eco Centre.

Public transport: BUS: Richards 412 Haverfordwest-Cardigan, and Poppit Rocket. RAIL: Fishguard Harbour 9 miles, Clarbeston Road 14.

Parking: Limited.

Nearest other hostels: Poppit Sands 11 miles (14 miles by coast path), Pwll Deri 13 (22 by coastal path), Trefin 15.

Price Band: B	Opening category: ❷

●● TREFIN ☆☆☆

Ffordd-yr-Afon, Trefin, Haverfordwest, Pembrokeshire SA62 5AU;
reservations@yha.org.uk
Tel: 0870 770 6074 Fax: 0870 770 6074
Bookings more than 7 days ahead: 0870 770 8868

In the centre of a small, friendly village, this hostel used to be a school and still retains a children's playground. Now refurbished, it's a good base for exploring Pembrokeshire Coast National Park. The sea is half a mile away, as is the coastal path. The fishing village of Abereiddy, famous for its Blue Lagoon and black-sand beaches, is two miles away, or head to St David's for safe swimming and sandcastles galore.

Location: OS 157, GR 840324.

Great for... a family holiday.

You need to know... it's self-catering accommodation only, although the hostel is close to a pub.

Accommodation: 26 beds: 5x4- and 1x6-bed rooms.

Family rooms: No. **FBR:** Yes. **Rent-a-Hostel:** No.

Explore the Pembrokeshire Coast National Park near YHA Trefin.

No credit cards accepted or hostel shop.
Daytime access: All public areas.
Reception open: 5pm.
Meals: Self-catering only.
Getting there: From Llanddewi–Brefi follow road southeast up Brefi Valley signed to hostel (not southwest to Farmers). Fork left at 4.75 miles. At signpost at 6 miles continue on rough track to hostel (1 mile).
Public transport: BUS: James 585/9 Aberystwyth-Tregaron, some calling, some with connections on James 588/9 to Llanddewi Brefi, then 7 miles or alight Tregaron on others, then 10 miles.
RAIL: Aberystwyth 28 miles.
Parking: Yes.
Nearest other hostels: Blaencaron 14 miles (8 by mountains), Dolgoch 19 (5 by mountains).

> **Price Band:** A   **Opening category:** 3

●● YSTRADFELLTE ☆☆
Tai'r Heol, Ystradfellte, Aberdare, CF44 9JF;
ystradfellte@yha.org.uk
Tel: 0870 770 6106 Fax: 0870 770 6106

These two charming cottages a mile south of the village make a good base for exploring the network of footpaths in the west of the Brecon Beacons National Park – don't miss the trail that leads to the spectacular waterfalls and natural swimming pool at Porth-yr-Ogof. The National Showcave Centre at Dan-yr-Ogof and cycle hire are also close by.
Location: OS 160, GR 925127.
Great for... walking, exploring and taking 'time out'.
You need to know... it's self-catering accommodation only; there's a small hostel shop; credit cards are not accepted.
Accommodation: 28 beds: 1x2-, 3x4-, 1x6- and 1x8-bed rooms.
Family rooms: Yes. **FBR:** Yes. **Rent-a-Hostel:** Yes.
Classroom: Yes. **Education packages:** No.
Facilities: Self-catering kitchen/dining room, lounge, showers, shop, cycle store, BBQ, drying room and camping.
Daytime access: All public areas.
Reception open: Before 10am and after 5pm.
Meals: Self-catering only.
Getting there: From M4, exit J43 and take A465 towards Merthyr Tydfil. Take slip road 1 mile past Glyneath roundabout signposted Onllwyn, A4019. At lights turn right, take second minor road on left to Pontneddfechan/waterfalls road. Continue to Ystradfellte hostel on left 1 mile before Ystradfellte village.
Public transport: BUS: Regular service from Neath and Swansea to Pontneddfechan/Glyneath (4m). Also service from Cardiff to Aberdare. Contact Traveline Cymru for latest info on 0870 6082 608.
RAIL: Aberdare 8 miles, Neath 20. **Parking:** Yes.
Nearest other hostels: Llwyn-y-Celyn 12 miles, Brecon 21, Llanddeusant 23.

> **Price Band:** A   **Opening category:** 2

Classroom: No.
Education packages: No.
Facilities: Lounge/dining room/self-catering kitchen, showers, cycle store, drying room and toilets. Picnic and BBQ area.
Daytime access: Public areas, via numbered pad.
Reception open: 5pm-7pm.
Meals: Self-catering only.
Getting there: From A487 take turning to Trefin. Hostel is in the village centre, near the pub.
Public transport: BUS: Richards 411 Haverfordwest-Fishguard (passes close to Fishguard Harbour station).
RAIL: Fishguard Harbour 12 miles, Haverfordwest 18.
Parking: Yes, six cars only.
Nearest other hostels: Penycwm 8 miles (by road), Pwll Deri 9, St David's 11, Trefdraeth 15.

> **Price Band:** A   **Opening category:** 2

● TYNCORNEL BUNKHOUSE ☆
Llanddewi-Brefi, Tregaron, Ceredigion
SY25 6PH; reservations@yha.org.uk
Tel: 0870 770 8868 Fax: 0870 770 6127

This isolated farmhouse is a favourite with folk in search of solitude. Walkers can explore the mountain terrain of the Elenydd while the Cors Caron Nature Reserve will thrill wildlife lovers. Wherever you wander, keep your eyes trained upwards to spot red kites.
Location: OS 147, GR 751534.
Great for... a retreat well away from it all.
You need to know... the hostel now has electricity but no phone; it's self-catering only.
Accommodation: 16 beds: 2x8-bed rooms.
Facilities: Self-catering kitchen/common room and shower.

Heart of England & The Wye Valley

Explore great historical towns or unwind in rolling countryside as you experience a region that is quintessentially English.

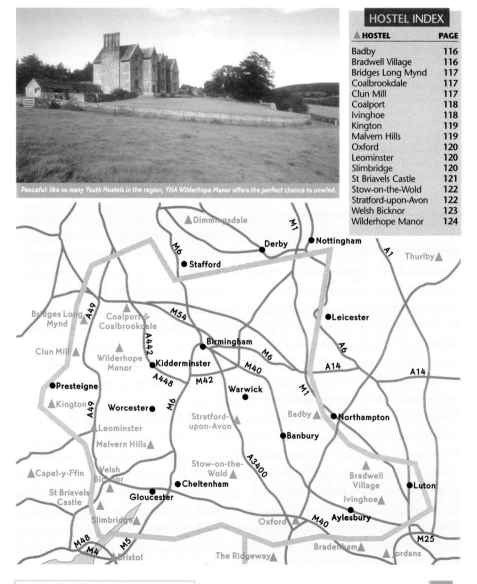

Peaceful: like so many Youth Hostels in the region, YHA Wilderhope Manor offers the perfect chance to unwind.

●● BADBY ☆☆

**Church Green, Badby, Daventry,
Northamptonshire NN11 3AS; badby@yha.org.uk
Tel: 0870 770 5680 Fax: 0870 770 5680**

Step into yesteryear and stay in the only thatched Youth Hostel in England and Wales. This cosy 17th century cottage is on the church green in the unspoilt village of Badby and has a large garden and orchard. But don't stand for too long – a sweeping landscape surrounds the hostel where a network of quiet lanes and footpaths will take eager walkers and cyclists to ancient churches and country houses.

Location: OS 152, GR 561588.

Great for... walkers seeking an idyllic break.

You need to know... the hostel is only minutes from the M1 and M40.

Accommodation: 20 beds: 2x2-, 2x4-(adjoining) and 1x8-bed rooms.

Family rooms: No. **FBR:** Yes. **Rent-a-Hostel:** Yes.

Classroom: No. **Education packages:** No.

Facilities: Lounge, self-catering kitchen, dining room, cycle store, shop and garden.

Daytime access: Public areas, via numbered lock.

Reception open: 5pm. **Meals:** Self-catering only.

Getting there: Turn off A361, main Daventry–Banbury road, at brown Youth Hostel sign. Follow main street into village. Just past Windmill pub, turn left onto Vicarage Hill until you reach church green. At T-junction turn left down hill and hostel is on left.

Public transport: BUS: Geoff Amos from Rugby station. RAIL: Long Buckby 6 miles, Rugby 12.

NATIONALEXPRESS Daventry bus station 3 miles.

Parking: There is no parking available directly outside hostel.

Nearest other hostels: Bradwell 21 miles, Stratford 24.

Price Band: B	Opening category: ❸

Walkers will enjoy the network of paths and lanes near YHA Badby.

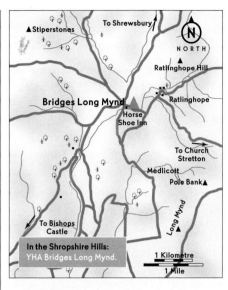

To Shrewsbury

▲Stiperstones

NORTH

Ratlinghope Hill

Bridges Long Mynd

Horse Shoe Inn

Ratlinghope

To Church Stretton

Medlicott

Pole Bank▲

Long Mynd

To Bishops Castle

In the Shropshire Hills: YHA Bridges Long Mynd.

1 Kilometre
1 Mile

●● BRADWELL VILLAGE ☆

**Vicarage Road, Milton Keynes, Bucks MK13 9AG;
bradwellvillage@yha.org.uk
Tel: 0870 770 5716 Fax: 0870 770 5717**

An attractive 18th century stone farmhouse, this Youth Hostel is within easy reach of Milton Keynes. The city boasts attractions including the UK's biggest indoor 'real' snow slope and a renowned contemporary gallery and theatre. It also has a multitude of parkland and lakes accessible by 200 miles of cycle routes. The home of the Enigma machine and Woburn Abbey and its safari park are nearby.

Location: OS 152, GR 831395.

Great for... year-round winter sports; cyclists of all abilities.

Accommodation: 37 beds: 1x1-, 3x4-, 1x5-, 1x9- and 1x10-bed rooms.

Family rooms: No. **FBR:** Yes. **Rent-a-Hostel:** Yes.

Classroom: No. **Education packages:** Yes.

Facilities: Lounge, dining room, self-catering kitchen, showers, drying room, cycle store and grounds.

Daytime access: All public areas via numbered lock.

Reception open: 5pm.

Meals: Breakfast only. Full catering for pre-booked parties of 10+.

Getting there: From A5 take A422 and turn right into Bradwell. From M1 J14 take A509 to central Milton Keynes. Take V6 (Grafton Street) right, follow signs to Bradwell. Hostel is next to the church.

Public transport: BUS: frequent from surrounding areas. RAIL: Milton Keynes Central 0.5 miles.

NATIONALEXPRESS Milton Keynes coachway 5 miles.

Parking: At rear of hostel.

Nearest other hostels: Ivinghoe 19 miles, Badby 21, Oxford 38.

Price Band: B	Opening category: ❸

●● BRIDGES LONG MYND ☆

Ratlinghope, Shrewsbury, Shropshire SY5 0SP;
Tel: 01588 650656 Fax: 01588 650531

You'll find this small hostel that was once the old village school hidden away in the Shropshire hills. Walkers will love it here, with the Shropshire Way passing close by and paths leading you to Long Mynd and Stiperstones. Remember to bring your binoculars as there's plenty of birdlife worth watching.

Location: OS 137, GR 395965.
Great for... keen walkers looking for uncrowded paths.
Accommodation: 37 beds: 1x5-, 1x8-, 1x10- and 1x14-bed rooms.
Family rooms: No. **FBR:** Yes. **Rent-a-Hostel:** No.
Classroom: No. **Education packages:** No.
Facilities: Lounge, self-catering kitchen, dining room, showers, drying room, cycle store and camping. No credit cards accepted (make cheques payable to Bridges Youth Hostel).
Daytime access: Shelter and toilet.
Reception open: 5pm.
Meals: Breakfast, picnic lunch, evening meal.
Getting there: From Church Stretton, take The Burway and fork right at top of Long Mynd (impassable in winter). From Shrewsbury, take road via Longden and Pulverbatch, then left by Horseshoe Inn.
Public transport: BUS: Boulton's 551 from Shrewsbury (Tue only). RAIL: Church Stretton 5 miles.
Parking: Yes.
Nearest other hostels: Wilderhope 13 miles, Clun Mill 16.

Price Band: A   Opening category: ❸

●● COALBROOKDALE ☆☆

c/o High Street, Coalport, Telford, Shropshire
TF8 7HT; ironbridge@yha.org.uk
Tel: 0870 770 5882 Fax: 0870 770 5883

Ironbridge was once the centre of British industry. This hostel at the 19th century Literary and Scientific Institute provides comfortable accommodation within walking distance of the first iron bridge in the world (constructed in 1777 to advertise iron-based technology) and the museum of iron. History buffs will be happy to indulge their inquisitive brains in no less than 10 industrial heritage museums.

Location: OS 127, GR 671043.
Great for... those interested in Britain's past, also for exploring the Shropshire hills.
You need to know... this is one of two Youth Hostels in Ironbridge (Coalport is the other); this hostel is available for pre-booked guests only.
Accommodation: 80 beds: 1x2-, 10x4-, 5x6- and 1x8-bed rooms.
Family rooms: No. **FBR:** Yes. **Rent-a-Hostel:** Yes.
Classroom: Yes. **Education packages:** Yes.
Facilities: Lounge, TV, games room, drying room, toilets, showers.
Daytime access: Toilet and members' kitchen only.
Reception open: 5pm.
Meals: Breakfast, picnic lunch, evening meal.
Getting there: From Telford centre, follow signs to Ironbridge. With the bridge on the left, turn right at the roundabout into Coalbrookdale. The hostel is half a mile on the right.
Public transport: BUS: Arriva 76/7 from Telford (pass close to Telford

● CLUN MILL ☆☆

The Mill, Clun, Craven Arms, Shropshire SY7 8NY Tel: 0870 770 5766 Fax: 0870 770 5766
Bookings more than 7 days ahead: 0870 770 5916

This restored watermill was once a focal point in the tiny town of Clun and you'll see much of the old machinery still in situ. It now offers accommodation to walkers and cyclists wanting to explore the environmentally sensitive area of the Clun Valley. There's a generous helping of history too, with hill forts and castles nearby.
Location: OS 137, GR 303812.
Great for... a walking break in rolling countryside.
You need to know... it's self-catering accommodation only.
Accommodation: 24 beds: 1x7-bed room and 1x4-, 1x8- and 1x5-bed rooms (en-suite).
Family rooms: No. **FBR:** Yes. **Rent-a-Hostel:** Yes.
Classroom: No. **Education packages:** No.
Facilities: Lounge/dining room, self-catering kitchen, showers, lockable cycle store, grounds and camping. New camping annexe with kitchen, drying room, toilet and shower.
Daytime access: Kitchen, drying room, toilet and shower.
Reception open: Staff available before 10am and after 5pm.
Meals: Self-catering only.
Getting there: From Clun High Street (B4368) go to the end of

Ford Street, turn right and then left. The hostel is 250 metres on the right, past the Memorial Hall.
Public transport: BUS: Whittlebus 745 from Ludlow and Craven Arms (passes close to Ludlow and Craven Arms stations), alight Clun 0.5 miles. RAIL: Broome 7 miles, Hopton 7, Craven Arms 10.
Parking: Yes.
Nearest other hostels: Bridges 16 miles, Wilderhope 20, Leominster 30.

Price Band: B   Opening category: ❷

YHA Clun Mill is ideal for those who want to explore Clun Valley.

Central). RAIL: Telford Central 5 miles, Wellington Telford West 5.
NATIONAL EXPRESS Town Centre, Telford.
Parking: Yes, limited.
Nearest other hostels: Coalport 3 miles, Wilderhope Manor 14.

Price Band: B **Opening category:** 4

●● COALPORT ☆☆☆
**John Rose Building, High Street, Coalport,
Shropshire TF8 7HT; ironbridge@yha.org.uk
Tel: 0870 770 5882 Fax 0870 770 5883**

Ironbridge was once the centre of British industry. Stay here and you'll be in the thick of its history, as the hostel (once the oldest china works in Europe) is set in the heart of the Ironbridge World Heritage site on the thickly wooded banks of the River Severn. History buffs will be happy to indulge their inquisitive brains in no less than 10 industrial heritage museums.
Location: OS 127, GR 671043.
Great for... visiting museums and the Shropshire hills.
You need to know... this is one of two Youth Hostels in Ironbridge.
Accommodation: 85 beds: 1x1-, 4x2-, 2x3-, 8x4-, 1x5-, 1x6-, 2x8-

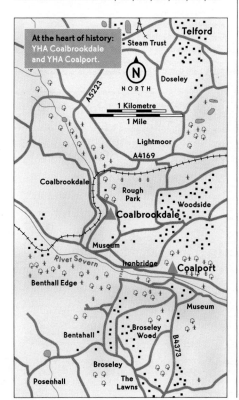

and 1x11-bed rooms, some en-suite.
Family rooms: Yes. **Rent-a-Hostel:** No.
Classroom: Yes. **Education packages:** Yes.
Facilities: Lounge, games rooms, cafeteria (10.00am–4pm except in winter), drying room and fully licensed bar.
Daytime access: All public areas.
Reception open: All day.
Meals: Breakfast, picnic lunch, evening meal. Buffets available if booked in advance. Fully licenced bar.
Getting there: From Telford, take A442 towards Kidderminster, then follow Ironbridge Museum signs past Blists Hill. Hostel is 1 mile on right at China Museum.
Public transport: BUS: Arriva 76/7 from Telford (pass close to Telford Central). RAIL: Shifnal 6 miles.
Parking: Museum car park.
Nearest other hostels: Coalbrookdale 3 miles, Wilderhope Manor 14.

Price Band: C **Opening category:** 4

Step back in time: YHA Coalbrookdale and Coalport.

●● IVINGHOE ☆
**High Street, Ivinghoe, Leighton Buzzard,
Bedfordshire LU7 9EP; ivinghoe@yha.org.uk
Tel: 0870 770 5884 Fax: 0870 770 5885**

The former home of a brewer, this Georgian mansion stands in the picturesque Bedfordshire village of Ivinghoe. It is an ideal base for walkers with the Ridgeway and Chilterns both nearby. Whipsnade Zoo is also in the area.
Location: OS 165, GR 945161.
Great for... walking, cycling and visiting London.
Accommodation: 50 beds: 2x5-, 2x6-, 1x8- and 2x10-bed rooms.
Family rooms: Yes. **Rent-a-Hostel:** No.
Classroom: No. **Education packages:** Yes.
Facilities: Lounge, TV, self-catering kitchen, showers, drying room and cycle store. **Daytime access:** Sorry, none until after 5pm.

●KINGTON

Victoria Road, Kington, Herefordshire HR5 3BX; kington@yha.org.uk
Tel: 0870 770 6128 Fax: 0870 770 6129

The hostel provides excellent modern accommodation including disabled facilities. A good base for walking at Offas Dyke and quiet border areas.

Location: OS 148 GR300568

Great for... exploring the borders and Offas Dyke. It's also a great gateway into South and Mid-Wales.

Accommodation: 27 beds: 3x2-, 4x4- and 1x5-bed rooms. Most rooms are en-suite including a ground floor room with disabled facilities.

Family rooms: Yes. **Rent-a-Hostel:** Yes.

Facilities: Common room, cycle store, laundry facilities, garden and wheelchair facilities.

Daytime access: All public areas, via numbered lock.

Reception open: 7am-10pm and 5pm-11pm.

Meals: Self-catering.

Getting there: In the town centre. The hostel is on Victoria Rd.

Public transport: BUS: Hereford 461/2, Leominster 497, Presteign and Knighton 468. RAIL: Leominster 14 miles, Hereford 25.

Parking: Yes. Space for 8 cars on site.

Nearest other hostels: Leominster 14 miles, Clun Mill 21.

Price Band: B	Opening category: ❷

YHA Kington is located within easy reach of Offa's Dyke and the quiet border areas, making it ideal for walkers.

Reception open: 5pm.

Meals: Breakfast, picnic lunch, evening meal.

Getting there: The hostel is in the village centre, next to the church and opposite the village green on the B489.

Public transport: BUS: Arriva 61 Aylesbury-Luton (passes close to Aylesbury and Luton stations). RAIL: Cheddington 2.5 miles.

Parking: Yes.

Nearest other hostels: Jordans 19 miles, Bradwell Village 19.

Price Band: B	Opening category: ❸

● MALVERN HILLS ☆

18 Peachfield Road, Malvern Wells, Worcestershire WR14 4AP; malvern@yha.org.uk
Tel: 0870 770 5948 Fax: 0870 770 5949

In Victorian times, wealthy socialites would visit the spa town of Great Malvern to take the water cure. Book a break here today and you'll still get a healthy holiday. This hostel, a fine Edwardian house, is adjacent to the Malvern commons, from where the Malvern Hills Area of Outstanding Natural Beauty stretches in a 10-mile ridge with views to 15 counties from the top. And of course, there are still opportunities to sample the famous spring water.

Location: OS 150, GR 774440.

Great for... walkers wanting a relaxed break.

Accommodation: 58 beds: 2x2- and 5x4–6-bed rooms, plus 3 larger rooms.

Family rooms: No. **Rent-a-Hostel:** No.

Classroom: No. **Education packages:** No.

Facilities: Lounge, TV, dining room, self-catering kitchen, games room, showers, drying room, cycle store, shop and garden.

Daytime access: Porch, toilet and games room.

Reception open: 5pm.

Meals: Breakfast, picnic lunch, evening meal.

Getting there: The hostel is 1.5 miles south of Great Malvern on the Wells Road (A449). Turn opposite the Railway Inn into Peachfield Road and the hostel is 400 metres on the right.

Public transport: BUS: frequent from surrounding areas. RAIL: Great Malvern 1 mile.

NATIONALEXPRESS Rosebank Gdns, Great Malvern, 1.25 miles.

Parking: Yes.

Nearest other hostels: Leominster 24 miles, Welsh Bicknor 28, Stow-on-the-Wold 33, Slimbridge 35.

Price Band: B	Opening category: ❸

YHA Leominster: ideal for history lovers.

LEOMINSTER ☆☆☆☆
The Old Priory, Leominster, Herefordshire HR6 8EQ
Tel: 0870 770 5916 Fax: 0870 770 5916

This new hostel is in a section of the Old Priory monastic complex, part of the Benedictine monastery that dates back to 1123. It was enlarged to form a workhouse in 1836 and now offers small, comfortable rooms from where you can wander the town's narrow streets and wonder at its medieval, Tudor and Georgian houses. The Lindlow and Kington Mortimer trails are close by.
Location: OS 149, GR 499593.
Great for... families in search of history.
You need to know... the hostel has self-catering facilities only.
Accommodation: 30 beds: 4x2-, 2x3- and 4x4-bed rooms.
Family rooms: Yes. **Rent-a-Hostel:** Yes.
Classroom: No. **Education packages:** No.
Facilities: Lounge, kitchen, toilets, showers, laundry and drying room. Facilities for people with disabilities.
Daytime access: Public areas, via numbered lock.
Reception open: 5pm.
Meals: Self-catering only.
Getting there: From all directions, enter town centre one-way system. At end of Burgess St, go straight across junction into Church St and follow road round left side of the church to end. From rail station, pedestrian access via Pinsley Road, park and churchyard.
Public transport: BUS: frequent from surrounding areas. RAIL: Leominster 0.25 miles.
Parking: Yes.
Nearest other hostels: Kington 14 miles, Clun Mill, Malvern Hills 24, Wilderhope Manor 25.

Price Band: B	Opening category: ❷

● OXFORD ☆☆☆☆
2a Botley Road, Oxford, Oxfordshire OX2 0AB;
oxford@yha.org.uk
Tel: 0870 770 5970 Fax: 0870 770 5971

This new, purpose-built Youth Hostel is located next to the railway station, close to the River Thames and only a few minutes' stroll from the historic city centre. It's the perfect base for exploring the multitude of attractions in the city or touring the Cotswolds, Ridgeway and the Chilterns. And with internet access, staying here is all too easy.
Location: OS 164, GR 486063.
Great for... a base to explore the Oxford area.
You need to know... there's no parking; park and ride nearby; breakfast is included in the overnight price.
Accommodation: 184 beds: 8x2- (2 with wheelchair access), 12x4- and 20x6-bed rooms.
Family rooms: Yes. **Rent-a-Hostel:** No.
Classroom: Yes. **Education packages:** Yes.
Facilities: Common room, lounge, TV room, café with table licence, wheelchair access, gardens, internet access, games room, laundry facilities, luggage store, payphone, smoking room.
Daytime access: All public areas.
Reception open: 24hrs (night security).
Meals: Breakfast, evening meal.
Getting there: From the station turn right and go under bridge. Hostel is on the right immediately behind the railway station (see map on page 173).
Public transport: RAIL: Oxford, adjacent.
NATIONALEXPRESS Gloucester Green 0.25 miles.
Parking: None except for disabled badge holders.
Nearest other hostels: Ridgeway 17 miles, Streatley 19.

Price Band: E	Opening category: ❶

● SLIMBRIDGE ☆☆☆
Shepherd's Patch, Slimbridge, Gloucestershire GL2 7BP; slimbridge@yha.org.uk
Tel: 0870 770 6036 Fax: 0870 770 6037

Birdwatchers will be in their element here, as a wide variety of wildfowl flocks to this area. The world famous WWT Wildfowl and Wetlands Centre is nearby and the hostel has an observation lounge so you can keep an eye on feathered visitors to the duck pond. Walkers will find plenty to do too, with long-distance footpath The Severn Way running past the hostel and the Cotswold Way four miles away. The National Waterways Museum and Berkeley Castle are also nearby.
Location: OS 162, GR 730043.
Great for... birdwatchers, cyclists, walkers and visiting historic Gloucester.
Accommodation: 56 beds: 5x2-, 4x4–8-, 1x8- and 1x10-bed rooms.
Family rooms: Yes. **Rent-a-Hostel:** No.
Classroom: Yes. **Education packages:** Yes.
Facilities: Lounge, games room, self-catering kitchen, showers, drying room, cycle store, shop and laundry facilities.
Daytime access: All public areas.
Reception open: 5pm.

Step back in time: YHA St Briavels Castle was once a moated Norman castle.

Meals: Breakfast, picnic lunch, evening meal.

Getting there: From M5 going south, exit at J13. Going north, exit J14. Follow signs to WWT Wetlands Centre from motorway and on A38. At Slimbridge roundabout on A38, follow signs to hostel. Continue through village of Slimbridge to Tudor Arms. The hostel is 250 metres down the lane to the right.

Public transport: BUS: Stagecoach in the Cotswolds 20 Stroud-Dursley, Stagecoach in Gloucester 91 Gloucester-Dursley (passes close to Gloucester station). On both alight Slimbridge roundabout 1.5 miles. RAIL: Cam & Dursley 3 miles, Stonehouse 8.5.

Parking: Yes.

Nearest other hostels: Bristol 25 miles, Bath 30, St Briavels Castle 30, Malvern Hills 35.

Price Band: **B**   Opening category: **4**

●● ST BRIAVELS CASTLE ☆☆

St Briavels, Lydney, Gloucestershire
GL15 6RG; stbriavels@yha.org.uk
Tel: 0870 770 6040 Fax: 0870 770 6041

You'll have no trouble thinking what to write on your postcards if you stay in this Youth Hostel, housed in a moated Norman castle. Originally built as a hunting lodge for King John in 1205 on the site of an earlier stronghold, its towers were added in 1293 as part of the Ring of Stone around Wales. It's a unique experience, especially when you enter into the ancient spirit with medieval banquets on Wednesdays and Saturdays in August.

Location: OS 162, GR 558045.

Great for... a unique experience for wannabe Norman knights.

You need to know... the building has no disabled access.

Accommodation: 70 beds: 1x4-, 3x6- and 2x8-bed rooms, plus 3 larger rooms.

Family rooms: No. **FBR:** Yes. **Rent-a-Hostel:** No.

Classroom: Yes. **Education packages:** Yes.

Facilities: Lounges, self-catering kitchen, dining room, showers, drying room, cycle store, shop and grounds. Medieval banquets on Wednesday and Saturday nights in August.

Daytime access: Shelter and toilets.

Meals: Breakfast, picnic lunch, evening meal.

Reception open: 5pm.

Getting there: From Chepstow take A466 towards Monmouth. After 6 miles, when the road crosses the River Wye, immediately take the right turn signposted St Briavels. After 0.5 miles, turn right again and follow St Briavels signs up the hill. The castle is right in front of you at the top of the hill. From Monmouth turn left before the bridge.

Public transport: BUS: Welcome Travel/Stagecoach in South Wales 69 from Chepstow (passes close to Chepstow station), alight Bigsweir Bridge 2 miles. RAIL: Lydney 7 miles.

Parking: Yes.

Nearest other hostels: Welsh Bicknor 12 miles, Slimbridge 30.

Price Band: **B**   Opening category: **4**

HOSTEL MANAGERS CHOOSE...
THE BEST VIEWS

River Wye YHA St Briavels Castle: "For the best way to see the beautiful tree-lined slopes of the Wye Valley, hire a kayak or canoe and paddle down the river."

Malvern Hills YHA Malvern Hills: "An Area of Outstanding Natural Beauty well worth exploring."

Clun Castle YHA Clun Mill: "An imposing ruin on the hill over the village."

Forest of Dean YHA Welsh Bicknor: "Biking for everyone on traffic-free trails with great views."

◉ ● STOW-ON-THE-WOLD ☆☆☆☆

The Square, Stow-on-the-Wold GL54 1AF;
stow@yha.org.uk
Tel: 0870 770 6050 Fax: 0870 770 6051

Stay in a listed 16th century townhouse in the market square of the Cotswold stone-built market town of Stow-on-the-Wold. Thanks to a Heritage Lottery grant, the hostel has been comfortably refurbished, with sympathetic restoration of the 17th century staircase. Despite the house's auspicious history, children are welcome here and you'll find a new play area and picnic tables in the garden.

Location: OS 163, GR 191258.
Great for... a family break in picturesque surroundings.
You need to know... parking in the square is restricted between 9am and 5pm.
Accommodation: 48 beds: 1x1-, 2x4-, 4x6-, 1x7- and 1x8- bed rooms, most en-suite.
Family rooms: Yes. **Rent-a-Hostel:** No.
Classroom: No. **Education packages:** Yes.
Facilities: Lounge, self-catering kitchen, TV, dining room, laundry facilities and cycle store. **Daytime access:** Public areas, via numbered lock.
Reception open: Staff available before 10am and after 5pm.
Meals: Breakfast, picnic lunch, evening meal.
Getting there: The hostel sits between the White Hart and the Old Stocks Hotel in Market Square.
Public transport: BUS: Pulhams P1 Cheltenham Spa-Moreton-in-Marsh (passes close to Cheltenham Spa station); Beaumont Travel 55 Moreton-in-Marsh-Cirencester. Both pass close to Moreton-in-Marsh station. RAIL: Moreton-in-Marsh 4 miles.
Parking: Car park at rear of hostel.
Nearest other hostels: Stratford-upon-Avon 20 miles, Oxford 30.

Price Band: C	Opening category: ❷

◉ ● STRATFORD-UPON-AVON ☆☆☆☆

Hemmingford House, Alveston, Stratford-upon-Avon, Warwickshire, CV37 7RG;
stratford@yha.org.uk
Tel: 0870 770 6052 Fax: 0870 770 6053

This splendidly refurbished Georgian mansion house is set in over three acres of grounds in a quiet village, just under two miles from Stratford-upon-Avon. It's a convenient place to stay if you're seeking a cultural weekend, visiting Shakespeare's birthplace and catching performances by the world renowned Royal Shakespeare Company at one of the town's three theatres. Warwick and Kenilworth Castles are also nearby.

Location: OS 151, GR 231562.
Great for... those who know Othello from Macbeth.

Special: YHA Stow-on-the-Wold is a listed 16th century townhouse.

● WELSH BICKNOR ☆☆☆

**near Goodrich, Ross-on-Wye, Herefordshire
HR9 6JJ; welshbicknor@yha.org.uk
Tel: 0870 770 6086 Fax: 0870 770 6087**

Outdoor folk will be spoilt for choice at this former Victorian rectory, set in 25 acres of relaxing riverside grounds with splendid views of the Royal Forest of Dean and Symonds Yat rock. Hire a canoe and take in the picturesque valley from the River Wye or choose pedal power to explore the Forest of Dean. Walkers will find miles of footpaths to follow – we recommend you start with the Wye Valley Walk which runs past the hostel.
Location: OS 162, GR 591177.

Great for... outdoor folk and families with plenty of energy.
Accommodation: 76 beds: 1x2-, 6x4-, 4x6-, 2x8- and 1x10-bed rooms.
Family rooms: Yes. **Rent-a-Hostel:** No.
Classroom: Yes. **Education packages:** No.
Facilities: Lounges, TV, games room, dining room, self-catering kitchen, showers, drying room, cycle store, laundry facilities, grounds, canoe landing stage and camping.
Daytime access: Public areas, via numbered lock.
Reception open: Staff available before 10am and after 5pm.
Meals: Breakfast, picnic lunch, evening meal.
Getting there: Leave A40 midway between Ross-on-Wye and Monmouth, follow signs to Goodrich/Goodrich Castle. From village, follow lane signed hostel 1.5 miles. Take second lane right after crossing cattle grid. It's a narrow, single track drive with sharp bend.

Set in 25 acres of riverside grounds: YHA Welsh Bicknor.

Public transport: BUS: Stagecoach in Wye & Dean 34 Monmouth-Ross-on-Wye, with connections from Gloucester and Hereford, alight Goodrich Village, 1.5 miles. RAIL: Lydney 12 miles, Gloucester 19.
Parking: Yes.
Nearest other hostels: St Briavels Castle 12 miles, Slmbridge 24.

Price Band: B   **Opening category:** ❷

You need to know... breakfast is included in the price.
Accommodation: 132 beds: 1x12-, 11x2-, 8x6-, 7x4-, 2x3- and 2x8-bed rooms, some en-suite.
Family rooms: Yes. **Rent-a-Hostel:** No.
Classroom: Yes. **Education packages:** Yes.
Facilities: TV lounge, games room, self-catering kitchen, showers, cycle store, laundry facilities, internet access, extensive grounds and foreign exchange. **Daytime access:** All public areas.
Reception open: 24hrs.
Meals: Breakfast, picnic lunch, evening meal.
Getting there: From Stratford-upon-Avon, at Clopton Bridge take B4086 Wellesbourne Road. Follow hostel signs and hostel is 1.5 miles on left. From M40, exit J15 and take A429 south, follow signs to Charlecote Park. Then turn right onto the B4086 and hostel is 1.5 miles on right (see map on page 173).
Public transport: BUS: Stagecoach in Warwickshire Red X18, 18 Leamington Spa-Stratford-upon-Avon-Coventry (pass close to Leamington Spa station). RAIL: Stratford-upon-Avon 2.5 miles. NATIONALEXPRESS» Riverside bus station 1.5 miles.
Parking: Large car park.
Nearest other hostels: Stow-on-the-Wold 20 miles, Badby 24.

Price Band: D   **Opening category:** ❸

Smart: YHA Stratford-upon-Avon is a refurbished Georgian mansion.

Walking in the Shropshire Hills near the National Trust-owned YHA Wilderhope Manor.

⬤⬤ WILDERHOPE MANOR ☆☆

Longville-in-the-Dale, Shropshire TF13 6EG;
wilderhope@yha.org.uk
Tel: 0870 770 6090 Fax: 0870 770 6091

Arrive along this hostel's sweeping drive and you may wonder if you've come to the wrong place. But this 16th century National Trust-owned manor house, with oak spiral staircases, timber-framed walls and grand dining hall, really can be your base. On Wenlock Edge in the Welsh Marches, you'll find plenty of walking in the Shropshire Hills. Sit a while in its extensive grounds with views across the Hope Valley and you may not want to go home.

Location: OS 137, GR 544928.

Great for... history lovers who want to live it up.

You need to know... for safety reasons, Wilderhope Manor is not suitable for children under five.

Accommodation: 70 beds: 4x4-, 1x6-, 2x10- and 2x14-bed rooms.

Family rooms: Yes. **Rent-a-Hostel:** No.

Classroom: No. **Education packages:** Yes.

Facilities: Lounge, games room, self-catering kitchen, showers, drying room and cycle store.

Daytime access: Shelter and toilets.

Reception open: 5pm.

Meals: Breakfast, picnic lunch, evening meal.

Getting there: From Much Wenlock, take B4371 towards Church Stretton for approx 7 miles to Longville-in-the-Dale. Take first left in village, after three-quarters of a mile turn into the drive on the left.

Public transport: Note: the days of operation of the 712 are Mon AND Fri, not Mon-Fri. BUS: Choice Travel 712 from Ludlow (Mon, Fri only); Shuttle bus operates from much Wenlock and Church Stretton straight to hostel door Sat & Sun only. Otherwise more frequent services from Ludlow or Bridgnorth to Shipton then 1.5 mile-walk (footpath). RAIL: Church Stretton 8 miles.

Parking: Yes. **Nearest other hostels:** Bridges 13 miles, Coalbrookdale 13, Coalport 13.

Price Band: B	Opening category: ❹

TRY RENT-A-HOSTEL

Many of the hostels in this guide can be booked through the Rent-a-Hostel scheme. For full details, turn to page 12.

Explore unspoilt coastlines and undisturbed countryside or treat the family to a traditional British seaside holiday on Norfolk's clean and safe beaches.

Near the coast: East of England Youth Hostels like YHA Great Yarmouth are perfect for a seaside break.

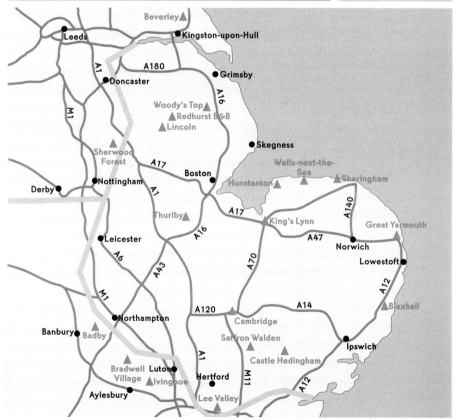

●● BLAXHALL ☆☆☆

**Heath Walk, Blaxhall, Woodbridge, Suffolk
IP12 2EA; blaxhall@yha.org.uk
Tel: 0870 770 5702 Fax: 0870 770 5703**

This 'Green Tourism' silver award-winning hostel has recently been refurbished to provide comfortable accommodation and good disabled access. This former village school is on the edge of Suffolk Sandlings, an Area of Outstanding Natural Beauty, which offers easy walking and flat cycling routes as well as many bird reserves including Minsmere and Orfordness.
Location: OS 156, GR 369570.
Great for... families, weekend walkers and birdwatchers.
You need to know... the nearest shop is 2 miles away.
Accommodation: 40 beds: 1x2-, 2x4- and 5x6-bed rooms.
Family Rooms: Yes. **Rent-a-Hostel:** Yes.
Classroom: Yes. **Education packages:** Yes.
Facilities: Dining room, two lounges, self-catering kitchen, showers, drying room and cycle store. **Daytime access:** Public areas, via numbered lock.
Reception open: Staff available before 10am and after 5pm.
Meals: Breakfast, picnic lunch, evening meal.
Getting there: Leave A12 at Wickham Market/Orford exit, follow signs to Tunstall (B1078) and then to hostel.
Public transport: BUS: First 180/1 Ipswich-Aldeburgh (pass Melton station) . RAIL: Wickham Market 3 miles, Saxmundham 5.
Parking: Yes.
Nearest other hostel: Great Yarmouth 41.

Price Band: B   **Opening category:** ❸

HOSTEL MANAGERS CHOOSE...

THE BEST SPOTS FOR RELAXING NEAR WATER

Punting on the Cam YHA Cambridge: "What could be finer? Enjoy the sights of the city as you glide along the River Cam in a chauffeured punt. For equally good views stroll along the riverbanks (known locally as the Backs). They are covered with daffodils in spring."
Blakeney Point YHA Sheringham: "Take a boat trip to Blakeney and see the large groups of common seals. Remember to keep a look out for lone seals swimming in the sea."
Winterton-on-Sea YHA Great Yarmouth: "Great secluded spot. It's backed by miles of sand dunes and has a conservation area to the north, perfect for walkers."
Wells beach YHA Wells-next-the-Sea: "Superb sand, very clean and great for families. The sea almost disappears out of sight at low tide!"

●● CAMBRIDGE ☆☆☆

**97 Tenison Road, Cambridge, Cambridgeshire
CB1 2DN; cambridge@yha.org.uk
Tel: 0870 770 5742 Fax: 0870 770 5743**

This busy international hostel is just minutes from the railway station and 15 minutes' walk from the city centre. The Victorian townhouse makes a great base for an English city break where you can relax by the river and visit colleges, museums and art galleries galore.
Location: OS 154, GR 460575.
Great for... a city break.
You need to know... breakfast is included in the overnight price; it's on-street parking only – metered and maximum stay two hours between 9am and 5pm.
Accommodation: 99 beds: 2-, 3-, 4-, 6- and 8-bed rooms.
Family rooms: No. **FBR:** Yes. **Rent-a-Hostel:** No.
Classroom: No. **Education packages:** No.
Facilities: Reception, lounges, games room, self-catering kitchen, bar, showers, luggage store, laundry facilities, cycle store and garden.
Daytime access: All public areas.
Reception open: 24hrs.
Meals: Breakfast, picnic lunch, evening meal.
Getting there: From city centre, follow signs to railway station. Take last left turning (at hostel sign) before the railway station (see map on page 172).
Public transport: BUS: frequent from surrounding areas. RAIL: Cambridge 0.5 miles.
NATIONALEXPRESS》 Drummer Street coach stop 1 mile.
Parking: Free parking for cars on roadside from 5pm to 9am (metered at other times).
Nearest other hostels: Saffron Walden 15 miles, Castle Hedingham 29, London 60.

Price Band: D   **Opening category:** ❶

●● CASTLE HEDINGHAM ☆

**7 Falcon Square, Castle Hedingham, Essex
CO9 3BU; castlehed@yha.org.uk
Tel: 0870 770 5756 Fax: 0870 770 5757**

If your idea of hostelling is basic bed and board, think again. Stay in this 16th century building and you'll enjoy substantial meals with the emphasis on home-cooked dishes and vegetarian fare. There are plenty of attractions to help you work up an appetite, and the hostel has a large lawned garden in which to relax afterwards. Bon appetit!
Location: OS 155, GR 786355.
Great for... home-cooked food.
Accommodation: 50 beds: 1x2-, 1x4-, 1x8-, 2x6- and 2x10+-bed rooms.
Family rooms: Yes. **Rent-a-Hostel:** No.
Classroom: Yes. **Education packages:** Yes.
Facilities: Lounge, self-catering kitchen, showers, drying room, cycle store and garden with BBQ. **Daytime access:** All public areas.
Reception open: 5pm.
Meals: Breakfast, picnic lunch, evening meal.
Getting there: Follow signs for Hedingham Castle. Opposite castle

All the fun of the fair: seaside amusements near YHA Great Yarmouth.

entrance, turn down Castle Lane. Hostel is on left at bottom of hill.
Public transport: BUS: Hedingham Omnibuses 89 from Braintree (passes close to Braintree station). RAIL: Sudbury 7miles, Braintree 8.
Parking: Nearby.
Nearest other hostels: Saffron Walden 20 miles, Cambridge 29.

Price Band: **B** Opening category: **❷**

● ● GREAT YARMOUTH ☆

2 Sandown Road, Great Yarmouth, Norfolk NR30 1EY; greatyarmouth@yha.org.uk
Tel: 0870 770 5840 Fax: 0870 770 5841

Once an Edwardian family hotel, this hostel makes a convenient base for that long-lost art – the traditional seaside holiday. The huge sandy shore of Great Yarmouth is minutes away and the town centre offers endless amusements for children. Visit the Maritime Museum of East Anglia or follow miles of broadland, coastal trails and cycle paths.
Location: OS 134, GR 529083.
Great for... families looking for a beach-based holiday exploring The Broads.
You need to know... the hostel stairs are steep.
Accommodation: 40 beds: 1x2-, 2x4-, 2x6-, 1x8- and 1x10-bed rooms.
Family rooms: No. **FBR:** Yes. **Rent-a-Hostel:** Yes.
Classroom: No. **Education packages:** No.
Facilities: TV lounge, self-catering kitchen, dining room, showers and cycle store. **Daytime access:** Sorry, none until 5pm.
Reception open: 5pm. **Meals:** Self-catering only.
Getting there: Enter Yarmouth from A12/A47 roundabout. Follow

road to lights, with Sainsbury's on the left. Bear left into Nicholas Road. Turn left at next lights (Nelson Road), then first right after coach station. **Public transport:** BUS: frequent from surrounding areas, also local services. RAIL: Great Yarmouth 0.5 miles.
NATIONALEXPRESS» Market Gates 0.5 miles.
Parking: On roadside by hostel.
Nearest other hostels: Sheringham 39, Blaxhall 41.

Price Band: **B** Opening category: **❷**

● ● HUNSTANTON ☆☆

15 Avenue Road, Hunstanton, Norfolk PE36 5BW; hunstanton@yha.org.uk
Tel: 0870 770 5872 Fax: 0870 770 5873

Hunstanton has consistently won seaside awards for its cleanliness and amenities that are just two minutes' walk from this hostel, a pair of Victorian townhouses built of warm red carstone. But don't spend all your time swimming and sunbathing – put on your walking boots and explore further afield for miles of easy striding. The Norfolk Coast Path will lead you along the famous striped cliffs, while Peddars Way follows an ancient route.
Location: OS 132, GR 674406.
Great for... quiet days spent walking, fun-packed family holidays, cycling, birdwatching, lazing on the beach and home-cooked meals with local themes.
Accommodation: 42 beds: 1x2-, 2x3-, 5x4-, 1x6 and 1x8-bed rooms.
Family rooms: Yes. **Rent-a-Hostel:** Yes.
Classroom: Yes. **Education packages:** Yes.

Facilities: Lounge/TV room, self-catering kitchen, dining room, meeting room with selection of games, showers, drying room, cycle store and small, private garden with patio.
Daytime access: Public areas, via numbered lock.
Reception open: 5pm.
Meals: Breakfast, picnic lunch, evening meal.
Getting there: From coast road (A149) turn into Sandringham Road, then take the third left into Avenue Road.
Public transport: BUS: First 410-413 from King's Lynn (passes close to King's Lynn station), Coast Hopper to Sheringham and Wells-next-the-sea. RAIL: King's Lynn 16 miles.
Parking: Roadside parking outside hostel.
Nearest other hostels: King's Lynn 16 miles, Wells-next-the-Sea 16, Sheringham 38.

> **Price Band:** B   **Opening category:** ❷

⚫ KING'S LYNN ☆
Thoresby College, College Lane, King's Lynn, Norfolk PE30 1JB; kingslynn@yha.org.uk
Tel: 0870 770 5902 Fax: 0870 770 5903

This traditional hostel is in a wing of the 500-year-old Chantry College building in the historic part of King's Lynn. Discover the heritage buildings and museums, as well as other local attractions such as the Queen's country residence at Sandringham, Houghton Hall and the Norman ruins of Castle Rising and Castle Acre. Walkers and cyclists will also enjoy the varied west Norfolk countryside.
Location: OS 132, GR 616199.
Great for... walking and cycling.
Accommodation: 35 beds: 1x1-, 1x3-, 2x6-, 1x9- and 1x10-bed rooms.
Family rooms: No. **FBR:** Yes. **Rent-a-Hostel:** Yes.
Classroom: No. **Education packages:** No.
Facilities: Lounge, self-catering kitchen, dining room, showers, drying room and cycle store. **Daytime access:** Public areas, via numbered lock.
Reception open: 5pm.
Meals: Breakfast only. Full meal service available for pre-booked groups of 10 or more.
Getting there: Follow signs to the Old Town. College Lane is opposite The Guildhall.
Public transport: BUS: frequent from surrounding areas. RAIL: King's Lynn 0.5 miles.
NATIONAL EXPRESS Vancouver Centre bus station 0.5 miles.
Parking: Follow signs to Old Town/South Quay. Free parking is on left of South Quay, north of College Lane, 50 metres from hostel.
Nearest other hostels: Hunstanton 16 miles, Wells-next-the-sea 32, Thurlby 38, Sheringham 39, Cambridge 45.

> **Price Band:** B   **Opening category:** ❷

⚫ SAFFRON WALDEN ☆
1 Myddylton Place, Saffron Walden, Essex CB10 1BB; saffron@yha.org.uk
Tel: 0870 770 6014 Fax: 0870 770 6015

Stay in the oldest inhabited building in Saffron Walden, a 600-year-old former maltings with oak beams, uneven floors and a walled garden. Saffron Walden is an ancient town with a rich heritage of old buildings set in rolling countryside, good for walking and cycling. It's also close to the Imperial War Museum's aviation collection at Duxford and the Jacobean mansion and gardens of Audley End House.
Location: OS 154, GR 535386.
Great for... walkers and cyclists — it makes an excellent base for exploring the area.
You need to know... there's no parking at the hostel.
Accommodation: 40 beds: 4x2-6- and 2x10-12-bed rooms.
Family rooms: No. **FBR:** Yes. **Rent-a-Hostel:** Yes.
Classroom: No. **Education packages:** Yes.
Facilities: Lounge, dining room, showers, self-catering kitchen, drying room, cycle store and garden. **Daytime access:** Due to the sensitive nature of this historic building, there is no access between 10am and 5pm. Nearest public toilets are on Hill Street, 500 yards from hostel.
Reception open: 5pm.
Meals: Breakfast, picnic lunch, evening meal.
Getting there: From the town centre follow High Street past the Saffron Hotel. The hostel is on the corner opposite Castle Street.

The oldest inhabited building in town: YHA Saffron Walden.

From the south take M11 J9 and from the north take M11 J10, and follow signs to Saffron Walden on B184. The hostel is on the right just past the Eight Bells pub as you come into the town.
Public transport: BUS: Village Link 5 from Stansted Airport. RAIL: Audley End 2.5 miles.
Parking: 800 metres to free car park.
Nearest other hostels: Cambridge 15 miles, Castle Hedingham 20.

> **Price Band:** B   **Opening category:** ❷

LINCOLN ☆

77 South Park, Lincoln, Lincolnshire LN5 8ES; lincoln@yha.org.uk
Tel: 0870 770 5918 Fax: 0870 770 5919

Lincoln has often been described as York in miniature, with its cathedral, castle, steep medieval streets and ancient Roman walls. With a range of modern shops and a cosmopolitan cluster of cafés, it's every bit as busy too. This hostel, a Victorian villa in a traffic-free area, has fine views from the dining room and conservatory across an open common, making it a suitably elegant base for rest and recuperation. It's also well-known for its home-cooked food using mainly local and organic produce.

Location: OS 121, GR 980700.
Great for... exploring Lincoln's city centre.
Accommodation: 41 beds: 1x2-, 1x3-, 1x4-, 1x6-, 2x8- and 1x10-bed rooms.
Family rooms: No. **FBR:** Yes. **Rent-a-Hostel:** Yes.
Classroom: Yes. **Education packages:** Yes.
Facilities: Lounge, TV room, self-catering kitchen, showers, drying room, cycle store, laundry facilities and grounds.
Daytime access: Public areas, via door keys. Access from 5pm on day of arrival.
Reception open: 5pm.
Meals: Breakfast, picnic lunch, evening meal.

Getting there: From the train station turn right onto St Mary's Street. Continue to Oxford Street. Go under flyover and up steps on the right. Go along Canwick Road and over lights. When the cemetery is on your left, South Park is on your right. (See map on page 172).
Public transport: BUS: frequent from surrounding areas.
RAIL: Lincoln 1 mile.
NATIONALEXPRESS» Lincoln City bus station 1 mile.
Parking: On site and additional parking opposite hostel.
Nearest other hostels: Woody's Top 25 miles, Sherwood Forest 30, Thurlby 35, Beverley Friary 54.

Price Band: B	Opening category: ❸

REDHURST B&B ◆◆◆

Redhurst B&B, Redhurst Holton cum Beckering, Market Rasen, Lincs LN8 5NG
Tel: 01673 857927 Fax: 01673 857927
Contact Mrs Vivienne Klockner

A warm welcome awaits guests at Redhurst B&B, set in gardens, orchard and copse in a small village nestling on the edge of the Lincolnshire Wolds. Enjoy swimming in the heated outdoor pool in summer and warmth from a crackling log fire in winter. An ideal centre from which to explore the many and varied attractions of Lincolnshire.

LEE VALLEY ☆☆☆☆☆

Windmill Lane, Cheshunt, Hertfordshire, EN8 9AJ; leevalley@yha.org.uk
Tel: 0870 770 6118 Fax: 0870 770 6119

Close to London, these six log cabins are situated on the shore of a lake in the 10,000 acres of Lee Valley Country Park. There are plenty of activities nearby — take your pick from sailing, kayaking, caving, climbing and canoeing to name but a few.
Location: OS 166, GR 368024.
Great for... outdoor enthusiasts, day trips to London and groups.
You need to know... breakfast is included in the price; the hostel has an alcohol license.
Accommodation: 114 beds: 2-, 3-, 4-, 6- and 8-bed rooms, facilities for the disabled. All rooms en-suite.
Family rooms: Yes. **Rent-a-Hostel:** Yes.
Classroom: Yes. **Education packages:** Yes.
Facilities: Meetings rooms, laundry, library, internet access, baggage room, Sky TV, seasonal café, cycle store, payphones, tourist information, licensed restaurant, showers.
Daytime access: All public areas.
Reception open: 24hrs.
Meals: Breakfast, lunch, evening meal.
Getting there: By train, travel from London Liverpool Street station. By road, leave the M25 at J25.
Public transport: BUS: frequent from surrounding areas to within 0.5 miles. RAIL: Cheshunt, adjacent.

Different: YHA Lee Valley comprises six log cabins on a lake shore.

Parking: Yes.
Nearest other hostels: Epping Forest 10 miles, London 16, Saffron Walden 37, Ivinghoe 36, Jordans 36.

Price Band: D	Opening category: ❶

Location: OS 121, GR 118814.

Great for... a countryside location to explore by car, cycle or walking.

You need to know... breakfast is included in the price.

Accommodation: 5 beds: 1x1- and 2x2 bed rooms.

Family rooms: No. **Rent-a-Hostel:** No.

Classroom: No. **Education packages:** No.

Facilities: Cycle store, laundry facilities, en-suite facilities for all rooms, garden, pool, BBQ and some disabled access.

Daytime access: All public areas.

Reception open: 2pm.

Meals: Packed lunches, light meals and dinners available on request.

Getting there: A158 from Lincoln to Skegness, then B1399 to Holton, turn left at crossroads and the B&B is on the right after the bend.

Public transport: BUS: Number 6 bus from Lincoln to Wragby. Owner will collect from Wragby.

Parking: Yes. On B&B grounds. Also has parking space for caravan/camper van and one electric hook-up.

Nearest other hostels: Lincoln 12 miles.

> **Price Band:** E   **Opening category:** ❸

● THURLBY ☆

16 High St, Thurlby, Bourne, Lincolnshire PE10 0EE

Tel: 0870 770 6066 Fax: 0870 770 6066

This homely hostel and its lovely garden enjoy a peaceful setting in an unspoilt Lincolnshire village. A 15th century forge and annexe, it offers a quiet haven to those seeking a tranquil base. Attractions in the area include the Wool Churches built by local sheep farmers, while cycling, fishing and watersports are on hand at Rutland Water.

Location: OS 130, GR 097168.

Great for... cycling, birdwatching and visiting Rutland Water.

You need to know... this hostel may close for refurbishment. Please enquire before planning your stay.

Accommodation: 24 beds: 1x3-, 2x4-, 1x5- and 1x8-bed rooms.

Family rooms: Yes. **Rent-a-Hostel:** Yes.

Classroom: No. **Education packages:** No.

Facilities: Lounge, self-catering kitchen, dining room, showers, drying room, cycle store, shop, grounds and camping.

Daytime access: Public areas, via numbered lock.

Reception open: 5pm.

Meals: Self-catering only.

Getting there: On the A15 between Peterborough and Bourne (don't confuse it with Thurlby near Lincoln). From Stamford take the A6121 to Bourne and turn south. The hostel is clearly signed from the road (0.25 miles).

Public transport: BUS: Delaine's from Peterborough (passes close to Peterborough station). RAIL: Peterborough 15 miles, Grantham 18. NATIONALEXPRESS» Bourne bus station 2.5 miles.

Parking: Yes, but limited.

Nearest other hostels: Lincoln 35 miles & King's Lynn 38.

> **Price Band:** B   **Opening category:** ❸

● SHERINGHAM ☆☆

1 Cremer's Drift, Sheringham, Norfolk NR26 8HX; sheringham@yha.org.uk

Tel: 0870 770 6024 Fax: 0870 770 6025

Extensive and spacious with a well-equipped conference centre, this hostel is set in an Area of Outstanding Natural Beauty on the heritage coastline of Norfolk. Sheringham is a fascinating example of a Victorian seaside resort where shellfishing remains an important industry. The hostel is ideally positioned for visiting beaches, the steam railway and the heavy horse centre.

Location: OS 133, GR 159428.

Great for... a traditional seaside holiday with lots of fresh air; activities without a car.

You need to know... the self-catering kitchen is very small and can be busy during school holidays. Breakfast included in the overnight price.

Accommodation: 100 beds: mostly 2-, 3-, 3x4- and a few 6–8-bed rooms. Ground floor accommodation for six wheelchair users.

Family rooms: Yes. **Rent-a-Hostel:** Yes.

Classroom: Yes. **Education packages:** Yes.

Facilities: Lounge/dining room, TV room, games room, bar and conference facilities, self-catering kitchen, drying room and cycle store.

Daytime access: All public areas.

Reception open: 1pm.

Meals: Breakfast, picnic lunch, evening meal.

Getting there: The hostel is off the main A149 behind St Joseph's Roman Catholic Church, only five minutes on foot from the railway and bus stations.

Public transport: BUS: First/Sanders X50, 4, 44 Norwich-Holt; Norfolk Green X98 King's Lynn-Cromer. RAIL: Sheringham 0.5 miles. NATIONALEXPRESS» Station Approach bus shelter 0.25 miles.

Parking: Yes.

Nearest other hostels: Wells-next-the-Sea 18 miles, Hunstanton 38, Great Yarmouth 39.

> **Price Band:** D   **Opening category:** ❹

Ideal location: YHA Sheringham in north Norfolk.

YHA Wells-next-the-Sea is surrounded by beautiful countryside.

● ● WELLS-NEXT-THE-SEA ☆☆☆☆

Church Plain, Wells, Norfolk NR23 1EQ;
wellsnorfolk@yha.org.uk
Tel: 0870 770 6084 Fax: 0870 770 6085

The quays still teem with yachts and fishing boats in the port of Wells, where you'll find this newly-opened hostel in the heart of the town. It's a fine base from which to indulge in flora and fauna forays into the surrounding countryside. Follow creeks and salt marshes busy with birdlife, enjoy miles of empty beaches or take a boat at high tide to see seals. Explore the network of footpaths leading inland and you'll discover ancient churches, flint villages and welcoming pubs. For the fit, the North Norfolk Coast Path is temptingly close.

Location: OS 132, GR 917433.

Great for... those with an interest in wildlife.

Accommodation: 32 beds: 3x2–3-bed rooms (double bed with bunk over; one is on the ground floor with disabled access and en-suite facilities), 1x3- and 5x4-bed rooms.

Family rooms: Yes. **Rent-a-Hostel:** Yes.

Classroom: No. **Education packages:** Yes.

Facilities: Lounges, TV, dining room, self-catering kitchen, meeting room, laundry, drying room and secure cycle store.

Daytime access: Public areas, via numbered lock.

Reception open: 5pm.

Meals: Self-catering only.

Getting there: On south side of town opposite church tower. From Hunstanton or Sheringham keep on A149 and turn into Church Plain next to church. From Fakenham (B1105), take first right on entering the town and turn left after 350 metres into Church Plain. By foot from waterfront take Staithe Street then High Street to Church Plain.

Public transport: BUS: Coast Hopper from King's Lynn, Sheringham; First 431 from Fakenham with connections from Norwich. RAIL: Sheringham 16 miles, King's Lynn 24.
NATIONALEXPRESS» Fakenham 8 miles.

Parking: Yes, behind and on forecourt of hostel building. One disabled space.

Nearest other hostels: Hunstanton 16 miles, Sheringham 18, King's Lynn 24.

Price Band: B	Opening category: ❷

● ● WOODY'S TOP ☆☆☆

Ruckland, Louth, Lincolnshire LN11 8RQ;
woodystop@yha.org.uk
Tel: 0870 770 6098 Fax: 0870 770 6098
Bookings more than 7 days in advance:
0870 770 5918.

This is one of YHA's quietest hostels, hidden well away from civilisation in the Lincolnshire Wolds. The converted farm buildings are surrounded by open fields so, if you don't want to see a soul, travel by foot or bike to explore the landscape. When you're ready to face the world again, ease yourself gently back into the rat race in the nearby market towns before making the 25-mile trip to Lincoln to ponder the might of its cathedral built on the orders of William the Conqueror.

Location: OS 122, GR 332786.

Great for... those seeking a peaceful rural retreat.

Accommodation: 20 beds: 1x2-, 3x4- and 1x6-bed rooms.

Family rooms: No. **FBR:** Yes. **Rent-a-Hostel:** Yes.

Classroom: No. **Education packages:** No.

Facilities: Self-catering kitchen/dining/sitting area, showers, drying room, cycle store and grounds. **Daytime access:** Public areas, via numbered lock. **Reception open:** 5pm.

Meals: Self-catering only.

Getting there: From A16 take minor road towards Ruckland, turn left and hostel is 300 metres from junction on right.

Public transport: BUS: Translinc 6C Louth-Horncastle, with connections for Grimsby, Skegness and Lincoln. RAIL: Thorp Culvert (not Sun) 18miles, Grimsby Town 22, Lincoln 25.
NATIONALEXPRESS» Louth and Horncastle.

Parking: Yes.

Nearest other hostels: Lincoln 25 miles, Beverley 50, Thurlby 55.

Price Band: B	Opening category: ❷

TRY RENT-A-HOSTEL

Many of the hostels in this guide can be booked through the Rent-a-Hostel scheme. For full details, turn to page 12.

South West England

Indulge your passion for the great outdoors. Whether it's watersports, pony trekking, cycling or exploring on foot, this is the region for you.

Ideal for youngsters: YHA Golant is typical of so many family-friendly Youth Hostels in the South West.

○ ● **BEER** ☆☆☆

**Bovey Combe, Beer, Seaton, Devon EX12 3LL;
beer@yha.org.uk**
Tel: 0870 770 5690 Fax: 0870 770 5691

On the edge of the fishing village of Beer, this light and airy country house has a large lawned garden. It's a relaxing hostel with child-friendly facilities. Activities nearby include mackerel fishing, a visit to the Quarry Caves or a ride on the steam train at Pecorama. Take a stroll along the South West Coast Path or head a little further to hunt for fossils on Charmouth Beach.

Location: OS 192, GR 223896.

Great for... quiet family holidays.

You need to know... the hostel's access road is steep and narrow.

Accommodation: 40 beds: 5x4-, 1x5-, 1x6- and 1x9-bed rooms.

Family rooms: Yes. **Rent-a-Hostel:** Yes.

Classroom: No. **Education packages:** No.

Facilities: Dining room, lounge, self-catering kitchen, residential licence, showers, drying room, cycle store and grounds.

Daytime access: All public areas.

Reception open: Staff available before 10am and after 5pm.

Meals: Breakfast, picnic lunch, evening meal.

Getting there: From Beer village go up Fore Street to Townsend and turn off to the track on the right, signposted.

Public transport: BUS: Axe Valley from Seaton with connections from Axminster station; First X53 Weymouth-Exeter. RAIL: Axminster 7 miles. **Parking:** Cars only (steep narrow access).

Nearest other hostels: Exeter 24 miles, Litton Cheney 28, Portland 44.

Price Band: **B** Opening category: **❸**

○ ● **BELLEVER** (DARTMOOR) ☆☆

**Bellever, Postbridge, Devon PL20 6TU;
bellever@yha.org.uk**
Tel: 0870 770 5692 Fax: 0870 770 5693

Escape the modern world at this hostel in the centre of Dartmoor National Park surrounded by open moorland with a network of off-road walking and cycling routes. Once part of a Duchy farm, this hostel makes a comfortable, child-friendly retreat.

Location: OS 191, GR 654773.

Great for... keen walkers and cyclists.

You need to know... parking is limited.

Accommodation: 38 beds: 3x6-, 3x4- and 1x8-bed rooms.

Family rooms: Yes. **Rent-a-Hostel:** Yes.

Classroom: Yes. **Education packages:** Yes.

● ● **BATH** ☆

Bathwick Hill, Bath BA2 6JZ; bath@yha.org.uk
Tel: 0870 770 5688 Fax: 0870 770 5689

A beautiful Italianate mansion in its own gardens, YHA Bath offers a comfortable base for exploring this elegant city. Buzzing with cosmopolitan energy, it enjoys all the facilities you would expect of such a prestigious location. Bath is a World Heritage City and famous for its hot springs, Roman Baths and Georgian architecture. Whatever time of year you choose to visit, you'll be sure to find a variety of festivals, theatre shows and exhibitions to keep you entertained.

Location: OS 172, GR 766644.

Great for... theatre, exhibition and festival goers.

You need to know... some beds are in an annexe; it's on-street parking with drop-off at the hostel.

Accommodation: 121 beds: 5x2-, 11x4-, 3x5-, 4x6-, 1x8- and 2x10-bed rooms.

Family rooms: Yes. **FBR:**Yes. **Rent-a-Hostel:** No.

Classroom: No. **Education packages:** Yes.

Facilities: Lounge with TV, self-catering kitchen, showers, cycle store, small shop, laundry facilities, fully licenced bar, internet access and foreign exchange.

Daytime access: All public areas. **Reception open:** 24hrs.

Meals: Breakfast, picnic lunch, evening meal.

Getting there: From London Road, follow signs to university and American Museum. From southwest, follow A36 to roundabout on Pulteney Road. (see map on page 171).

Public transport: BUS: First 18 from Bath Spa.
RAIL: Bath Spa 1.25 miles.
NATIONAL EXPRESS» Manvers St bus station 1.25 miles.
Parking: On Bathwick Hill.

Nearest other hostels: Bristol 14 miles, Cheddar 27, Slimbridge 37, Street 30.

Price Band: **B** Opening category: **❶**

Famous throughout the world: the historic Roman Baths, near YHA Bath.

Facilities: Dining room/self-catering kitchen, showers, drying room and cycle store. **Daytime access:** All public areas.
Reception open: 5pm.
Meals: Breakfast, picnic lunch, evening meal.
Getting there: From Postbridge (B3212) take road marked Bellever.
Public transport: BUS: First 98 from Tavistock; otherwise 82 Exeter-Plymouth, alight Postbridge, 1 mile. Reduced winter service (Oct-May weekends only). RAIL: Plymouth 24 miles.
Parking: Limited.
Nearest other hostels: Steps Bridge 18 miles, Dartington 19, Exeter 25, Okehampton 25.

Price Band: **B**   Opening category: **3**

●● BOSCASTLE HARBOUR
Palace Stables, Boscastle, Cornwall PL35 0HD
Tel: 0870 770 5710 Fax: 0870 770 5711
Bookings more than 7 days ahead: 0870 770 8868

Experience the unique character of this cosy retreat. Originally a stable for the horses that pulled the boats ashore in the National Trust-protected harbour, the hostel is now popular with walkers on the South West Coast Path that runs right past its door. Superb coastal scenery ensures excellent walking country while lovers of literature will appreciate the local Thomas Hardy connections.
Location: OS 190, GR 096915.
Great for... walkers on the South West Coast Path.
You need to know... there's no parking by the hostel. Public car park 250 metres away.
Accommodation: 25 beds: 4x4–9-bed rooms.
Family rooms: No. **FBR:** Yes. **Rent-a-Hostel:** Yes.
Classroom: No. **Education packages:** No.
Facilities: Lounge/dining area, self-catering kitchen, showers and cycle store.
Daytime access: All public areas except drying room.
Reception open: 5pm.
Meals: Self-catering only.
Getting there: Walk from bridge on the B3263 towards harbour alongside river. Hostel is last building on the right at top of slipway.
Public transport: BUS: Western Greyhound 522/3 Wadebridge-Bude. RAIL: Bodmin Parkway 24 miles.
Parking: Public car park for cars and coaches, 250 metres (overnight free).
Nearest other hostels: Tintagel 5 miles, Elmscott 28, Golant 30.

Price Band: **B**   Opening category: **2**

●● BOSWINGER ☆☆☆
Boswinger, Gorran, St Austell, Cornwall PL26 6LL
Tel: 0870 770 5712 Fax: 0870 770 5712

If you're planning on visiting the Eden Project and the Lost Gardens of Heligan this year, then YHA Boswinger makes a convenient base. A cosy mix of old farm buildings with a courtyard and veranda, it enjoys excellent sea views and is surrounded by a wide choice of beaches. On the Coast Path, walkers will find a multitude of routes

and cyclists will enjoy the Cornish Trail.
Location: OS 204, GR 991411.
Great for... a convenient base with sea views.
You need to know... only breakfast is available unless a group has pre-booked.
Accommodation: 40 beds: 3x2-, 4x4- and 3x6-bed rooms.
Family rooms: Yes. **Rent-a-Hostel:** Yes.
Classroom: No. **Education packages:** No.
Facilities: Lounge, dining room, self-catering kitchen, showers, drying room, cycle store and BBQ. **Daytime access:** All public areas.
Reception open: Staff available before 10am and after 5pm.
Meals: Breakfast only.
Getting there: From St Austell take B3273 towards Mevagissey. After 5 miles turn right at top of hill and follow signs for Gorran, passing Heligan Gardens on the left. Fork right just before Gorran to follow brown hostel signs. The hostel is situated in Boswinger hamlet near Seaview international campsite.
Public transport: BUS: Western Greyhound 526 X St Austell-Gorran Churchtown, then 1 mile. RAIL: St Austell 10 miles. **Parking:** Yes.
Nearest other hostels: Golant 17 miles, Perranporth 25.

Price Band: **B**   Opening category: **2**

●● BRISTOL ☆☆
14 Narrow Quay, Bristol BS1 4QA;
bristol@yha.org.uk
Tel: 0870 770 5726 Fax: 0870 770 5727

This hostel makes the perfect base to explore the vibrant city of Bristol. With views over the waterways, it has been sympathetically restored to create a relaxing yet cosmopolitan atmosphere. Visit the magnificent Avon Gorge, Brunel's suspension bridge or one of the many theatres, museums and art galleries in the city.
Location: OS 172, GR 586725.
Great for... city activities.
You need to know... breakfast is included in the overnight price.
Accommodation: 92 beds: mostly 2–4-bed rooms, plus 1x5- and 2x6-bed rooms.
Family rooms: Yes. **Rent-a-Hostel:** No.
Classroom: Yes. **Education packages:** Yes.
Facilities: Lounge, TV room, games room, self-catering kitchen and cafe bar, showers, cycle store, luggage store and laundry facilities.
Daytime access: All public areas. **Reception open:** 24 hrs.
Meals: Breakfast only. Full meal service available to pre-booked groups of 10+.
Getting there: From London or South Wales, exit M4 at J19, then take M32. From Birmingham or South West, exit M5 at J18, then A4. (see map on page 171).
Public transport: Bus: frequent from surrounding areas. RAIL: Bristol Temple Meads 0.5 miles.
NATIONAL EXPRESS Marlborough Street bus station 1 mile.
Parking: At NCP Prince Street. Meter parking behind hostel.
Nearest other hostels: Bath 14 miles, Cheddar 20, Slimbridge 25.

Price Band: **D**   Opening category: **1**

● BURLEY ☆☆☆

**Cott Lane, Burley, Ringwood, Hampshire
BH24 4BB**
Tel: 0870 770 5734 Fax: 0870 770 5735

A former family home, this hostel stands in extensive grounds with immediate access to the New Forest and within easy reach of the Beaulieu Motor Museum and the beaches of Bournemouth. With cycling, pony trekking and watersports all possible to arrange locally, it's the ideal base for a get-away-from-it-all break close to the seaside.

Location: OS 195, GR 220028.

Great for... cyclists, horseriders and nature lovers.

You need to know... the hostel is at the end of an unsurfaced track and can be hard to find in the dark. Watch out for cattle and ponies.

Accommodation: 36 beds: 1x4-, 1x6-, 2x8- and 1x10-bed rooms.

Family rooms: Yes. **FBR:** Yes. **Rent-a-Hostel:** Yes.

Classroom: No. **Education packages:** No.

Facilities: Lounge, dining room, self-catering kitchen, showers, drying room, grounds and camping.

Daytime access: All public areas.

Reception open: 5pm.

Meals: Breakfast, picnic lunch, evening meal.

Getting there: Follow Lyndhurst Road past Burley School on left and past golf course for 0.5 miles to a crossroads. Follow signpost to White Buck Inn and turn left into Cott Lane. Follow signs for hostel.

Public transport: BUS: Wilts & Dorset X34/5 Bournemouth-Southampton (passes Ashurst New Forest and Southampton stations), alight Durmast Corner 0.5 miles; 105 Poole-Ringwood, alight Burley 0.5 miles. RAIL: Sway 5.5 miles, New Milton 6.

Parking: Yes.

Nearest other hostels: Totland Bay 17 miles (via ferry), Salisbury 21, Winchester 23.

Price Band: B	Opening category: ❷

Walking in the New Forest near YHA Burley.

◌● CHEDDAR ☆☆☆

**Hillfield, Cheddar, Somerset BS27 3HN;
cheddar@yha.org.uk**
Tel: 0870 770 5760 Fax: 0870 770 5761

Cheddar Gorge is an adventure playground for all and this hostel is in the thick of the action. The modernised Victorian house sits in the village below the dramatic gorge that has the highest limestone cliffs in England. There's an exciting underground world to discover in Cheddar's incredible caves and Wookey Hole, just six miles away. The Mendip Hills and Somerset Levels will keep walkers busy while families will want to travel the 12 miles to the traditional seaside resort of Weston-super-Mare.

Location: OS 182, GR 455534.

Great for... an action-packed family holiday.

Accommodation: 45 beds: mostly 2-, 4- and 6-bed rooms.

Family rooms: Yes. **Rent-a-Hostel:** No.

Classroom: No. **Education packages:** No.

Facilities: Lounge, self-catering kitchen, conservatory, showers, drying room, cycle store and laundry. **Daytime access:** Annexe with toilets, seating area and kitchen.

Reception open: Staff available before 10am and after 5pm.

Meals: Breakfast, picnic lunch, evening meal.

Getting there: From M5 exit at J22. Take A38 and A371 to Cheddar. In village turn left at war memorial into The Hayes. Just beyond school, turn left into Hillfield to hostel. From Wells follow A371, turning right into The Hayes in village.

Public transport: BUS: First 126, 826 Weston-super-Mare-Wells (pass close to Weston Milton and Weston-super-Mare stations). RAIL: Weston Milton 10 miles, Weston-super-Mare 11.

Parking: Yes.

Nearest other hostels: Street 17 miles, Bristol 20, Bath 27.

Price Band: B	Opening category: ❷

● CHOLDERTON (STONEHENGE)
Cholderton Rare Breeds Farm, Amesbury Road, Cholderton, Wiltshire SP4 0EW; pam@rabbitworld.co.uk
Tel: 0870 770 6134 Fax: 0870 770 6135

Situated on the edge of the village of Cholderton and part of the rare breeds farm, this bunkhouse offers excellent facilities. During your stay you will have free access to the farm where there are pygmy goats, lambs, piglets, chicks, rabbits and an Iron Age farm. Stonehenge and Woodhenge are close by, as is the city of Salisbury.
Location: OS 130, 209423
Great for... visiting Stonehenge, Woodhenge, Salisbury and Winchester.
Accommodation: 18 beds: 2x3-bed rooms (with travel cots) and 2x6+-bed rooms.
Family rooms: Yes. **Rent-a-Hostel:** Yes.
Classroom: Yes. **Education packages:** Yes.
Facilities: Cafe bar, common room, lockers, luggage store, games room, garden, tour office and wheelchair facilities.
Daytime access: All public areas.
Reception open: Between 5pm and 9pm.
Meals: Limited selection of cafe meals.
Getting there: Situated just off the A303 between Amesbury and Andover.
Public transport: BUS: Wilts & Dorset 63 from Salisbury-Tidworth then 15 min walk, (Wed & Fri) 63 straight to farm. RAIL: Grately station 3.75 miles (Salisbury-Waterloo line), Penryn 18, Penmere 18.
Parking: Yes.
Nearest other hostels: Salisbury 8 miles.

Price Band: B   Opening category: ❶

Spend some time on the farm at YHA Cholderton.

Walking on the Tarka Trail near Chenson Camping Barn.

CHENSON CAMPING BARN
campingbarns@yha.org.uk
Booking: 0870 770 8868
Arrival time: Mr & Mrs Chandler, 01363 83236

This cob and timber camping barn, formerly used for cider pressing, is on a working farm in the beautiful Taw Valley. It's just half a mile from the Tarka Trail and close to the Forestry Commission's Eggesford Forest with its many walks and mountain bike routes. And when you return from a full day's workout, you'll be pleased to know that cream teas are available to order.
Accommodation: Sleeps 8 in two areas.
Facilities: Cooking facilities, sitting area, wood-burning stove, showers (hot water included), electric light and metered electricity. Breakfast and cream teas available to order.
Nearest pub: 2 miles. **Nearest shop:** 2 miles.
Location: OS 191, GR 705099.

Price Band: C   Opening category: ❸

● ● COVERACK ☆☆
Parc Behan, School Hill, Coverack, Helston, Cornwall TR12 6SA; coverack@yha.org.uk
Tel: 0870 770 5780 Fax: 0870 770 5781

The Lizard Peninsula will delight all outdoor lovers. Amateur geologists will be fascinated by rocks forced up from under the Earth's crust. Walkers will love the ever-changing scenery of the South West Coast Path. Fishermen will take to the sea and adrenaline junkies will try their hands at new watersports. This hostel is ideally placed to explore it all with panoramic views of dramatic cliffs and deserted coves. A Victorian country house, it also boasts spacious grounds for games and camping.
Location: OS 204, GR 782184.
Great for... families willing to try their hands at new sports.
Accommodation: 37 beds: 1x3-, 3x4-, 1x6- and 2x8-bed rooms.
Family rooms: Yes. **Rent-a-Hostel:** Yes.

Classroom: No. **Education packages:** No.
Facilities: Dining room, pool table, self-catering kitchen, lounge with open fire, showers, camping and grounds with volleyball court.
Daytime access: Public areas, via numbered lock.
Reception open: 5pm.
Meals: Breakfast, picnic lunch, evening meal.
Getting there: From Helston, follow signs to St Keverne and Coverack. At Zoar garage turn right and follow signs to hostel and Coverack village.
Public transport: BUS: Truronian T2 or T3 from Helston with connections from Redruth. RAIL: Penryn or Penmere, both 18 miles.
Parking: Yes.
Nearest other hostels: Lizard 12 miles (9 by coastal path), Penzance 25, Land's End 31.

Price Band: B	Opening category: ❷

● CROWCOMBE ☆☆

Crowcombe Heathfield, Taunton, Somerset TA4 4BT
Tel: 0870 770 5782 Fax: 0870 770 5782

If you have young children and want a relaxing break, come to Crowcombe. It's on a quiet country lane with high earth banks and fences surrounding the garden, so you can let the kids play safely. Families will find plenty to do – easy walking on the Quantock Hills, mountain biking, the West Somerset Steam Railway and the coast are all nearby.
Location: OS 181, GR 138339.
Great for... families who enjoy countryside activities.
You need to know... this hostel may close during 2005. Please contact the hostel prior to your visit.
Accommodation: 47 beds: all 4–6-bed rooms, plus 1x2-bed rooms
Family rooms: Yes. **Rent-a-Hostel:** Yes.
Classroom: Yes. **Education packages:** Yes.
Facilities: Lounge, TV room, large self-catering kitchen and dining room, showers, drying room, central heating, laundry facilities, cycle store, small shop, garden, games field and camping.
Daytime access: All public areas, via numbered lock.
Reception open: Staff available before 10am and after 5pm.
Meals: Breakfast, picnic lunch, evening meal.
Getting there: Follow A358 from Taunton for 10 miles. Turn left at Triscombe Cross (Red Post Cottage), signposted Crowcombe Station. The hostel is 0.75 miles on right after the railway bridge.
Public transport: BUS: First 28/C, 928 Taunton-Minehead (passes Taunton station), alight Red Post 0.5 miles. RAIL: Taunton 10 miles, Crowcombe (West Somerset Rly) 0.5.
NATIONAL EXPRESS Taunton 10 miles. **Parking:** Yes.
Nearest other hostels: Quantock Hills 10 miles (7 by path), Minehead 16.

Price Band: B	Opening category: ❸

Ideal for families: Crowcombe's large garden is just part of its appeal for parents and young children.

●● DARTINGTON ☆☆

Lownard, Dartington, Totnes, Devon TQ9 6JJ
dartington@yha.org.uk
Tel: 0870 770 5788 Fax: 0870 770 5789

This traditional 16th century cottage hostel comes complete with exposed beams, log-burning stove and its own babbling brook. It's an ideal base for exploring the River Dart and South Hams countryside. The historic town of Totnes, with a Norman castle and medieval guildhall, is a couple of miles away. Dartmoor National Park and the south Devon coastal resorts are all within easy reach.

Location: OS 202, GR 782622.
Great for... a quiet countryside break.
You need to know... showers, toilets and bedrooms are external, a few steps away from the main building.
Accommodation: 30 beds: 5x6-bed rooms.
Family rooms: Yes. **Rent-a-Hostel:** Yes.
Classroom: No. **Education packages:** No.
Facilities: Sitting/dining area, two self-catering kitchens, showers, cycle store, drying room and garden. **Daytime access:** Shelter and WC.
Reception open: Staff available before 10am and after 5pm.
Meals: Self-catering only.
Getting there: Take A385 from Shinner's Bridge roundabout in centre of Dartington. Turn right after quarter of a mile into a narrow lane unsuitable for coaches. The hostel is 200 metres on right.
Public transport: BUS: First X80 Torquay-Plymouth (passes Paignton and Totnes), alight Shinner's Bridge 0.5 miles. RAIL: Totnes 2 miles.
NATIONAL EXPRESS» Royal Seven Stars Hotel 2 miles.
Parking: Yes. Please park cars in car park and not in lane.
Nearest other hostels: Maypool 11 miles, Bellever 19.

Price Band: B **Opening category:** ❷

●● ELMSCOTT ☆

Elmscott, Hartland, Bideford, Devon EX39 6ES;
reservations@yha.org.uk
Tel: 0870 770 5814 Fax: 0870 770 5815
Bookings more than 7 days ahead: 0870 770 8868

Expect a windswept but warm welcome at the remote YHA Elmscott. This newly renovated Victorian school is in a wild, next-to-nature location close to Clovelly with sea views of Lundy Island. You'll find amazing rock formations, a profusion of wild flowers and many lanes on this unspoilt section of coastline plus easy access to the South West Coast Path. And, after exhilarating walks, a well-equipped kitchen and comfortable lounge will restore your spirits.

Location: OS 190, GR 231217.
Great for... walkers wanting a remote retreat.
You need to know... it's self-catering accommodation only.
Accommodation: 32 beds: all 2-, 4- and 6-bed rooms, most in an annexe.
Family rooms: No. **FBR:** Yes. **Rent-a-Hostel:** Yes.
Classroom: No. **Education packages:** No.
Facilities: Self-catering kitchen, sitting room, dining room, showers, washrooms and cycle store. **Daytime access:** Toilet and shelter.
Reception open: 5pm.
Meals: Self-catering only.

Getting there: Leave A39 just north of West Country Inn and follow signs. On foot from Hartland, continue to far west end of Fore Street and pick up footpath to Elmscott through The Vale (3.5 miles).
Public transport: BUS: First 319 Barnstaple-Hartland (passes close to Barnstaple station), alight Hartland 3.5 miles.
RAIL: Barnstaple 25 miles.
Parking: Yes.
Nearest other hostels: Boscastle 28 miles, Tintagel 32, Lynton 35.

Price Band: B **Opening category:** ❷

●● EXETER ☆☆☆

Mount Wear House, 47 Countess Wear Road, Exeter, Devon EX2 6LR; exeter@yha.org.uk
Tel: 0870 770 5826 Fax: 0870 770 5827

This spacious 17th century building is tucked away on the edge of the city and is surrounded by tranquil grounds. A walk along the historic ship canal or expansive River Exe (where herons and kingfishers sometimes linger) will lead you towards the Quay and the beautiful cathedral in the heart of the city. The centre is only a 10-minute bus ride away and has many intriguing attractions to explore – the Royal Albert Memorial Museum to name just one. Safe cycle routes, Powderham Castle, the east and south Devon coasts and rugged Dartmoor are all within easy visiting distance.

Location: OS 192, GR 941897.
Great for... a family break close to both city and countryside.
Accommodation: 66 beds: 1x2-, 6x4-, 2x5-, 1x6- and 3x8-bed rooms.
Family rooms: Yes. **Rent-a-Hostel:** Yes.
Classroom: No. **Education packages:** No.
Facilities: Lounge, TV, self-catering kitchen, showers, drying room, cycle store, lockers, laundry, garden and camping.
Daytime access: Public areas, via numbered lock.
Reception open: Staff available before 10am and after 5pm.

HOSTEL MANAGERS CHOOSE...

THE BEST SITES FOR LOCAL HISTORY

Bath Spa YHA Bath: "The only place in the UK where you can bathe in natural, hot spring water. It's been used for thousands of years for healing, relaxation and leisure."
Clifton Suspension Bridge YHA Bristol: "Brunel's 214-metre bridge spanning the Avon Gorge is one of the most spectacular in England."
Stonehenge YHA Salisbury: "Britain's greatest prehistoric monument is a World Heritage Site."
Glastonbury Abbey YHA Street: "Set in 36 beautifully peaceful acres of parkland in the centre of the ancient market town of Glastonbury."
Dunster YHA Minehead: "This medieval village is a short but spectacular walk away from the hostel. Visit the castle, watermill and indulge in a West Country cream tea."

Meals: Breakfast, picnic lunch, evening meal.
Getting there: From M5, J30, follow signs for city centre. Turn right at Countess Wear roundabout, then first left into School Lane. From A30, join M5 at J29 southbound and follow instructions above. From A379, follow signs for Topsham, turn left at Countess Wear round-about then left into School Lane. From Exeter city centre follow signs for Topsham. (see map on page 172).
Public transport: BUS: Stagecoach Devon K, T, 57, 85 (pass close to Exeter Central), alight Countess Wear post office 0.5 miles. RAIL: Topsham 2 miles, Exeter Central 3, Exeter St David's 4. NATIONAL EXPRESS Paris Street bus station 3 miles.
Parking: Yes.
Nearest other hostels: Steps Bridge 10 miles, Beer 24, Dartington 27.

Price Band: C   **Opening category:** 3

● EXFORD (EXMOOR) ☆☆
Exe Mead, Exford, Minehead, Somerset TA24 7PU
Tel: 0870 770 5828 Fax: 0870 770 5829

This Victorian house stands in its own grounds on the bank of the River Exe in Exford village. In the centre of Exmoor National Park, it's the ideal base to explore the open hills and wooded valleys all around. You may even be lucky enough to spot a red deer. Dunkery Beacon, Porlock Weir and Dunster Castle are all nearby while Exmoor and the Somerset coast are on the doorstep.
Location: OS 181, GR 853383.
Great for... a central base to explore Exmoor.
Accommodation: 51 beds: some 2x2-bed rooms, mostly 4-6-bed options (3 en-suite).
Family rooms: Yes. **Rent-a-Hostel:** Yes.
Classroom: No. **Education packages:** No.
Facilities: Lounge, self-catering kitchen, dining room, drying room and cycle store. **Daytime access:** All public areas.
Reception open: Staff available before 10am and after 5pm.
Meals: Breakfast, picnic lunch, evening meal. In winter, meals are only available if booked in advance.
Getting there: The hostel is in the centre of the village by the bridge over the river.
Public transport: BUS: Exmoor Bus 285 from Minehead (summer Sun only); otherwise First 38 from Minehead, alight Porlock 7 miles. RAIL: Taunton 28 miles, Minehead (West Somerset Rly) 13.
Parking: Yes.
Nearest other hostels: Minehead 13 miles, Lynton 15, Crowcombe 22.

Price Band: B   **Opening category:** 3

FOX AND HOUNDS CAMPING BARN
campingbarns@yha.org.uk
Booking: 0870 770 8868
Arrival time: Mr Ward, 01822 820206

This camping barn, close to the village of Lydford, has direct access onto the western edge of Dartmoor.
You need to know... this barn has no catering area.
Accommodation: Sleeps 12 in two areas, each with six bunk beds.

Beautiful: Exmoor National Park surrounds YHA Exford.

Facilities: Electric light. No catering area but adjacent pub serves breakfast and other meals. Some facilities shared with campers.
Nearest pub: Next door. **Nearest shop:** 0.5 miles.
Location: OS 191, GR 525866.

Price Band: C   **Opening category:** 3

● GOLANT ☆☆☆
Penquite House, Golant, Fowey, Cornwall
PL23 1LA; golant@yha.org.uk
Tel: 0870 770 5832 Fax: 0870 770 5833

Set in three acres of grounds with a further 14 acres of woodland to explore, YHA Golant is ideally suited to children. Overlooking the Fowey Estuary, it's just four miles from the sea and an excellent base for discovering the Cornish coastline. There's plenty of good walking on Bodmin Moor where you can't miss the ancient standing stones and circles. The Lost Gardens of Heligan and the Eden Project are both nearby, as is Dobwalls Family Adventure Park.
Location: OS 200, GR 116556.
Great for... an active family holiday.
You need to know... the approach is down a long single-track lane.
Accommodation: 94 beds: 1x2-, 4x4-, 7x6-bed rooms, plus two larger dormitories.
Family rooms: Yes. **Rent-a-Hostel:** No.
Classroom: Yes. **Education packages:** Yes.
Facilities: TV lounge, games room, self-catering kitchen, dining room, drying room, cycle store, dinner licence, laundry and shop.
Daytime access: All public areas.
Reception open: Staff available before 10am and after 5pm.
Meals: Breakfast, picnic lunch, evening meal.
Getting there: Leave A30 at Bodmin and follow signs for B3268 (Lostwithiel) until signs for B3269 (Fowey). Take B3269 (Fowey) from A390 1.5 miles west of Lostwithiel. The hostel is signposted from Castle Dore Crossroads after 2 miles.
Public transport: BUS: First 25 St Austell-Fowey (passes Par station), alight Castle Dore Crossroads 1.5 miles. RAIL: Par 3 miles. NATIONAL EXPRESS St Blazey 4.5 miles.
Parking: Yes.
Nearest other hostels: Boswinger 17 miles, Boscastle Harbour 28, Tintagel 28, Treyarnon Bay 28.

Price Band: C   **Opening category:** 3

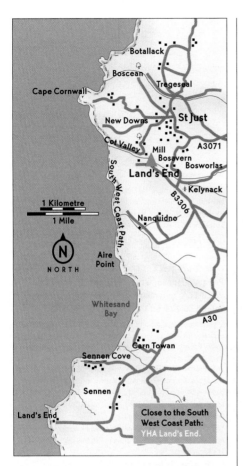

Botallack
Boscean
Cape Cornwall
Tregeseal
New Downs
St Just
Cot Valley
Mill
Bosavern
A3071
Land's End
Bosworlas
Kelynack
1 Kilometre
1 Mile
B3306
Nanquidno
NORTH
Aire Point
South West Coast Path
Whitesand Bay
A30
Carn Towan
Sennen Cove
Sennen
Land's End

Close to the South West Coast Path: YHA Land's End.

GREAT HOUNDTOR CAMPING BARN

campingbarns@yha.org.uk
Booking: 0870 770 8868
Arrival time: Mrs Moreton, 01647 221202

On the eastern edge of Dartmoor near the village of Manaton, this camping barn stands in the shadow of Houndtor and close to Haytor and Widecombe in the Moor.

You need to know... dogs are not allowed. There are no three-point plug sockets.
Accommodation: Sleeps 14 in two upstairs sleeping galleries.
Facilities: Electric light, shower (both on meter), cooking area with two Calor gas rings and open fire (wood available).
Nearest pub: 1.5 miles.
Location: OS 191, GR 749795.

Price Band: G   Opening category: ❸

LAND'S END ☆☆

Letcha Vean, St Just-in-Penwith, Penzance, Cornwall TR19 7NT
Tel: 0870 770 5906 Fax: 0870 770 5907

The closest hostel to Land's End with more than half of the rooms commanding fine views of the sea. This peaceful location provides a haven for rare migratory birds in spring and autumn and, in summer, visitors should make the four-mile trip to the fine surfing and swimming beach at Sennen Cove. The South West Coast Path is just five minutes away or, for a day out with a difference, take a flight to the Isles of Scilly from the airport that's just 10 minutes' drive away. A pint and live music at the local pub will round off your stay.
Location: OS 203, GR 364305.
Great for... active families with older children.
You need to know... parking is limited.
Accommodation: 36 beds: 2x2-, 1x3-, 3x4-, 1x5- and 2x6-bed rooms.
Family rooms: Yes. **Rent-a-Hostel:** Yes.
Classroom: No. **Education packages:** No.
Facilities: Lounge, self-catering kitchen, cycle store, grounds and camping. **Daytime access:** All public areas except 10am-12pm. Access 12-5pm will be unmanned. **Reception open:** 5pm.
Meals: Breakfast, picnic lunch, evening meal.
Getting there: By car from B3306, turn right at Kelynack through farmyard and down lane marked No Access For Motors. By foot from St Just bus station, walk past library and turn left to follow a surfaced road past the chapel to the end. Cross a stile, go through field following hedge and through gate at bottom. Path comes out on road above hostel. Bring a torch.
Public transport: BUS: First 17/A from Penzance (passes Penzance station), alight St Just 0.5miles. RAIL: Penzance 8 miles.
Parking: Limited.
Nearest other hostels: Penzance 8 miles, Coverack 31.

Price Band: B   Opening category: ❷

LITTON CHENEY ☆☆☆

Litton Cheney, Dorchester, Dorset DT2 9AT;
reservations@yha.org.uk
Tel: 0870 770 5922 Fax: 0870 770 5923
Bookings more than 7 days ahead: 0870 770 8868

In a traditional Dorset village in an Area of Outstanding Natural Beauty, YHA Litton Cheney is surrounded by excellent walking and cycling country. This comfortable Dutch barn, once a cheese factory, makes a good family base and is close to Chesil Beach, Abbotsbury Swannery and subtropical gardens.
Location: OS 194, GR 548900.
Great for... walkers and cyclists keen to explore Dorset.
You need to know... only self-catering accommodation is offered.
Accommodation: 22 beds: 2x2-, 3x4- and 1x6-bed rooms.
Family rooms: Yes. **Rent-a-Hostel:** Yes.
Classroom: No. **Education packages:** No.
Facilities: Self-catering kitchen, lounge/diner, showers, cycle store and drying room. **Daytime access:** Public areas, via numbered lock.
Reception open: 5pm.

Meals: Self-catering only.
Getting there: From A35 into village, follow hostel signs. The hostel is next door to White Horse pub.
Public transport: BUS: First 31 Weymouth-Axminster (passes Axminster, Dorchester South and close to Dorchester West stations), alight Whiteway 1.5 miles. RAIL: Dorchester South or West, 10 miles.
Parking: Limited.
Nearest other hostels: Portland 19 miles, Lulworth Cove 25, Beer 28, Street 40.

Price Band: B   Opening category: ❷

LOPWELL CAMPING BARN
campingbarns@yha.org.uk
Booking: 0870 770 8868 (owners will contact guests to arrange key collection)

This camping barn sits on the banks of the River Tavy in an Area of Outstanding Natural Beauty. On the edge of Dartmoor, it's an ideal location for walking, cycling, canoeing and birdwatching. The Tamar Valley Discovery Trail runs close by.
You need to know... you cannot hire the barn for celebrations; dogs are allowed downstairs if you book sole usage; also book sole usage if you have children under five years of age.
Accommodation: Sleeps 16 on first floor.
Facilities: Shower, toilets adjacent, cooking area with microwave and fridge, sitting areas, hot water and metered electricity.
Nearest pub: 2.5 miles. **Nearest shop:** 2.5 miles.
Location: OS 201, GR 475650.

Price Band: C   Opening category: ❸

LULWORTH COVE ☆☆
School Lane, West Lulworth, Wareham, Dorset BH20 5SA; lulworth@yha.org.uk
Tel: 0870 770 5940 Fax: 0870 770 5941

YHA Lulworth Cove is a single storey purpose-built timber building on the edge of the tranquil fishing village of West Lulworth. Surrounded by fields and wonderful views of the Dorset hills, it's a mile's walk to the oyster-shaped Lulworth Cove and dramatic coastline. Children will enjoy a day out at Monkey World and Bovington Tank Museum.
Location: OS 194, GR 832806.
Great for... families looking for a mix of coast and countryside.
Accommodation: 34 beds: 2x4-, 2x5 and 2x6-bed rooms. 1x4 ensuite. **Family rooms:** Yes. **Rent-a-Hostel:** Yes.
Classroom: No. **Education packages:** No.
Facilities: Lounge/diner, self-catering kitchen, showers, drying room, cycle store and grounds. **Daytime access:** Public areas, via numbered lock.
Reception open: 5pm.
Meals: Breakfast, picnic lunch, evening meal.
Getting there: 100 metres east of B3070, turn opposite Castle Inn into School Lane.
Public transport: BUS: First 103 Dorchester-Bovington; Dorset Linkrider from Weymouth (both pass Wool station). RAIL: Wool 5 miles.
Parking: Yes.
Nearest other hostels: Swanage 17 miles, Portland 23, Litton Cheney 25.

Price Band: B   Opening category: ❷

LIZARD ☆☆☆☆☆
Lizard Point, Cornwall, TR12 7NT
Tel: 0870 770 6120 Fax: 0870 770 6121

Formerly a Victorian hotel acquired by the National Trust to preserve and protect this most unique location, this newly-restored building now offers first-class facilities and has stunning views out to sea over Lizard Point. Almost the most southerly building in England, it provides a superb base for exploring the spectacular coastline of this historic peninsula. This hostel is also within easy reach of all the exciting attractions west Cornwall has to offer.
Location: OS 204, GR 704116.
Great for... families, walkers and disabled guests.
You need to know... there is no external shelter.
Accommodation: 30 beds: 2x3- (en-suite, suitable for wheelchairs), 2x4-, 2x5- and 1x6-bed rooms.
Family rooms: Yes. **Rent-a-Hostel:** Yes.
Classroom: Yes. **Education packages:** No.
Facilities: Lounge, self-catering kitchen, dining room, showers, toilets, cycle store, parking. **Daytime access:** None until 5pm. For guests staying: all public areas, via numbered lock.
Reception open: 5pm. **Meals:** Self-catering only.

Five-star: YHA Lizard boasts amazing views over Lizard Point.

Getting there: From Helston, take the A3083, signposted to Lizard. When you arrive at the village, follow the signs for the most southerly point along narrow lane. Turn left at signpost and the hostel is next to the lighthouse.
Public transport: BUS: Truronian T1 from Truro station. RAIL: Penryn 18 miles.
NATIONAL EXPRESS Request stop at Helston.
Parking: Yes.
Nearest other hostels: Coverack 8 miles, Penzance 25, Land's End 33.

Price Band: C   Opening category: ❷

Kid's play: prepare for a fun-filled activity holiday at YHA Okehampton.

◉◉ LYNTON ☆☆☆

Lynbridge, Lynton, Devon EX35 6AZ
lynton@yha.org.uk
Tel: 0870 770 5942 Fax: 0870 770 5943

This tranquil hostel, a former country house, sits on the side of a steep wooded gorge and is a good base for discovering Exmoor. Close to the sea and the National Trust estate of Watersmeet, there are plenty of child-friendly attractions nearby. A wildlife park, dinosaur park and the Big Sheep Theme Park are all a short drive away. For quieter days out, there are also lots of riverside and cliff walks leading from the hostel.

Location: OS 180, GR 720487.
Great for... an energetic family holiday.
You need to know... parking is limited.
Accommodation: 36 beds: 2x2-, 2x4- and 4x6-bed rooms.
Family rooms: Yes. **Rent-a-Hostel:** Yes.
Classroom: No. **Education packages:** Yes.
Facilities: Lounge, self-catering kitchen, dining room, drying room, cycle store, shop and laundry. **Daytime access:** All public areas.
Reception open: Staff available before 10am and after 5pm.
Meals: Breakfast, picnic lunch, evening meal.
Getting there: From A39 at Lynmouth, follow Lynton sign right up

steep hill (B3234), turn left to Lynbridge and right at the Bridge Inn. From Barbrook, turn off A39 at petrol station and follow B3234 (Lynmouth Road) for 1 mile (do not turn off). In Lynbridge, turn left at The Bridge Inn up a steep, narrow road.
Public transport: BUS: First 309, 310 from Barnstaple (passes close to Barnstaple station); also 300 Barnstaple-Minehead (Sat & Sun all year and daily Jun-Sep only). RAIL: Barnstaple 20 miles.
Parking: Limited.
Nearest other hostels: Exford 15 miles, Minehead 21, Elmscott 35.

Price Band: B	Opening category: ❸

◉◉ OKEHAMPTON (DARTMOOR) ☆☆☆

Klondyke Road, Okehampton EX20 1EW;
okehampton@yha.org.uk
Tel: 0870 770 5978 Fax: 0870 770 5979

Prepare for serious fun in this uniquely preserved Victorian railway goods shed, now offering modern accommodation. On the edge of Dartmoor National Park, this licensed adventure centre specialises in providing activity holidays. Have a go at rock climbing, gorge scrambling, pony trekking, archery, treasure hunts and lots more. Or opt for a more relaxed pace and put on your walking boots to explore the surrounding moors.

Location: OS 191, GR 591942.
Great for... improving your skills in a fun-filled atmosphere.
Accommodation: 124 beds: all 2-, 4-, 6- and 8-bed rooms.
Family rooms: Yes. **Rent-a-Hostel:** Yes.
Classroom: Yes. **Education packages:** Yes.
Facilities: Lounge, dining room, self-catering kitchen, laundry, showers, toilets and camping. Outdoor activities (book in advance).
Daytime access: All public areas.
Meals: Breakfast, picnic lunch, evening meal.
Reception open: Staff available before 10am and after 5pm.
Getting there: From A30, head into Okehampton. In town centre at traffic lights turn into George Street and then right into Station Road. Bear left at monument and continue under bridge. The hostel is on the left.
Public transport: BUS: First X9/10 Exeter-Bude (passes Exeter St David's station), alight Okehampton town centre, then 0.5 miles; 187 Gunnislake station-Okehampton station (Sun, Jun-Sep only). RAIL: Okehampton adjacent (Sun, Jun-Sep only); otherwise Copplestone 13 miles, Exeter St David's 22.
NATIONALEXPRESS» West Street 0.5 miles.
Parking: Yes.
Nearest other hostels: Steps Bridge 18 miles, Bellever 20 (13 over moors), Exeter 24.

Price Band: **C**	Opening category: **❸**

● ● MINEHEAD ☆☆☆
Alcombe Combe, Minehead, Somerset TA24 6EW
Tel: 0870 770 5968 Fax: 0870 770 5969

Combine a traditional seaside holiday with a blast of outdoor activity at Minehead. This attractive country house sits high in the Exmoor hills of Somerset, just two miles from sandy beaches where children will love the funfair and swimming pools. Plenty of easy walking routes leave from the hostel's back door (with the South West Coast Path nearby), leading you to spectacular hill views that inspired the hymn All Things Bright and Beautiful. Mountain bikers will also find exciting trails.
Location: OS 181, GR 973442.
Great for... walking and seaside fun.
You need to know... the hostel is at the end of a private track with limited parking.
Accommodation: 35 beds: 1x3- (double bed with single over), 5x4- and 2x6-bed rooms.
Family rooms: Yes. **Rent-a-Hostel:** Yes.
Classroom: No. **Education packages:** Yes.
Facilities: Lounge, self-catering kitchen, dining room, drying room, cycle store and grounds.
Daytime access: Public areas, via numbered lock.
Reception open: Staff available before 10am and after 5pm.
Meals: Breakfast, picnic lunch, evening meal.
Getting there: Turn off the A39 at Alcombe into Brook Street or Church Street and follow this road to Britannia Inn on Manor Road, continuing when it becomes a private track for the last half-mile. Turn sharp left up to the hostel. The hostel can be difficult to find after dark.
Public transport: BUS: First 28, 928 Taunton-Minehead (passes Taunton station), alight Alcombe 0.5 miles. RAIL: Taunton 25 miles, Minehead or Dunster (both West Somerset Rly) 2.
Parking: Limited.
Nearest other hostels: Exford 13 miles (10 on foot), Quantock Hills 14, Crowcombe Heathfield 16, Lynton 21.

Price Band: **B**	Opening category: **❸**

MULLACOTT FARM CAMPING BARN
campingbarns@yha.org.uk
Booking: 0870 770 8868
Arrival time: Mrs Homa, 01271 866877

These newly-renovated former stables are on a small working farm in an Area of Outstanding Natural Beauty in Exmoor. Free-range eggs and sausages are available from the farm.
Great for... exploring north Devon, Tarka country, Exmoor and nearby beaches. Riding and quad bike riding next door.
You need to know... the main sleeping areas are above-ground platforms (14) and bunkbeds (6).
Accommodation: Sleeps 8 in one large area, plus small stalls each sleeping 2-4. Accommodates 20 in total.
Facilities: Electric light, dining area, kitchen area with full-size oven, hob, fridge-freezer, microwave, toaster, kettle, sinks with hot water (all on coin-operated meters), basic cooking equipment and cutlery. Separate toilets and shower (coin operated) adjacent, covered storage area, picnic area and car parking. Dogs welcome.
Nearest pub: 0.25 mile. **Nearest shop:** 0.25 miles.
Location: OS 180, GR 514455.

Price Band: **C**	Opening category: **❸**

HOSTEL MANAGERS CHOOSE...
THE BEST VIEWS IN THE WEST COUNTRY

West Somerset Steam Railway YHA Crowcombe: "Enjoy 20 miles of Somerset scenery as the train rolls beside the Quantock Hills and the Bristol Channel coast."
Cheddar gorge & caves YHA Cheddar: "Views with a difference. The cathedral-like caves and Britain's biggest gorge are million-year-old Ice Age riverbeds."
The Quantocks and Exmoor YHA Quantock Hills: "These are now virtually the only places in England where red deer can be seen in large numbers."
Durlston Country Park YHA Swanage: "For stunning views and wildlife, visit this fabulous 280-acre countryside paradise."
Tintagel YHA Tintagel: "Breakfast outside the hostel on the picnic benches and drink in the 180-degree view of the sea and north Cornwall's craggy coastline."

NORTHCOMBE CAMPING BARN
campingbarns@yha.org.uk
Booking: 0870 770 8868

This attractive camping barn has been converted from a watermill. Just a mile from Dulverton, a network of footpaths and bridleways leads onto Exmoor and to the Barle River valley where you'll find good canoeing.
Great for... riding, canoeing, cycling and walking.
Accommodation: Sleeps 15 in bunk beds in two areas.
Facilities: Fully equipped cooking area, hot water, fridge, shower, electric light (all on meter), wood-burning stove. Stabling available.
Nearest pub: 1 mile. **Nearest shop:** 1 mile.
Location: OS 181, GR 915292.

Price Band: G   **Opening category:** ❸

Set in beautiful landscaped gardens: YHA Penzance.

●● PENZANCE ☆
Castle Horneck, Alverton, Penzance, Cornwall TR20 8TF; penzance@yha.org.uk
Tel: 0870 770 5992 Fax: 0870 770 5993

This early Georgian manor stands in landscaped gardens and commands sweeping views of Mounts Bay and the Lizard Peninsula. Visit St Michael's Mount and the home of the Tate Gallery (St Ives), or take a boat to the Isles of Scilly. Enjoy a wide choice of meals, from speciality fresh-baked pizzas to Cornish fish pie and sticky toffee pudding.
Location: OS 203, GR 457302.
Great for... coastal views and lovely beaches.
You need to know... this hostel has facilities for camping.
Accommodation: 80 beds: mostly 4–10-bed rooms.
Family rooms: No. **FBR:** Yes.
Rent-a-Hostel: No.
Classroom: No. **Education packages:** Yes.
Facilities: Lounge, TV room, self-catering kitchen, showers, drying room, cycle store, lockers, grounds and camping with dedicated facilities.
Daytime access: All public areas.
Reception open: Staff available before 10am and after 5pm.
Meals: Breakfast, picnic lunch, evening meal.
Getting there: Drivers, follow A30 around Penzance by-pass and

turn at Castle Horneck sign to avoid town centre. Walkers/cyclists, go through town centre and past YMCA. Turn right onto Castle Horneck Road and cross A30. Continue through trees; hostel is on left.
Public transport: BUS: 343 from bus station; 5/6 to The Pirate pub. RAIL: Penzance 1.5 miles. FERRY: Isles of Scilly 1.5 miles.
NATIONAL EXPRESS Penzance bus station 1.5 miles.
Parking: Yes.
Nearest other hostels: Land's End 8 miles, Coverack 19, Perranporth 29.

Price Band: G   **Opening category:** ❸

●● PERRANPORTH ☆☆
Droskyn Point, Perranporth, Cornwall TR6 0GS
Tel: 0870 770 5994 Fax: 0870 770 5994

Once a coastguard station, this hostel is perched in a clifftop location on the rugged north coast of Cornwall, a surfer's paradise. Expect spectacular views of untamed Atlantic seas and three miles of lifeguarded sandy beaches. Walkers will want to follow the South West Coast Path, while nature lovers should look out for seals and dolphins in the St Agnes Marine Conservation Area.
Location: OS 204, GR 752544.
Great for... active people in need of an adrenalin rush.
You need to know... there's a charge for daytime parking between June and September.
Accommodation: 24 beds: 2x4- and 2x8-bed rooms.
Family rooms: No. **FBR:** Yes. **Rent-a-Hostel:** Yes.
Classroom: No. **Education packages:** No.
Facilities: Lounge/dining room, self-catering kitchen, garden, cycle and surfboard store and drying room (suitable for wetsuits).
Daytime access: All public areas.
Reception open: 5pm.
Meals: Self-catering only.
Getting there: From A30 turn right onto B3285 signposted Perranporth. Continue into Perranporth centre and turn right then immediately left on to St George's Hill signposted St Agnes. Turn

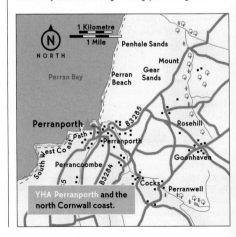
YHA Perranporth **and the north Cornwall coast.**

right into Tywarnhayle Road at hostel sign. Turn left on to Tregundy Lane at car park following hostel sign. Continue on Droskyn Point beyond Cellar Cove Hotel. On South West Coast Path from St Agnes, fork left at trail marker to Perranporth and hostel is 100 metres down footpath.

Public transport: BUS: First 85, 87/A/B Truro-Newquay (pass close to Truro and Newquay stations). RAIL: Truro 10 miles, Newquay 10 (not Sun, except Jun-Sept).

NATIONALEXPRESS Beach Road 0.25 miles.

Parking: Free overnight parking 250 metres (charge for daytime parking June–Sept).

Nearest other hostels: Treyarnon Bay 22 miles, Boswinger 25.

Price Band: 🅱	Opening category: ❷

●● PORTLAND ☆☆☆

Hardy House, Castle Road, Portland, Dorset DT5 1AU; portland@yha.org.uk
Tel: 0870 770 6000 Fax: 0870 770 6001

During the heyday of the Royal Navy's presence in Portland, this early Edwardian building belonged to the First Admiral and was later used as the headquarters for the MOD police. It benefits from extensive views over Lyme Bay and is a good base to explore the island's heritage, including Portland Castle and Portland Lighthouse. The South West Coastal Footpath will give you a good look at the

flora and fauna, or visit Chesil beach or nearby Weymouth to enjoy its award-winning beaches.

Location: OS 194, GR 685741.

Great for... a look into Portland's past, exploring the Jurassic Coast and Thomas Hardy country, walking and watersports.

Accommodation: 28 beds: 1x4- and 4x6-bed rooms.

Family rooms: Yes. **Rent-a-Hostel:** Yes.

Classroom: No. **Education packages:** Yes.

Facilities: Self-catering kitchen, quiet room, day room with showers and toilets. Tourist information centre.

Daytime access: Day room with tea/coffee facilities, shower and WC.

Reception open: 5pm.

Meals: Self-catering only. Meals available for pre-booked groups of 10+.

Getting there: On arriving at Portland, from Victoria Square turn left into Victory Road, then left again into Castle Road. The hostel is on the right-hand side.

Public transport: BUS: First 1/A, 7/A, Sureline 1X, X10 from Weymouth. RAIL: Weymouth 4.5 miles.

NATIONALEXPRESS Weymouth 4 miles.

Parking: Yes.

Nearest other hostels: Litton Cheney 19 miles, Lulworth Cove 23, Beer 44.

Price Band: 🅱	Opening category: ❸

From YHA Portland, visit nearby Chesil Beach and search for 'Hag' pebbles, which have a hole in them made by the action of the waves.

Ideal base: YHA River Dart.

● RIVER DART ☆☆

Galmpton, Brixham, Devon TQ5 0ET;
riverdart@yha.org.uk
Tel: 0870 770 5962 Fax: 0870 770 5963

Whether you are looking for an energetic family holiday, a relaxing break or to celebrate a special occasion, the imposing YHA River Dart Centre is an ideal base from which to explore the English Riviera. Enjoy Torbay's attractions or explore the natural splendour of Dartmoor. Relax on award-winning beaches, learn to dive or sail, visit the historic port of Plymouth or Roman city of Exeter. After a busy day you can return to the tranquility of the YHA River Dart Centre to enjoy a superb choice of adult and children's meals overlooking the Dart estuary or relax in our galleried halls by an open fire.

Location: OS 202, GR 877546.

Great for... large groups, schools and wedding receptions in our four acres of gardens overlooking the River Dart.

Accommodation: 70 beds: all 4-, 5-, 6-, 8- and 12-bed rooms.

Family rooms: Yes. **Rent-a-Hostel:** Yes.

Classroom: Yes, ICT suite. **Education packages:** Yes.

Facilities: TV lounge, quiet room/leader lounge, games room, ICT suite and classroom, meeting room, self-catering kitchen, drying room, cycle store and camping.

Daytime access: All public areas.

Reception open: Before 10am and after 5pm.

Meals: Breakfast, picnic lunch, evening meal and special event catering.

Getting there: At A38, A380 and A3022 intersection with A379, take second turning on right (Manor Vale Road) following Greenway Road through the village, towards National Trust Greenway bearing left at YHA sign.

Public transport: BUS: Stagecoach Devon 12 Paignton station-Brixham, alight Churston Pottery 2 miles.
RAIL: Paignton 5 miles, Churston (Dart Valley Railway) 2.
NATIONALEXPRESS Brixham, Bank Lane 4 miles.

Parking: Yes, 30 cars and coach park.

Nearest other hostels: Dartington 11 miles, Salcombe 26, Exeter 32.

> **Price Band:** B   **Opening category:** ❷

●● QUANTOCK HILLS ☆☆

Sevenacres, Holford, Bridgwater, Somerset
TA5 1SQ; reservations@yha.org.uk
Tel: 0870 770 6006 Fax: 0870 770 6006
Bookings more than 7 days ahead: 0870 770 8868

Head off the beaten track to this traditional country house high on the Quantock Hills with views across the Bristol Channel to Wales. Walk straight from the hostel onto the hills to see a wealth of wildlife or venture down to Kilve beach to hunt for fossils. History lovers will enjoy exploring the nearby town of Dunster, dominated by the towers and turrets of a Victorian castle.

Location: OS 181, GR 146416.

Great for... keen walkers wanting a country retreat.

You need to know... it's self-catering accommodation only.

Accommodation: 24 beds: 1x2-, 1x4- and 3x6-bed rooms.

Family rooms: No. **FBR:** Yes. **Rent-a-Hostel:** Yes.

Classroom: No. **Education packages:** No.

Facilities: Lounge, dining room, self-catering kitchen, showers, central heating, wood-burning stove, drying room, grounds and camping. **Daytime access:** Sorry, none until after 5pm.

Reception open: 5pm.

Meals: Self-catering only.

Getting there: From Kilve, take lane opposite post office and, after 1 mile, follow a rough track. From Holford, take road through Hotel (1.5 miles), cross second cattle grid, go uphill to a sharp bend and take rough track on right to hostel.

Public transport: BUS: First 15, 915, 927 Bridgwater-Minehead (passing close to Bridgwater station). RAIL: Bridgwater 13 miles.
NATIONALEXPRESS Bridgwater 13 miles.

Parking: Limited.

Nearest other hostels: Crowcombe 10 miles (7 on foot), Minehead 14.

> **Price Band:** B   **Opening category:** ❸

RUNNAGE CAMPING BARNS

campingbarns@yha.org.uk
Booking: 0870 770 8868
Arrival time: Christine Coaker, 01822 880222

A former hay loft and stable block has been converted to form these two camping barns. They are situated on a working farm in the very heart of Dartmoor, close to Soussons and Bellever forest. This is an ideal location for schools and groups that enjoy walking, cycling, climbing and canoeing.

You need to know... it's a minimum of 12 people for weekend bookings; minimum two nights on weekends and Bank Holidays; sole use booking for weekends and Bank Holidays. Mountain bikes available for hire on site.

Accommodation: Sleeps 15x2.

Facilities: Hot water, cooker, microwave, toaster, kettle, fridge and hot showers. Electricity for cooking and heating extra.

Nearest pubs: 1.5 miles.

Location: OS 191, GR 667792.

> **Price Band:** G   **Opening category:** ❸

●● SALCOMBE ☆☆

Sharpitor, Salcombe, Devon TQ8 8LW
Tel: 0870 770 6016 Fax: 0870 770 6017

If you love the sea, Salcombe is the place for you. Test out your sea legs on one of the sailing packages available at the hostel or be brave and try your hand at a range of watersports. Safe sandy beaches are just a few minutes away, or venture further on the coastal path to Bolthead, Hope Cove and beyond. After a busy day, this Edwardian National Trust property set in six acres of semi-tropical gardens makes an elegant spot in which to recuperate.

Location: OS 202, GR 728374.

Great for... groups with a passion for the sea and the outdoors.

You need to know... there's no parking at the hostel 10am-5pm.

Accommodation: 52 beds: 1x2-, 5x4-, 1x6-, 1x7-, 1x8- and 1x9-bed rooms.

Family rooms: Yes. **Rent-a-Hostel:** No.

Classroom: Yes. **Education packages:** No.

Facilities: Lounge, TV room, dining room, self-catering kitchen, showers, drying room and cycle store.

Daytime access: To foyer. Guests staying over have access via numbered lock. National Trust tea rooms with toilet nearby.

Meals: Breakfast, picnic lunch, evening meal.

Reception open: 5pm.

Getting there: From Kingsbridge, follow A381 to Salcombe, then follow brown YHA and Overbecks signs to hostel.

Public transport: BUS: Tally Ho! from Kingsbridge (connects from Plymouth, Dartmouth and, for trains, from Totnes; through buses from Totnes Sun), alight Salcombe 2 miles. RAIL: Totnes 20 miles.

Parking: Convenient National Trust car park available between 5pm and 10am. During the day, please park at South Sands Hotel (15 minutes by foot) or North Sands (20 minutes).

Nearest other hostels: Dartington 21 miles, River Dart 26 (via Dart Ferry or Totnes).

Price Band: 8	Opening category: ❷

YHA Salcombe: a sea-lover's paradise.

● SALISBURY ☆☆

Milford Hill, Salisbury, Wiltshire SP1 2QW;
salisbury@yha.org.uk
Tel: 0870 770 6018 Fax: 0870 770 6019

This is a 200-year-old building in secluded grounds. It's just a short walk into the heart of the historic city of Salisbury and makes a good base for groups seeking to explore the multitude of attractions throughout Wiltshire. It's just minutes from Salisbury Cathedral and nine miles from Stonehenge.

Location: OS 184, GR 149299.

Great for... off-road cycling; history enthusiasts.

You need to know... the hostel's 20-bedded lodge is available for private hire; breakfast is included in the overnight price.

Accommodation: 70 beds. Main house, 50 beds: 1x1-, 1x2-, 3x4-bed rooms, plus larger rooms; Lodge: 2x3-, 4x4-bed rooms including lounge, showers and toilets.

Family rooms: Yes. **Rent-a-Hostel:** No.

Classroom: No. **Education packages:** Yes.

Facilities: TV room, lounge, showers, self-catering kitchen, coin-operated laundry, cycle store and garden.

Daytime access: All public areas.

Reception open: 7.30am–10.30pm.

Meals: Bed and breakfast package only. Full meals service only available to pre-booked groups.

Getting there: Motorists, follow A36 signposts. Follow brown signs on A36 by Salisbury college roundabout. On foot, walk east from tourist information centre following black footpath signs, leading into Milford Street and up hill (see map on page 173).

Public transport: BUS: frequent from surrounding areas. RAIL: Salisbury 1 mile.

NATIONALEXPRESS>> Endless Street, Salisbury 1.2 miles.

Parking: Yes.

Nearest other hostels: Burley 21 miles, Winchester 24, Bath 39.

Price Band: D	Opening category: ❶

HOSTEL MANAGERS CHOOSE...
THE BEST BEACH EXPERIENCES

Durdle Door Archway YHA Lulworth Cove: "A steep climb up the hill above Durdle Door gives the most spectacular views of the coastline."

Treyarnon Bay YHA Treyarnon Bay: "Treyarnon boasts one of the most unspoilt beaches in North Cornwall and is ideal for surfing."

Coverack YHA Coverack: "The picturesque bay is ideal for windsurfing. Go on, anyone can try."

Perran Sands YHA Perranporth: "Surfers' paradise with the added bonus of spectacular views over the rugged coastline."

Walk the coast path to Land's End YHA Land's End: "It's an absolute must."

Hostels ideally situated for walking on Dartmoor are YHA Bellever, Steps Bridge and Okehampton.

● STEPS BRIDGE (DARTMOOR)

**Steps Bridge, near Dunsford, Exeter, Devon
EX6 7EQ; bellever@yha.org.uk
Tel: 0870 770 6048 Fax: 0870 770 6049
Bookings over 7 days ahead: 0870 770 5692**

If you feel the need for peace and tranquillity, this unpretentious chalet is a quiet haven in a secluded woodland location on the edge of East Dartmoor. From this steep hillside overlooking the Teign Valley, there are endless walks leading across the rugged Dartmoor Tors and onto the lower slopes where you'll discover rare wildflowers, birds and butterflies. Although facilities are basic, the bunkrooms are comfortable.

Location: OS 191, GR 802882.

Great for... active walkers who want to avoid the crowds.

You need to know... the toilets, showers and some bunkrooms are outside the main building.

Accommodation: 24 beds: 1x2-, 2x4-, 1x6- and 1x8-bed rooms.

Family rooms: No. **Rent-a-Hostel:** Yes.

Classroom: No. **Education packages:** No.

Facilities: Sitting/dining area, self-catering kitchen, showers, drying room and cycle store. **Daytime access:** All public areas.

Reception open: Staff available before 10am and after 5pm.

Meals: Self-catering only.

Getting there: On the B3212 Exeter to Moretonhampstead road, the hostel is opposite Steps Bridge Tea Rooms. The hostel drive is very steep so please take care.

Public transport: BUS: Stagecoach 359 from Exeter Central. RAIL: Exeter Central 9 miles, Exeter St David's 9.

Parking: Please park in the public car park opposite end of hostel drive; no parking on drive.

Nearest other hostels: Exeter 11 miles, Bellever 18, Okehampton 18, Dartington 26.

Price Band: A	Opening category: ❷

●● STREET ☆

**The Chalet, Ivythorn Hill, Street, Somerset
BA16 0TZ street@yha.org.uk
Tel: 0870 770 6056 Fax: 0870 770 6057**

Overlooking Glastonbury Tor, this basic Swiss-style chalet is surrounded by National Trust land and feels like a quiet retreat. However, it's within easy reach of the Mendip Hills, Somerset Levels, mystical Glastonbury and historic Wells. The amenities of the town of Street are also close by.

Location: OS 182, GR 480345.

Great for... a quiet base for touring Somerset.

Accommodation: 28 beds: 2x3-, 4x4- and 1x6-bed rooms.

Family rooms: Yes. **Rent-a-Hostel:** Yes.

Classroom: No. **Education packages:** No.

Facilities: Lounge/diner, self-catering kitchen, showers, drying room, cycle store and camping ground.

Daytime access: All public areas.
Reception open: Staff available before 10am and after 5pm.
Meals: Self-catering only.
Getting there: From Street, take the B3151 towards Somerton for 2 miles. Turn right at Marshalls Elm crossroads and follow signs to hostel which is 500 metres on your right.
Public transport: BUS: First 376/7, 976/7, 929 Bristol-Yeovil (passes Bristol Temple Meads station), alight Marshalls Elm then 500m. RAIL: Castle Cary 11 miles, Bridgwater 13.
NATIONALEXPRESS Leigh Road 1.25 miles.
Parking: Yes.
Nearest other hostels: Cheddar 17 miles, Quantock Hills 28, Bristol 33.

Price Band: B	Opening category: ❸

●● SWANAGE ☆☆☆

Cluny, Cluny Crescent, Swanage, Dorset
BH19 2BS; swanage@yha.org.uk
Tel: 0870 770 6058 Fax: 0870 770 6059

For an activity-packed holiday, Swanage is the place to be. The town boasts safe, sandy beaches, spectacular coastal scenery, high sunshine ratings and festivals galore. And just a few minutes' walk from the town centre is this elegant Victorian house offering fine views across the bay. Don't miss exploring the Jurassic Coast, a World Heritage Site that tells a geological story covering 200 million years.
Location: OS 195, GR 031785.
Great for... sunbathers, swimmers and walkers.
You need to know... breakfast is included in the overnight price.
Accommodation: 100 beds in small bedrooms.
Family rooms: Yes. **Rent-a-Hostel:** No.
Classroom: Yes. **Education packages:** No.
Facilities: Lounge, TV, games room, self-catering kitchen, showers, drying room, laundry facilities, residential licence and cycle store.
Daytime access: All public areas. **Reception open:** All day.
Meals: Breakfast, picnic lunch, evening meal.
Getting there: From Bournemouth, take Sandbanks ferry, then travel on to Swanage via Studland village. From Wareham, take A351 to Swanage via Corfe Castle. From Swanage town centre, go up Stafford Road (next to White Swan Inn in High Street) which runs into Cluny Crescent. The hostel is at the top of the hill on the right.
Public transport: BUS: Wilts & Dorset 150 from Bournemouth (passes Branksome station); 142-4 from Poole (pass Wareham station). Alight Swanage bus station on all services then 0.25 mile.
RAIL: Wareham 10 miles.
NATIONALEXPRESS Swanage bus station 0.25 miles.
Parking: Yes.
Nearest other hostels: Lulworth Cove 17 miles, Burley 29.

Price Band: D	Opening category: ❹

TREYARNON BAY ☆☆☆

Tregonnan, Treyarnon, Padstow, Cornwall
PL28 8JR; treyarnon@yha.org.uk
Tel: 0870 770 6076 Fax: 0870 770 6077

Enjoy a traditional seaside break at this hostel situated above a beautiful sandy bay. Formerly a 1930s summer residence, the hostel is virtually on the beach so you can build sandcastles, surf and watch sunsets to your heart's content. Beach games and the obligatory buckets and spades are available at the hostel. Walkers and cyclists will find plenty to do or, if you're feeling energetic, try the all-inclusive surf package offered by the hostel.
Location: OS 200, GR 859741.

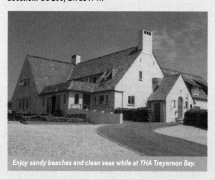
Enjoy sandy beaches and clean seas while at YHA Treyarnon Bay.

Great for... a quiet seaside break.
You need to know... due to health and safety and noise considerations, we are not suitable for under-3s.
Accommodation: 70 beds: 5x3-bed rooms containing 1x family bunk (double bed), 3x5-bed rooms containing 1x family bunk (double bed), 4x4- and 4x6-bed rooms. Many rooms en-suite.
Family rooms: Yes. **Rent-a-Hostel:** Yes.
Classroom: Yes. **Education packages:** Yes.
Facilities: Dining/sitting room, cafeteria (10am-4pm except in winter), self-catering kitchen, drying room, showers, cycle store and garden. **Daytime access:** All areas.
Reception open: Staff available before 10am and after 5pm.
Meals: Breakfast, picnic lunch, evening meal.
Getting there: From A30 southbound, take A389 to Padstow, then B3276 to St Merryn and on towards Newquay. Then turn off at third right turn to Treyarnon. From Newquay, take B3276 towards Padstow and, after Porthcothan, follow hostel signs. From Treyarnon beach follow lane marked Private Residents Only. Hostel is on right.
Public transport: BUS: First 55 Bodmin Parkway station-Padstow, then Western Greyhound 556 Padstow-Newquay to Constantine, 0.5 miles. RAIL: Newquay (not Sun, except Jun-Sep) 10 miles, Bodmin Parkway 21.
Parking: Yes.
Nearest other hostels: Perranporth 22 miles, Tintagel 23, Boscastle Harbour 24.

Price Band: C	Opening category: ❸

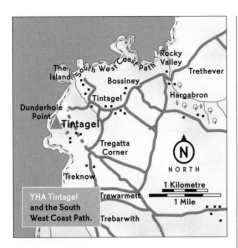

YHA Tintagel and the South West Coast Path.

●● TINTAGEL ☆☆

Dunderhole Point, Tintagel, Cornwall PL34 0DW;
reservations@yha.org.uk
Tel: 0870 770 6068 Fax: 0870 770 6069
Bookings more than 7 days ahead: 0870 770 8868

Have you had enough of 21st century Britain? Then stay in this remote, well-equipped and comfortable hostel, perched on Glebe Cliff with stunning coastal views over Dunderhole Point. Walk the South West Coast Path, explore the 13th century remains of Tintagel Castle or just watch the wild seas crash over the rocks below.

Location: OS 200, GR 047881.

Great for... Arthurian legend lovers, walkers and families.

You need to know... access to the hostel is along a narrow, rough and unlit track and parking is limited.

Accommodation: 22 beds, 1x2-, 2x4- and 2x6-bed rooms.

Family rooms: No. **FBR:** Yes. **Rent-a-Hostel:** Yes.

Get away from it all as you relax at YHA Tintagel.

Classroom: No. **Education packages:** No.

Facilities: Self-catering kitchen, sitting/dining area, showers and cycle store. **Daytime access:** Public areas, via numbered lock.

Reception open: 5pm.

Meals: Self-catering only.

Getting there: By car, from Tintagel village take B3263 to Tregatta (0.75 miles). Turn right along a narrow lane, then a very rough, unlit track to the hostel. On foot, follow road to Tintagel church, then path for 300 metres to hostel.

Public transport: BUS: Western Greyhound 522/3 Wadebridge-Bude, alight Tintagel 0.5 miles. RAIL: Bodmin Parkway 20 miles.

Parking: Limited.

Nearest other hostels: Boscastle Harbour 5 miles, Treyarnon Bay 23 (18 by ferry), Golant 28.

Price Band: B   Opening category: ②

Brave the steep descent to Tintagel Cove near YHA Tintagel.

WOODADVENT CAMPING BARN

campingbarns@yha.org.uk
Booking: 0870 770 8868
Arrival time: Mrs Brewer, 01984 640920

You'll find this camping barn in a quiet, unspoilt corner of Exmoor National Park. In the farmyard a mile outside Roadwater village, the former cider barn still has the original cider press in situ.

Great for... walking, pony riding and the nearby steam railway.

Accommodation: Sleeps 12 in two areas.

Facilities: Electric light and shower (both metered), heating, cooking and recreation area and BBQ area. Breakfast available.

Nearest pub: 2 miles. **Nearest shop:** 2 miles.

Location: OS 181, GR 037374.

Price Band: C   Opening category: ③

TRY RENT-A-HOSTEL

Many of the hostels in this guide can be booked through the Rent-a-Hostel scheme. For full details, turn to page 12.

South East England

Take your pick from the natural splendour of the New Forest and the South Downs, great seaside resorts and attractive towns alive with history.

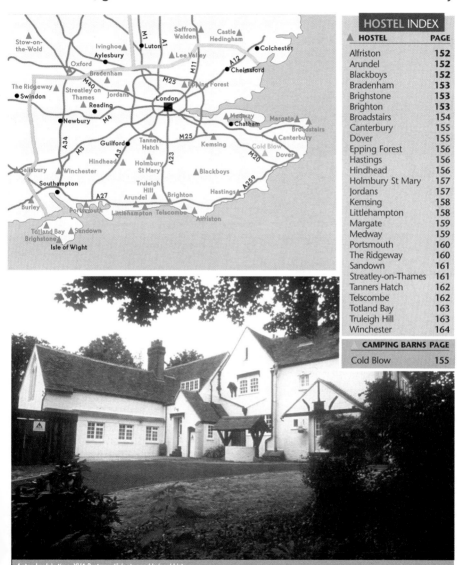

A step back in time: YHA Portsmouth is steeped in local history.

● ALFRISTON ☆

Frog Firle, Alfriston, Polegate, East Sussex BN26 5TT; alfriston@yha.org.uk
Tel: 0870 770 5666 Fax: 0870 770 5667

Relax in the Tudor beamed lounge or the large walled garden of this comfortable historic house. The network of footpaths and bridleways, National cycle route 2 and good public transport links make Alfriston an ideal Youth Hostel for exploring the South Downs and Sussex towns. It is three miles from the sea and the Seven Sisters cliffs, with castles, houses, galleries and nature reserves to discover. Pretty Alfriston village offers teashops and the National Trust's Clergy House.

Location: OS 199, GR 518019.
Great for... families; walking and cycle hire.
You need to know... the hostel is popular with families not needing day access.
Accommodation: 66 beds: 7x2–4-, 6x6–8- and 1x10-bed rooms.
Family rooms: No. **FBR:** Yes. **Rent-a-Hostel:** No.
Classroom: Yes. **Education packages:** Yes.
Facilities: Two common rooms, internet access, self-catering kitchen, showers, drying room, cycle store and garden.
Daytime access: Basic shelter and toilet facilities.
Reception open: 5pm.

Historic YHA Alfriston is ideal for active families.

Meals: Breakfast, picnic lunch, evening meal.
Getting there: On foot, follow river to Litlington footbridge, take bridlepath west for 400 metres. By road, the hostel is 0.75 miles south of Alfriston on east side where road narrows.
Public transport: BUS: Renown 126 Seaford-Alfriston-Eastbourne (passes close to Seaford and Polegate stations); RDH 125 from Lewes station to within 0.5 miles. RAIL: Seaford 3 miles, Berwick 3. FERRY: New Haven to Dieppe 6 miles.
Parking: Yes.
Nearest other hostels: Telscombe 11, Blackboys 17.

Price Band: B	Opening category: ❸

●● ARUNDEL ☆☆☆☆

Warningcamp, Arundel, West Sussex BN18 9QY; arundel@yha.org.uk
Tel: 0870 770 5676 Fax: 0870 770 5677

Enjoy the best of both worlds in this handsome Georgian mansion. Situated at the end of a private road with a spacious front lawn, it's well away from the busy traffic of Arundel yet just over a mile from the town centre. If you're bringing the family, you'll be pleased to know the sandy beaches of Littlehampton and West Wittering are nearby, where the kids can run riot with buckets and spades. There's also walking aplenty – the Monarch's Way will lead you onto the expansive South Downs or, for an evening stroll, follow the riverside path to Arundel.

Location: OS 197, GR 032076.
Great for... families with young children.
You need to know... it's a children's paradise, a home away from home; breakfast is included in the price.
Accommodation: 65 beds: 2-, 3-, 4-, 5- and 6-bed rooms, 3 rooms en-suite with double beds.
Family rooms: Yes. **Rent-a-Hostel:** No.
Classroom: Dining room seats 60. **Education packages:** No.
Facilities: TV lounge and games room, dining room, two self-catering kitchens, showers, drying room, pool table, table-tennis table, internet access and bar football, cycle store, grounds, camping and BBQ. **Daytime access:** Public areas, via numbered lock.
Reception open: 5pm.
Meals: Breakfast, picnic lunch, evening meal.
Getting there: Follow A27 around Arundel towards Littlehampton.

Turn left down small road past station, signposted to hostel and Warningcamp. Continue to first crossroads and turn left. Follow lane around two right-hand turns.
Public transport: BUS: Stagecoach in the South Downs 702 from Brighton, alight Arundel Station then 1 mile. RAIL: Arundel 1 mile. **NATIONALEXPRESS** A27 Arundel 1.25 miles.
Parking: Yes.
Nearest other hostels: Littlehampton 4 miles, Truleigh Hill 16, Brighton 20.

Price Band: D	Opening category: ❸

●● BLACKBOYS ☆

Blackboys, Uckfield, East Sussex TN22 5HU
Tel: 0870 770 5698 Fax: 0870 770 5699

With just 30 beds, this wooden cabin set in woodland is a quiet escape from the hurly-burly of southern England. A walk along the Weald Way will be high on your priority list if you stay here, as will a visit to Batemans at Burwash, a National Trust property and once the home of Rudyard Kipling. It's also ideal for exploring the Bluebell Railway and Cuckoo Trail.

Location: OS 199, GR 521215.
Great for... small groups wanting a quiet weekend away.
You need to know... you should bring provisions — Blackboys only offers self-catering accommodation.
Accommodation: 30 beds: 1x2-, 3x3-, 1x4- and 3x5-bed rooms.
Family rooms: No. **FBR:** Yes. **Rent-a-Hostel:** Yes.
Classroom: No. **Education packages:** No.

Facilities: Lounge/dining room, self-catering kitchen, showers, laundry, drying room, cycle store, luggage store, camping and grounds. **Daytime access:** Enclosed front porch and toilet.
Reception open: 5pm. **Meals:** Self-catering only.
Getting there: From Cross-in-Hand take right fork at Blackboys village then second right following signs to hostel at crossroads. From Uckfield take Heathfield Road B2102. After 4 miles turn left at crossroads, turn down Gun Road and go across stream. Hostel is in woods on right next to farmhouse. From Lewes Road fork left at Blackboys Inn. Follow hostel sign and keep straight on.
Public transport: BUS: Stagecoach/Renown 318 Etchingham-Uckfield (pass Etchingham and close to Uckfield stations), alight Blackboys 0.5 miles. RAIL: Buxted 2.5 miles, Lewes 11.
NATIONALEXPRESS▶ Uckfield bus terminal 4 miles.
Parking: Cars and minibuses only.
Nearest other hostels: Alfriston 17 miles, Brighton 17, Telscombe 17, Eastbourne 18, Kemsing 30.

Price Band: B	Opening category: ❸

○● BRADENHAM ☆☆
Bradenham Woods Lane, Bradenham, High Wycombe, Buckinghamshire HP14 4HF; bradenham@yha.org.uk
Tel: 0870 770 5714 Fax: 0870 770 5715

Once the village hall and schoolhouse, Bradenham was previously the central focus of this National Trust village. It now offers modest

Keen walkers will have plenty of paths to explore near YHA Bradenham.

accommodation to keen walkers and cyclists wanting to explore the surrounding maze of waymarked paths.
Location: OS 165, GR 828972.
Great for... keen walkers who want to explore the Chiltern beechwoods on foot.
You need to know... it's open all year to groups.
Accommodation: 14 beds: 1x6-, and 2x4-bed rooms.
Family rooms: No. **FBR:** Yes. **Rent-a-Hostel:** Yes.
Classroom: No. **Education packages:** No.
Facilities: Lounge/dining room, self-catering kitchen, showers, drying room and cycle store. **Daytime access:** Sorry, none until after 5pm. Further details on website.
Reception open: 5pm. **Meals:** Self-catering only.

Getting there: Leave M40 at J4, follow A4010 (signed Aylesbury) to Bradenham. Turn off at Red Lion and hostel is opposite church.
Public transport: BUS: 2/5/321/322 High Wycombe-Princes Risborough (Mon-Fri only), alight Bradenham Red Lion 0.5 miles; Arriva 323/324 High Wycombe-Princes Risborough (daily), alight Walters Ash — Bradenham turn 1 mile. RAIL: Saunderton 1.5 miles (hourly to London Marylebone and Birmingham New Street), High Wycombe 4.5.
NATIONALEXPRESS▶ High Wycombe bus station 4.25 miles.
Parking: Roadside lay-by.
Nearest other hostels: Jordans 12 miles, Ivinghoe 17, Streatley on Thames 31.

Price Band: B	Opening category: ❹

○● BRIGHSTONE
Please direct all enquiries for YHA Brighstone through YHA Totland Bay, Hurst Hill, Totland Bay, Isle of Wight PO39 0HD; totland@yha.org.uk
Tel: 0870 770 6070 Fax: 0870 770 6071

This newly built seasonal hostel owned by the Scouting Association and tucked behind the village church hall is just one mile away from the beach and Isle of Wight Pearl. Also close by are Moltistone Manor and Gardens, Dinosaur farm, Hanover Point Fossil Forest and Blackgang Chine.
Location: OS 196, GR 832428.
Great for... walking the quiet paths of West Wight.
You need to know...only available mid July-August.
Accommodation: 12 beds: 2x6-bed rooms.
Family rooms: No. **FBR:** Yes. **Rent-a-Hostel:** No.
Classroom: No. **Education packages:** No.
Facilities: Laundry, members' kitchen, showers and toilets, disabled showers and toilets, dining room and lounge.
Reception open: 8am-10am and 5pm-10pm.
Meals: Self-catering only.
Getting there: In the centre of the village of Brighstone behind the church hall.
Public transport: FERRY: Lymington to Yarmouth 10 miles, Southampton to Cowes 14, Portsmouth to Fishbourne 17. BUS: 7B from Three Bishops pub opposite church hall. RAIL: Seaford 3 miles, Berwick 3.
Parking: Yes, 200 yards from hostel.
Nearest other hostels: Totland Bay 8 miles, Sandown 16.

Price Band: B

●● BRIGHTON ☆☆☆
Patcham Place, London Road, Brighton, East Sussex BN1 8YD; brighton@yha.org.uk
Tel: 0870 770 5724 Fax: 0870 770 5725

With so much to do, Brighton is an exciting city to visit. No one can resist the traditional seaside pursuits at the world-famous pier and pavilion. Then there's a cosmopolitan range of shops to explore before you even contemplate an energetic night on the town. Just as well then, that this 16th century manor house offers a retreat from the city in open parkland on the outskirts of Brighton. And, when you're rested, the staff will be only too happy to help plan your activities for tomorrow.

Location: OS 198, GR 300088.

Great for... a base to explore Brighton and the South Downs.

You need to know... the hostel is on the outskirts of Brighton, 3 miles from the city centre; breakfast is included in the price.

Accommodation: 56 beds: 1x4-, 3x6-, 1x10- and 2x12-bed rooms.

Family rooms: No. **FBR:** Yes. **Rent-a-Hostel:** No.

Classroom: No. **Education packages:** Yes.

Facilities: Lounge/TV room, self-catering kitchen, showers, cycle shed and laundry facilities.

Reception open: 1pm–11pm (closes 12 midnight).

Meals: Breakfast, evening meal and picnic lunch.

Daytime access: All public areas.

Getting there: Public transport from city centre. From train station walk down Queens Road to clock tower, turning right to Churchill Square bus stops. Stage Coach bus 770 stops outside hostel (Patcham–Black Lion) or take 5A bus to Patcham (Co-op). The bus also stops on North Road, pavilion on Old Steine, Preston Park and all stops on London Road. From Patcham village Co-op, follow Old London Road round to left past Post Office to London Road. Hostel is opposite Black Lion pub. By road, hostel is 3 miles north of Brighton city centre on London Road (A23) adjacent to A23/A27 junction (see map on page 171).

Public transport: BUS: Brighton & Hove 5/A; otherwise Stagecoach in the South Downs 107 Brighton-Horsham, Stagecoach Coastline 770, Metrobus 87 Brighton-Haywards Heath (pass close to Preston Park and Haywards Heath stations). RAIL: Preston Park 2 miles, Brighton 3.5.

NATIONALEXPRESS Opposite hostel outside Black Lion pub.

Parking: Yes.

Nearest other hostels: Truleigh Hill 6 miles, Telscombe 10, Alfriston 14.

Price Band: D	Opening category: ❸

● ● ● **BROADSTAIRS** ☆☆

3 Osborne Road, Broadstairs, Kent CT10 2AE;
broadstairs@yha.org.uk
Tel: 0870 770 5730 Fax: 0870 770 5730

If you're always complaining that the world isn't what it used to be, a stay at Broadstairs should restore your faith in old-time England. A traditional hostel with a personal atmosphere, it's centrally located in this historic seaside resort. Gentle pursuits are the name of the day and a stroll along the award-winning beach half a mile away is a must. Or, if you're looking for a dash of culture, book during the Charles Dickens week in June or the folk week in August.

Location: OS 179, GR 390679.

Great for... short breaks to blow away the cobwebs!

You need to know... there are two cats at the hostel.

Accommodation: 23 beds: 1x2-, 1x3 and 3x6-bed rooms.

Family rooms: No. **FBR:** Yes. **Rent-a-Hostel:** No.

Classroom: No. **Education packages:** No.

Facilities: Lounge, dining room with TV and video, self-catering kitchen, showers, drying room, cycle store, laundry facilities and garden with BBQ.

Daytime access: None until after 5pm. Public toilets at station.

Reception open: 5pm.

Meals: Self-catering only; full meals service available for pre-booked groups of 15 or more.

Getting there: From town centre and beach, head uphill along High Street, under railway bridge and left at traffic lights. The hostel is first building after the row of shops (see map on page 171).

Public transport: BUS: From surrounding areas. RAIL: Broadstairs 100 metres. FERRY: Ramsgate 2 miles, Dover 19. AIRPORT: London (Manston) 3 miles. **NATIONALEXPRESS** Pierremont Hall, High Street 0.25 miles. **Parking:** Roadside.

Nearest other hostels: Margate 4 miles (7 along coast), Canterbury 18, Dover 19, Medway 45.

Price Band: B	Opening category: ❷

Stunning retreat: YHA Brighton is a 16th century manor house on the outskirts of the city.

●● CANTERBURY ☆

54 New Dover Road, Canterbury, CT1 3DT;
canterbury@yha.org.uk
Tel: 0870 770 5744 Fax: 0870 770 5745

This splendid Victorian villa is near the centre of the early Christian city of Canterbury, with good access onto the Kent Downs. The hostel is popular with groups and individuals alike, who enjoy the friendly atmosphere. It's within easy reach of the North Downs Way and Pilgrims' Way, while the city itself has a cathedral, St Augustine's Abbey, various museums, guided tours and theatres.

Location: OS 179, GR 157570.

Great for... cathedral lovers and those who want to explore Kent.

You need to know... parking is limited; breakfast is included in the price.

Accommodation: 68 beds: 1x1-, 2x2-, 1x3-, 1x4-, 4x5-, 1x6- and 3x10-bed rooms.

Family rooms: No. **FBR:** Yes. **Rent-a-Hostel:** Yes.

Classroom: No. **Education packages:** Yes.

Facilities: Lounge, TV, cycle shed, laundry, self-catering kitchen, showers, bureau de change, internet access and garden.

Daytime access: All public areas.

Reception open: 3pm.

Meals: Full meals service available for pre-booked groups of 10+.

Getting there: Follow signs for Dover and the hostel is on the A2050, 1 mile from the city centre (see map on page 172).

Public transport: BUS: frequent from surrounding areas. RAIL: Canterbury East 0.5 miles, Canterbury West 1.5.
NATIONALEXPRESS Canterbury bus station 0.75 miles.

Parking: Yes.

Nearest other hostels: Dover 14 miles, Margate 15, Broadstairs 18, Medway 30, Kemsing 42.

Price Band: D	Opening category: ❸

COLD BLOW CAMPING BARN

campingbarns@yha.org.uk
Booking: 0870 770 8868
Arrival time: Dora Pilkington, 01622 735038

These two bunkhouses and camping barn, between Maidstone and Sittingbourne in Kent, are on the North Downs and close to the Pilgrim's Way. They are also near to YHA Kemsing and YHA Medway, making them a convenient stop on a short walking tour.

You need to know... the toilets and shower for the camping barn are in an adjoining barn.

Accommodation: The camping barn sleeps up to 18; there are two bunk barns sleeping up to 10 and 32.

Facilities: Camping barn: fully equipped kitchen, log burner, radiators, BBQ, some sleeping mats, showers on 50p meter, drying and laundry. Bunk barns: self-contained, though smaller barn shares toilet/showers with camping barn; fully equipped kitchen, toilets, showers; all electricity included. Showers on meters; bring sleeping bag and pillow case.

Nearest pub: 1 mile. **Nearest shop:** 2 mile.

Location: OS 188, GR 822580.

Price Band: G	Opening category: ❸

Convenient: YHA Dover is perfect for the town and the port.

●● DOVER ☆

306 London Road, Dover, Kent CT17 0SY;
dover@yha.org.uk
Tel: 0870 770 5798 Fax: 0870 770 5799

This Georgian listed building is a convenient stop for those hopping across the Channel to France and Belgium. Situated close to the town centre shops, public transport terminals and ferry ports, it offers foreign exchange, some cross-Channel transport ticket sales and internet access should you wish to check sailing times. If you've a few hours to spare before you leave these shores, then a visit to nearby Dover Castle will keep that holiday excitement afloat.

Location: OS 179, GR 311421.

Great for... a stress-free night en-route to the Continent.

You need to know... the hostel is on two sites, 0.5 miles apart; breakfast is included in the price.

Accommodation: 120 beds: 5x2-, 1x4-, 5x6-, 9x8–10-bed rooms.

Family rooms: Yes. **Rent-a-Hostel:** Yes, at one site.

Classroom: Dining rooms both seat 45. **Education packages:** Yes.

Facilities: Lounge, TV, games room, dining rooms, self-catering kitchen, showers, pool table, internet access, cycle store, garden with pond, bureau de change and discount ferry tickets.

Daytime access: All public areas.

Reception open: All day. **Meals:** Breakfast included.

Getting there: From Dover Priory station turn left to roundabout, take first exit and hostel is 0.5 miles on left. From M20/A20, at fourth roundabout, take first exit. At next roundabout, take second exit and hostel is 0.5 miles on left.

Nearest other hostels: Canterbury 14 miles, Broadstairs 20, Medway 40, Kemsing 50.

Public transport: BUS: Frequent from surrounding areas. RAIL: Dover Priory 1 mile. FERRY: P&O Stena (tel: 0870 5 202020), Hoverspeed (tel: 0870 5 240241), Eurostar (tel: 0870 5 186186).
NATIONALEXPRESS Pencester Road bus station 0.25 miles.

Parking: On street nearby.

Price Band: D	Opening category: ❶

●● EPPING FOREST ☆

**Wellington Hill, High Beach, Loughton,
Essex IG10 4AG; epping@yha.org.uk
Tel: 0870 770 5822 Fax: 0870 770 5823**

Combine hectic days in the big city with a generous dose of tranquillity in Epping Forest. With London just 10 miles away on the Central Line, a day trip to the capital is an easy option, made all the better by your return to this woodland retreat. For a more relaxed day out, Waltham Abbey, Connaught Water and Loughton Iron Age Camp are all nearby. Or for ultimate peace, follow the miles of paths that criss-cross the 6,000 acres of uncrowded ancient woodland surrounding the hostel.

Location: OS 167, GR 408983.

Great for... the best of both worlds; and for mixed groups wanting a variety of activities.

You need to know... there's a pub next door.

Accommodation: 36 beds: 6x4- and 2x6-bed rooms.

Family rooms: Yes. **Rent-a-Hostel:** Yes.

Classroom: No. **Education packages:** No.

Facilities: Lounge/dining room, self-catering kitchen, showers, cycle store, garden with BBQ and camping. **Daytime access:** Covered verandah, entrance hall, shower, toilet, drying and washbasin.

Reception open: 5pm.

Meals: Self-catering only; breakfast trolley available.

Getting there: From the M25, exit at J26 and take the A121 to Loughton. Turn right after Volunteer Inn. Continue on this road for approx 500 metres then turn right, then left up Wellington Hill. The hostel is on the right. From Loughton tube station, take a minicab or walk (40 minutes).

Public transport: BUS: Arriva 240, 250 (Waltham Cross station–Loughton Underground), alight Volunteer Inn 1.5 miles. UNDERGROUND: Loughton 2 miles. RAIL: Chingford 3.5 miles.

Parking: Car park available (don't park on rough track); not suitable for coaches.

Nearest other hostels: City of London 13 miles, Saffron Walden 29.

Price Band: B	Opening category: ❷

The well-preserved might of Bodiam Castle near YHA Hastings.

●● HASTINGS ☆☆☆

**Guestling Hall, Rye Road, Guestling, Hastings,
East Sussex TN35 4LP; hasting@yha.org.uk
Tel: 0870 770 5850 Fax: 0870 770 5851**

A great base for exploring this activity-packed area. Children in particular will love it here. With one-and-a-half acres of land and lots of trees, there's plenty of room for children to run around. Cots and highchairs are available, as is a special menu catering for the tastes of under-10s. A host of attractions will keep the kids entertained by day – Bodiam Castle, Camber Sands, Underwater World and Smugglers Adventure, set in a labyrinth of caves, are a few favourites.

Location: OS 199, GR 848133.

Great for... a family holiday.

You need to know... there's a small lake in the grounds so keep a close eye on the children.

Accommodation: 55 beds: 5x4-, 1x5-, 1x6-, 2x7 and 1x10-bed rooms.

Family rooms: Yes. **Rent-a-Hostel:** Yes.

Classroom: No. **Education packages:** Yes.

Facilities: Lounge, dining room, table-tennis room, self-catering kitchen, showers, drying room, cycle store and grounds. Camping is usually available if booked in advance. **Daytime access:** Small shelter and outside toilet. **Reception open:** 5pm.

Meals: Breakfast, picnic lunch, evening meal.

Getting there: From Hastings, take A259 Folkestone/Rye for 5 miles and hostel is 200 metres past White Hart on left. From Rye, it is 8 miles on the right, 300 metres after road changes to double lane.

Public transport: BUS: Stagecoach in Hastings 711 Hastings station-Dover (passes Rye station), Empress/Rambler 347 Hastings station-Pett. RAIL: Hastings 5 miles.

NATIONALEXPRESS Queen's Parade 5 miles (town centre).

Parking: Limited to 12 cars.

Nearest other hostels: Blackboys 25 miles, Alfriston 33.

Price Band: B	Opening category: ❷

●● HINDHEAD ☆

**Devil's Punchbowl, off Portsmouth Road, Thursley,
Godalming, Surrey GU8 6NS;
reservations@yha.org.uk
Tel: 0870 770 5864 Fax: 0870 770 5864
Bookings more than 7 days ahead: 0870 770 8868**

A break at Hindhead is an experience all of its own and you'll forget that the rest of the world even exists. You'll be staying in sympathetically restored National Trust cottages that are chock-full of character. They're situated in an Area of Outstanding Natural Beauty so expect an abundance of flora and fauna among the heath and woodland-rich countryside. Walkers will be in heaven, with trails to the dramatic Devil's Punchbowl, nearby Frensham Common and The Pilgrims' Way.

Location: OS 186, GR 892368.

Great for... walkers wanting a rural retreat.

You need to know... you will have to walk half a mile from the car park to the hostel. Bring a torch.

Accommodation: 12 beds: 2x2-, 2x4-bed rooms.

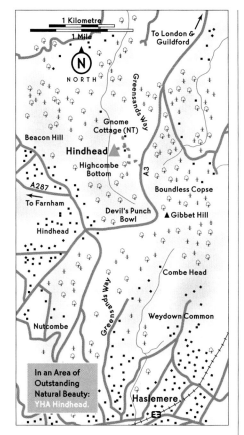

Family rooms: No. **FBR:** Yes. **Rent-a-Hostel:** Yes.
Classroom: No. **Education packages:** No.
Facilities: Lounge/dining area, self-catering kitchen, toilets, shower.
Daytime access: Public areas, via numbered lock. Pre-bookings only.
Reception open: 5pm.
Meals: Self-catering only.
Getting there: Turn off A3 (Portsmouth Road) onto track between Brook turning and Hindhead crossroads.
Public transport: BUS: Stagecoach in Hants & Surrey 18/9 Aldershot-Haslemere (pass close to Haslemere station); 71 from Guildford (pass close to Godalming and Farnham stations). Alight in Hindhead area up to 1 mile according to stops.
RAIL: Haslemere 2.5 miles by path (4.5 by road).
NATIONAL EXPRESS ▶▶ A3 lay-by near traffic lights 1.5 miles.
Parking: National Trust 0.5 miles, no access by car to hostel, unload by arrangement.
Nearest other hostels: Holmbury St Mary 20 miles, Tanners Hatch 25, Portsmouth 29.

Price Band: **B**   Opening category: **❸**

●● HOLMBURY ST MARY ☆

Radnor Lane, Dorking, Surrey RH5 6NW;
holmbury@yha.org.uk
Tel: 0870 770 5868 Fax: 0870 770 5869

In 4,000 acres of woodland in an Area of Outstanding Natural Beauty, this cosy hostel with small rooms enjoys quiet surroundings. Set in grounds perfect for playing and relaxing, it's also ideally suited as a base to explore the Surrey Hills or walk the North Downs Way and Greensand Way. There's an orienteering course and treasure hunt to try, mountain bikes and guided walks can be arranged locally and National Trust properties such as Polesden Lacey are nearby.
Location: OS 187, GR 104450.
Great for... walking, mountain biking and orienteering.
You need to know... The café is open summer weekends 12-4pm.
Accommodation: 52 beds: 2x2- and 12x4-bed rooms.
Family rooms: No. **FBR:** Yes. **Rent-a-Hostel:** Yes.
Classroom: Yes. **Education packages:** Yes.
Facilities: Lounge, self-catering kitchen, showers, drying room, cycle store, grounds and camping. **Daytime access:** Information Centre only. **Reception open:** 5pm.
Meals: Breakfast, picnic lunch, evening meal.
Getting there: The hostel is 2 miles south of Abinger Hammer on A25 between Guildford and Dorking. Follow signs to Holmbury St Mary on B2126 and hostel is 1 mile north of village.
Public transport: BUS: Arriva 21. RAIL: Gomshall 3 miles, Dorking 6.
Parking: Yes.
Nearest other hostels: Tanners Hatch 6 miles, Hindhead 20.

Price Band: **B**   Opening category: **❸**

●● JORDANS ☆

Welders Lane, Jordans, Beaconsfield,
Buckinghamshire HP9 2SN; jordans@yha.org.uk
Tel: 0870 770 5886 Fax: 0870 770 5887

Hunt for history in this traditional hostel in a quiet village with an impressive heritage. Closely associated with the early Quaker movement, the village is home to the Mayflower Barn, William Penn's grave and a 17th century meeting house. A trip to Milton's Cottage in the next village is recommended and Windsor is within visiting distance. The hostel enjoys quiet surroundings with a garden and all-day access available for families.
Location: OS 175, GR 975910.
Great for... a quiet break just outside London.
You need to know... the London Underground is 5 miles away.
Accommodation: 22 beds: 2x5- and 2x6-bed rooms.
Family rooms: No. **FBR:** Yes. **Rent-a-Hostel:** Yes.
Classroom: No. **Education packages:** No.
Facilities: Well-equipped self-catering kitchen, lounge/dining area, showers, cycle store, grounds, camping, BBQ and patio area.
Daytime access: Private/family rooms have all-day access. Other guests arriving before 5pm have access to the washrooms and the verandah.
Reception open: 5pm.
Meals: Light breakfast.

Getting there: Leave the M40 at J2, A355 to Beaconsfield. At second roundabout (A40) head for Gerrard's Cross. After half a mile, turn left onto Potkiln Lane. After 1 mile, turn right onto Welders Lane. From Seer Green station turn right onto Long Bottom Lane, left into Potkiln Lane and take first right onto Welders Lane.
Nearest other hostels: Bradenham 12 miles, Ivinghoe 19, Hampstead Heath 25.
Public transport: BUS: Arriva 305 Beaconsfield station-Uxbridge, alight Seer Green 0.5 miles. RAIL: Seer Green 0.5 miles.
NATIONALEXPRESS Beaconsfield.
Parking: 8 cars maximum.

Price Band: B	Opening category: ❶

● KEMSING ☆

Church Lane, Kemsing, Sevenoaks, Kent
TN15 6LU; kemsing@yha.org.uk
Tel: 0870 770 5890 Fax: 0870 770 5891

Commanding fine views, this former 19th century vicarage set in its own grounds lies at the foot of the North Downs. There is plenty to do nearby, including the attractions of Knole House, Ightham Mote, Chartwell, Whitbread hop farm and Lullingstone Park Visitor Centre. It's also handy for the famous Pilgrims' Way.
Location: OS 188, GR 555588.
Great for... a base to explore the North Downs.
Accommodation: 50 beds: 2x4-, 4x6-, 1x8- and 1x10-bed rooms.

Family rooms: No. **FBR:** Yes. **Rent-a-Hostel:** No.
Classroom: No. **Education packages:** No.
Facilities: Lounge and quiet room, self-catering kitchen, dining room, TV, showers, cycle store, grounds and camping.
Daytime access: Limited public areas, via numbered lock.
Reception open: 5pm.
Meals: Breakfast, picnic lunch, evening meal.
Getting there: From Otford station turn right, take first right to

A former 19th century vicarage: YHA Kemsing.

LITTLEHAMPTON ☆☆☆☆

Littlehampton, West Sussex, BR17 5AW;
littlehampton@yha.org.uk
Tel: 0870 770 6114 Fax: 0870 770 6115

This new hostel is part of a redevelopment of Fisherman's Wharf on the east bank of the River Arun. Set in a traditional seaside resort just five minutes from the beach, it's a great base for all the family to explore the south coast, with family rooms throughout. Although the hostel offers self-catering accommodation, the complex includes a bistro, as well as a tourist information centre and the Look & Sea Centre.
Location: Sheet 197, GR 025019
Great for... sandy beaches and traditional seaside fun.
You need to know... it's a cosy, fun hostel with nautical charm.
Accommodation: 32 beds: 3-, 4- and 5-bedded rooms.
Classroom: No. **Education packages:** No.
Facilities: Lounge, dining room, self-catering kitchen, showers, cycle shed, laundry, TV room and video.
Daytime access: All public areas, via numbered lock.
Reception open: 5pm.
Meals: Self-catering only on site. Meals available at YHA Arundel, 4 miles away.
Getting there: Follow signs for Look & Sea from town centre.
Public transport: BUS: 700 service every 30 minutes from

Worthing–Portsmouth, 702 service Mon-Sat only.
RAIL: Littlehampton 0.5 miles.
FERRY: Portsmouth to Newhaven 27 miles.
NATIONALEXPRESS London–Chichester service 027.
Parking: Nearby.
Nearest other hostels: Arundel 4 miles, Truleigh Hill 18, Brighton 22.

Price Band: C	Opening category: ❷

Fun days at the beach await you at YHA Littlehampton.

junction with Childsbridge Lane and turn right again. Turn left at crossroads into West End and continue to Church Lane (2 miles).
Public transport: BUS: Arriva 425/6, 433 from Sevenoaks (pass close to Sevenoaks station), alight Kemsing post office 250 yards. RAIL: Kemsing (not Sun) 1.5 miles, Otford 1.5.
Parking: Yes.
Nearest other hostels: London 26 miles, Medway 26, Canterbury 42, Dover 60.

Price Band: B   **Opening category:** ❷

● ● MARGATE ☆☆☆

3-4 Royal Esplanade, Westbrook Bay, Margate, Kent CT9 5DL; margate@yha.org.uk
Tel: 0870 770 5956 Fax: 0870 770 5956

Pack your bucket and spade because traditional seaside holidays don't get better than this. The hostel, converted from a hotel, is on the beachfront at Westbrook Bay, which boasts a gently shelving sandy beach. A five-minute stroll along the promenade takes you to Margate's main beach with its lively attractions and arcades. Be warned – with Dreamland Fun Park and arcades galore, you'll have trouble dragging the kids away from their candyfloss.
Location: OS 179, GR 342706.
Great for... traditional family holidays by the sea.
You need to know... it's self-catering accommodation only.
Accommodation: 55 beds: 2x6- and 2-, 3-, 4- and 5-bed rooms.
Family rooms: Yes. **Rent-a-Hostel:** Yes.
Classroom: No. **Education packages:** No.
Facilities: Lounge, dining room, quiet room, self-catering kitchen, cycle store, limited laundry facilities and currency exchange.
Daytime access: None until 5pm. Keys arranged for pre-booked families.
Reception open: 5pm.
Meals: Self-catering; meals available to pre-booked parties of 10+.
Getting there: From Main Beach and railway station take A28 Canterbury Road, passing Royal Sea Bathing Hospital, and turn right into Westbrook Gardens after the Dog and Duck pub. Hostel is third building along Royal Esplanade seafront.
Public transport: BUS: frequent from surrounding areas. RAIL: Margate 500 metres.
NATIONALEXPRESS» Clock Tower, Marine Parade 0.5 miles.
Parking: No.
Nearest other hostels: Broadstairs 4 miles (7 along coast), Canterbury 15, Dover 20, Medway 42.

Price Band: B   **Opening category:** ❶

● ● MEDWAY ☆☆☆

Capstone Road, Gillingham, Kent ME7 3JE; medway@yha.org.uk
Tel: 0870 770 5964 Fax: 0870 770 5965

Make this beautiful Kentish oast house your base for a busy break that will appeal to all the family. The area is rich with history and you'll find everything from a Napoleonic fort to a Norman castle in the area. The nearby towns of Rochester and Chatham are both worth a day's

Different: YHA Medway is a Kentish oast house in a history-rich area.

wander or, for more rural entertainment, Capstone Country Park is opposite the hostel and has nature trails, picnic areas and a fishing lake. And, for the energetic, the nearby ski slope, toboggan run and rink offers icy excitement.
Location: OS 178, GR 783653.
Great for... all the family.
You need to know... there's a country park on the doorstep.
Accommodation: 40 beds: 4x2-, 1x3-, 6x4- and 1x5-bed rooms.
Family rooms: Yes. **Rent-a-Hostel:** Yes.
Classroom: Yes. **Education packages:** Yes.
Facilities: TV lounge, self-catering kitchen, dining room, showers, drying room, cycle store, lockers and laundry facilities.
Daytime access: Shelter and toilet.
Reception open: 5pm.
Meals: Breakfast, picnic lunch, evening meal.
Getting there: Exit M2 at J4 and take A278 to Gillingham. Turn left at first roundabout signed to hostel, Capstone Country Park and Ski Centre. From Chatham railway station, take taxi or walk to Pentagon Shopping Centre for regular services to the Wheatsheaf pub or 114 to Waggon at Hale pub. All services alight on Capstone Road and follow hostel signs.
Public transport: BUS: Nu Venture 113/4 from Gillingham to within two miles, alight Luton Rec Ground. RAIL: Chatham (Kent) 2 miles.
NATIONALEXPRESS» Hempstead Valley Shopping Centre 2 miles.
Parking: Yes.
Nearest other hostels: Kemsing 23 miles, Canterbury 25, Broadstairs 40, Dover 40.

Price Band: B   **Opening category:** ❷

● PORTSMOUTH ☆

**Old Wymering Lane, Cosham, Portsmouth,
Hampshire PO6 3NL; portsmouth@yha.org.uk
Tel: 0870 770 6002 Fax: 0870 770 6003**

Step back in time at this hostel with a history dating back to the 11th century. This old manor house has a homely atmosphere, encouraging you to relax in the wood-panelled hall at the end of a day exploring the historic dockyards where you can visit the Mary Rose and stand on the deck of The Victory, Nelson's flagship.

Location: OS 196, GR 640955.

Great for... history aplenty.

Accommodation: 48 beds, 3x6-, 2x8- and 1x14-bed rooms.

Family rooms: No. **FBR:** Yes. **Rent-a-Hostel:** Yes.

Classroom: No. **Education packages:** No.

Facilities: Lounge, self-catering kitchen, showers, drying room and cycle store. **Daytime access:** None, until after 5pm.

Reception open: 5pm

Meals: Breakfast, picnic lunch, evening meal.

Getting there: From Cosham police station, take Medina Road, then seventh turning on the right, Old Wymering Lane. The hostel is opposite the church entrance (see map on page 173).

Public transport: BUS: frequent from surrounding areas. RAIL: Cosham 1 mile.

NATIONALEXPRESS» The Hard Interchange, Portsmouth 2.5 miles.

Parking: Yes.

Nearest other hostels: Sandown 10 miles (via ferry), Winchester 25, Arundel 26.

Price Band: B	Opening category: ❸

●● THE RIDGEWAY ☆☆☆

**Court Hill, Wantage, Oxfordshire OX12 9NE;
ridgeway@yha.org.uk
Tel: 0870 770 6064 Fax: 0870 770 6065**

Set on the edge of the Berkshire Downs with views over the Vale of

Extensive grounds and a conservation area: YHA The Ridgeway.

the White Horse, this is a heaven-sent base for walkers with Britain's oldest route, the Ridgeway National Trail, just 500 metres away. The well-maintained hostel is a collection of converted timber barns built around a courtyard. If you appreciate the countryside then you'll also enjoy spending time in the extensive grounds that include a beechwood conservation area.

Location: OS 174, GR 393851.

Great for... walkers and cyclists looking for a comfortable base.

You need to know... the disabled toilet is separate from the sleeping accommodation.

Accommodation: 59 beds, 1x2-, 6x4-, 1x5-, 1x6-, 1x9- and 1x13-bed rooms.

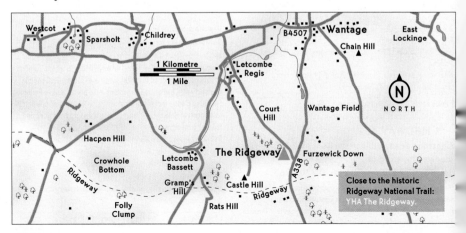

Close to the historic Ridgeway National Trail: YHA The Ridgeway.

Family rooms: Yes. **Rent-a-Hostel:** No.

Classroom: Yes. **Education packages:** Yes.

Facilities: Lounge, TV, self-catering kitchen, dining room, showers, drying room, cycle store, laundry facilities, grounds and camping.

Daytime access: Public areas, via numbered lock.

Reception open: 5pm.

Meals: Breakfast, picnic lunch, evening meal.

Getting there: From the M4, exit at J14, take the A338 towards Wantage for 9 miles and the hostel is signposted and on the left. From Wantage, take A338 towards Hungerford — the hostel is signposted and on the right at the brow of the hill. From Ridgeway National Trail east, follow signs. From Ridgeway west, follow A338 (left from trail) and then take first left.

Public transport: BUS: Stagecoach Oxford 32/A/B from Didcot Parkway; 31, X31 from Oxford, alight Wantage 2 miles. RAIL: Didcot Parkway 10 miles.

Parking: Yes.

Nearest other hostels: Streatley 14 miles, Oxford 17.

Price Band: **C**	Opening category: **②**

● SANDOWN ☆☆☆

The Firs, Fitzroy Street, Sandown, Isle of Wight PO36 8JH; sandown@yha.org.uk

Tel: 0870 770 6020 Fax: 0870 770 6021

This hostel is ideally placed to explore the Isle of Wight, an adventure playground for children and adults alike. With a spacious sandy beach and the bustling town centre of Sandown both a few minutes away, it won't be long before your holiday begins in earnest. You'll find plenty to do, with well-maintained trails to explore on foot or by bike, as well as a range of watersports. The hostel even offers free loans of buckets and spades!

Location: OS 196, GR 597843.

Great for... action-packed family breaks.

You need to know... there's street parking only.

Accommodation: 47 beds: 3x2-, 6x4-, 1x5- and 2x6-bed rooms.

Family rooms: Yes. **Rent-a-Hostel:** Yes.

Classroom: No. **Education packages:** Yes.

Facilities: Open plan lounge, dining area with TV, self-catering kitchen, showers, drying room, cycle store and small garden.

Daytime access: Public areas, via numbered lock.

Reception open: 5pm.

Meals: Breakfast, picnic lunch, evening meal.

Getting there: By car, follow A3055 to Sandown and turn down Melville Street then 2nd left down Fitzroy Street. The hostel is signed from A3055. On foot, the hostel is signposted from the railway station.

Public transport: BUS: frequent from surrounding areas. RAIL: Sandown 0.5 miles. FERRY: Ryde Pierhead 6 miles (Wightlink, tel: 0870 5827744), East Cowes 12 (Red Funnel, tel: 023 8033 4010), Ryde 5 (Hovertravel, tel: 01983 811000).

NATIONALEXPRESS High St 0.5 miles.

Parking: Small car park. Room for 4 cars only.

Nearest other hostels: Portsmouth 10 miles (via ferry), Totland Bay 24.

Price Band: **B**	Opening category: **②**

Kids and parents alike will love a break at YHA Streatley.

● STREATLEY-ON-THAMES

☆☆☆ **Reading Road, Streatley, Berkshire RG8 9JJ; streatley@yha.org.uk**

Tel: 0870 770 6054 Fax: 0870 770 6055

If you're coming to Streatley-on-Thames with the children, you'd better make sure you book a long break. There are so many kid-friendly attractions to squeeze into your stay, including Legoland (Windsor), Beale Adventure Park and Wyld Court Rainforest Centre. At the end of each day frazzled parents will be glad to return to this comfortable Victorian house, close to one of the prettiest stretches of the River Thames, with plenty of walking on the nearby Ridgeway and Thames paths.

Location: OS 174, GR 591806.

Great for... energetic children.

Accommodation: 48 beds: 1x2-, 3x4-, 2x5- and 4x6-bed rooms.

Family rooms: Yes. **Rent-a-Hostel:** No.

Classroom: Yes. **Education packages:** Yes.

Facilities: TV room, self-catering kitchen, dining room, showers, drying room and grounds.

Daytime access: All public areas.

Reception open: 5pm.

Meals: Breakfast, picnic lunch, evening meal.

Getting there: Hostel is on A329 north of M4 (exit J12), 50 metres south of traffic lights in village.

Public transport: BUS: Thames Travel 132/7 Goring & Streatley station-Wallingford. RAIL: Goring & Streatley 1 mile.

Parking: Yes.

Nearest other hostels: Ridgeway 14 miles, Oxford 19.

Price Band: **C**	Opening category: **③**

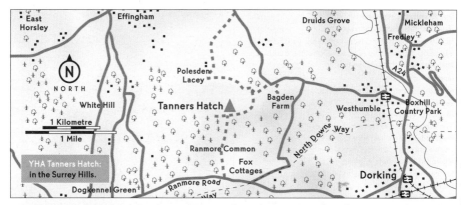

YHA Tanners Hatch: in the Surrey Hills.

● TANNERS HATCH ☆

off Ranmore Road, Dorking, Surrey RH5 6BE;
tanners@yha.org.uk
Tel: 0870 770 6060 Fax: 0870 770 6060

If you're looking for a charming and unique country cottage to stay in, easily accessible from London, with easy access to Gatwick Airport, you've found it at Tanners Hatch. Within its ancient whitewashed walls, you'll relax in front of an open fire with a handful of other guests. If you're a walker, you won't have to wait long to stretch your legs as the hostel is only accessible on foot through National Trust woods. There's an extensive network of footpaths that explore the Surrey Hills Area of Outstanding Natural Beauty – don't miss a stroll to Polesden Lacey, a National Trust Regency mansion.

Location: OS 187, GR 140515.

Great for... walkers, cyclists and getting away from it all.

You need to know... Tanners Hatch has outside toilet and showering facilities; there is no access for cars to the hostel, unloading only.

Accommodation: 25 beds: 1x7- and 2x9-bed rooms.

Family rooms: No. **Rent-a-Hostel:** On request.

Classroom: No. **Education packages:** Yes.

Facilities: Lounge, dining room with resource library, herb garden, extensive grounds, self-catering kitchen, shower, cycle store and camping. **Daytime access:** Public areas, via numbered lock, pre-bookings only. **Reception open:** 5pm. **Meals:** Self-catering.

Getting there: From Box Hill station turn left and follow road for 2 miles before turning left at Bagden Farm. Turn right past barn and follow signs along the pedestrian route. By car from A24, take Ashcombe Road straight over mini-roundabout and turn right at T-junction. Follow the road until you reach the National Trust car park. Turn left and take third track on the right-hand side (by 4 Fox cottages) and follow signs.

Public transport: BUS: Surrey Explorer (weekends and Bank Holidays during main season). Pick up from Dorking town, drop off at Ranmore Road; 465 Teddington-Dorking, alight West Humble 2.5 miles. RAIL: Box Hill & Westhumble 2.5 miles. Dorking Main/Deapdene 3.5.

Parking: Park at NT car park (£2).

Nearest other hostels: Holmbury St Mary 6 miles, London 23, Hindhead 25.

Price Band: B   **Opening category:** ❸

●● TELSCOMBE ☆

Bank Cottages, Telscombe, Lewes, East Sussex
BN7 3HZ; reservations@yha.org.uk
Tel: 0870 770 6062 Fax: 0870 770 6062
Bookings more than 7 days ahead: 0870 770 8868

The South Downs offer countryside lovers miles of well-drained chalk paths with uninterrupted views over rolling grassland. These 18th century cottages in the minuscule village of Telscombe are ideally placed for exploring the area. If you're looking for a few days of quiet wandering around picturesque villages, then this hostel is for you. If you feel like venturing further afield, then Virginia Woolf's house, Rodmell, is nearby.

Location: OS 198, GR 405033.

Great for... a quiet retreat into the countryside.

You need to know... parking in the village is not permitted.

Accommodation: 22 beds: 1x2- and 5x4-bed rooms.

Beautiful 18th century cottages: YHA Telscombe.

Family rooms: No. **FBR:** Yes.
Rent-a-Hostel: Yes.
Classroom: No. **Education packages:** No.
Facilities: Lounge/dining area, reading room, self-catering kitchen, showers, drying room, cycle store, shop for basic provisions and grounds.
Daytime access: Outside toilet.
Reception open: 5pm.
Meals: Self-catering only.
Getting there: On foot, the South Downs Way footpath passes 1.5 miles north of Telscombe village.
Public transport: BUS: Brighton & Hove 14/A, 712-4 Brighton-Eastbourne (passes close to Brighton station), alight Heathy Brow 0.5 miles. RAIL: Southease 2.5 miles, Lewes 6.5, Brighton 7. NATIONALEXPRESS Newhaven 5 miles.
Parking: By arrangement with warden.
Nearest other hostels: Brighton 10 miles, Alfriston 11, Blackboys 17.

Price Band: B **Opening category:** ❷

● TOTLAND BAY ☆☆☆

Hurst Hill, Totland Bay, Isle of Wight PO39 0HD;
totland@yha.org.uk
Tel: 0870 770 6070 Fax: 0870 770 6071

Lord Mountbatten opened this Youth Hostel in 1975, once a large private Victorian house. It is situated in West Wight, an Area of Outstanding Natural Beauty much of which is owned by the National Trust. You'll find a wealth of wildlife all around whether you choose to walk on the downs or along the impressive chalk cliffs. Search for sealife in rock pools, brave the chairlift to explore Alum Bay, take the obligatory snapshot of the Needles or head inland on foot to escape the summer crowds.
Location: OS 196, GR 324865.
Great for... wildlife lovers and beach bathers.
You need to know... parking is limited, although there is additional on-street parking.
Accommodation: 56 beds: 1x2-, 7x4-, 3x6- and 1x8-bed rooms.
Family rooms: Yes. **FBR:** Yes. **Rent-a-Hostel:** Yes.
Classroom: No. **Education packages:** No.
Facilities: Lounge, TV room, dining room, self-catering kitchen, showers, drying room, cycle store and shop.
Daytime access: All public areas.
Reception open: 5pm. From 1pm during school holidays.
Meals: Breakfast, picnic lunch, evening meal.
Getting there: From roundabout in centre of Totland, take left fork past garage up Weston Road. At the end, turn left up Hurst Hill and hostel is at top of a short hill on the left.
Parking: Yes.
Public transport: BUS: Southern Vectis 7/A Newport-Yarmouth-Ryde, 7B from Newport via Brighstone, 42 from Yarmouth, alight Totland War Memorial 0.5 miles. FERRY: Yarmouth 3 miles (Wightlink, tel: 0870 5827744), West Cowes 15 (Red Funnel, tel: 020 8033 334010).
Nearest other hostels: Burley 17 miles (by ferry), Sandown 24.

Price Band: B **Opening category:** ❸

HOSTEL MANAGERS CHOOSE...
THE BEST FAMILY EXPERIENCES

Drusillas Park YHA Alfriston: "The best small zoo in England, with lots of animals and hands-on activities."
Broadstairs Beach YHA Broadstairs: "Relax at our award-winning sandy beach and beautiful bay."
Legoland YHA Jordans: "Lots to do and see for all the family including amazing Lego models, rides and car racing."
Black Park country park, Chilterns YHA Jordans: "Safe cycling for families just eight miles from the hostel."
'Look & Sea' tower YHA Littlehampton: "Enter the fantastic circular glass tower to enjoy spectacular panoramic views of the Sussex coastline."
South Downs YHA Truleigh Hill: "Family groups on mountain bikes will cope with all bridlepaths in the area."
Winchester Cathedral YHA Winchester: "Discover the history and heritage of this impressive 7th century cathedral."
Hastings YHA Hastings: "Attractions include the Shipwreck Heritage Centre, a wreck preserved in the sands of Hastings beach and, for the children, the Smugglers Adventure in the cave system of the West Hill."
Sandown YHA Sandown: "Surfboards, jetskis and pedalos can all be hired at this lively beach."

● TRULEIGH HILL ☆☆☆

Tottington Barn, Shoreham-by-Sea, West Sussex
BN43 5FB; truleighhill@yha.org.uk
Tel: 0870 770 6078 Fax: 0870 770 6079

This hostel sits within the boundaries of the newly designated South Downs National Park and so offers a good base for walkers and cyclists. There are a variety of routes to choose from, but one of guests' favourites is the Devil's Dyke walk that leads you to an Iron Age fort. Families with youngsters will also be comfortable here, as cots, highchairs and a child-oriented menu are available.
Location: OS 198, GR 220105.
Great for... walkers wanting to explore the South Downs.
Accommodation: 56 beds: some 2-4-, mostly 6-bed rooms.
Family rooms: Yes. **Rent-a-Hostel:** Yes.
Classroom: No. **Education packages:** No.
Facilities: Lounge, self-catering kitchen, dining room, showers, drying room, cycle store, shop and grounds.
Daytime access: Day shelter and toilet available all day. Access to main hostel by prior arrangement.
Reception open: 5pm.
Meals: Breakfast, picnic lunch, evening meal.
Getting there: From the A27, take the A283 Shoreham exit and turn left at the Red Lion pub. Look for the first hostel sign on the left-hand

Situated in the South Downs National Park: YHA Truleigh Hill.

side after approx 300 metres. From here, it's 3 miles to hostel.
Public transport: BUS: Compass 100 Pulborough station-Henfield, alight junction of the Edburton road then 1 mile; otherwise Brighton & Hove/Stagecoach Coastline 20/X from Shoreham-by-Sea station, alight 0.5 miles south of Upper Beeding then 1.5 miles by bridlepath.
RAIL: Shoreham-by-Sea 4 miles.
NATIONALEXPRESS Shoreham 5 miles.
Parking: Yes.
Nearest other hostels: Brighton 6 miles (by path), Arundel 16, Littlehampton 18, Holmbury 35.

Price Band: B	Opening category: ❸

●● WINCHESTER ☆
1 Water Lane, Winchester, Hampshire SO23 0EJ;
Tel: 0870 770 6092 Fax: 0870 770 6093

This 18th century water mill is a National Trust property spanning the River Itchen. A hostel since 1931, it offers simple, unusual accommodation. Its low beams, mill machinery and impressive lofty hall make this a unique hostel, from where you can enjoy relaxing riverside walks. It's also close to Winchester's imposing guildhall, cathedral and King Arthur's Round Table, while it's close enough to London for a day trip to the capital.
Location: OS 185, GR 486293.
Great for... sites of historic interest; day trips to London.
You need to know... the hostel offers modest facilities. Due to the structural restrictions of this historic building, this hostel is limited to a one-star ETC rating.

Accommodation: 31 beds: 1x4-, 1x9- and 1x18-bed rooms.
Family rooms: No. **FBR:** Yes. **Rent-a-Hostel:** No.
Classroom: No. **Education packages:** No.
Facilities: Lounge/dining area, self-catering kitchen, showers, cycle store and garden. **Daytime access:** None, until 5pm but public toilets, cafes, shops and shelter all within 500m.
Reception open: 5pm.
Meals: Breakfast only.
Getting there: From guildhall, walk over the Eastgate Bridge and take the first left into Water Lane (no vehicle entry). The hostel is the third door on the left.
Public transport: BUS: frequent from surrounding areas.
RAIL: Winchester 1 mile.
NATIONALEXPRESS King Alfred's Statue 150 metres.
Parking: Chesil Street car park 0.25 miles.
Nearest other hostels: Burley 23 miles, Salisbury 24, Portsmouth 25.

Price Band: B	Opening category: ❷

TRY RENT-A-HOSTEL
Many of the hostels in this guide can be booked through the Rent-a-Hostel scheme. For full details, turn to page 12.

Jersey

New for 2005, the YHA reaches the Channel Islands. Be among the first members to discover what hostelling in Jersey is really like!

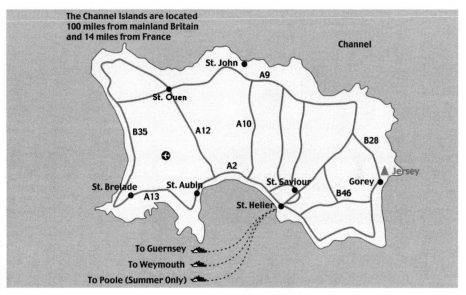

The Channel Islands are located 100 miles from mainland Britain and 14 miles from France

Channel

St. John
A9
St. Ouen
B35 A12 A10
B28
A2
St. Brelade St. Aubin St. Saviour Gorey
A13 B46
St. Helier

To Guernsey
To Weymouth
To Poole (Summer Only)

● ● ● JERSEY

Haut de la Garenne, La rue de la Poucle et des Quatre Chemins, St Martin, Jersey JE3 6DU;
jersey@yha.org.uk
Tel: 0870 770 6130 Fax: 0870 770 6131

Jersey's first Youth Hostel! A major refurbishment has transformed the former Victorian school and orphanage into a 105-bed Youth Hostel, situated on the island's east coast with views towards France and a short stroll from the majestic Mont Orgueil Castle. The building is famous to millions as the office of TV detective Jim Bergerac! Jersey has superb beaches and countryside along with an extensive network of walking and cycling routes, it has something for everyone.
Location: Jersey Leisure Map 1:25,000 GR 710505.
Great for... walking, cycling, clean beaches and birdwatching. Day trips to France and sunshine.
You need to know... breakfast is included in the price.
Accommodation: 105 beds: 3x2-, 4x4-, 1x5-, 2x6- and 6x6+ bed rooms. Some with en-suite and disabled access.
Family rooms: Yes. **Rent-a-Hostel:** No.
Classroom: Yes. **Education packages:** Yes.
Facilities: BBQ, garden, common room, luggage store, cycle store, storage heaters, conference room, games room, TV lounge and laundry.
Daytime access: All public areas, via numbered lock.
Reception open: 7am-10am, 5pm-11pm.
Meals: Breakfast, picnic lunch and evening meal.

The first youth hostel on the island: YHA Jersey.

Getting there: Ferry from Poole, Weymouth or Portsmouth. Flights from many UK airports.
Public transport: BUS: catch the 3a from St Helier to Ransoms Garden Centre then follow signs to the hostel. After 5.45pm you have to catch the No1 to Gorey Pier then climb the steep hill, bearing right to Castle Green pub. The hostel is about half a mile up Le Mont de la Garenne path.
Parking: Yes. On site.
Nearest other hostels: Portsmouth, Portland and Swanage (all via ferry) and Granville (France, via ferry).

Price Band: D **Opening category:** ❸

London

Eight hostels that bring you to the very centre of one of the most exciting, vibrant, cosmopolitan cities in the world. What are you waiting for?

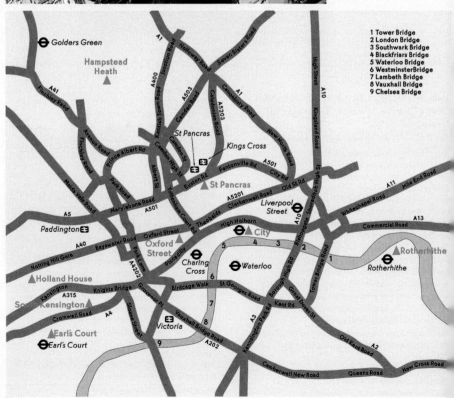

1 Tower Bridge
2 London Bridge
3 Southwark Bridge
4 Blackfriars Bridge
5 Waterloo Bridge
6 WestminsterBridge
7 Lambeth Bridge
8 Vauxhall Bridge
9 Chelsea Bridge

Safe and centrally located: YHA City of London.

In the heart of a lively area: YHA Earl's Court.

● ● CITY OF LONDON ☆☆☆

36 Carter Lane, London EC4V 5AB;
city@yha.org.uk
Tel: 0870 770 5764 Fax: 0870 770 5765

Just 100 metres from St Paul's Cathedral, this hostel is centrally located for exploring London. Formerly the choir boys' school for the Cathedral, it's in London's business area, which is both safer and quieter than many city parts. With plenty of public transport nearby, internet access and lockers, it makes a practical base for sightseers.
Location: OS 176, GR 319811.
Great for... exploring the city from a central location.
You need to know... there's no self-catering kitchen; no groups accepted; no cycle storage; breakfast included in the overnight fee.
Accommodation: 190 beds: several 1-, 2- and 3-bed rooms, mainly 4–8-bed, plus 2x9-bed and 2x10-bed options.
Family rooms: Yes. **Rent-a-Hostel:** No.
Classroom: No. **Education packages:** No.
Facilities: Reception, restaurant, TV lounge, showers, luggage room, laundry and meeting room. **Daytime access:** All public areas.
Reception open: 24hrs.
Meals: Breakfast, picnic lunch, evening meal.
Getting there: At Blackfriars Underground, turn right onto Queen Victoria Street and take second left into St Andrews Hill. Carter Lane is at the top and the hostel is on the right.
Public transport: BUS: frequent TfL services.
UNDERGROUND: St Paul's 0.5 miles, Blackfriars 0.5, City Thameslink 0.5, Liverpool Street 1. **NATIONALEXPRESS** Victoria Coach Station 3.25 miles. **Parking:** NCP Queen Victoria Street.
Nearest other hostels: Oxford Street 2 miles, South Kensington 2 Rotherhithe 3, Earl's Court 5.

Price Band: 🔲   **Opening category:** ❶

● EARL'S COURT ☆☆☆

38 Bolton Gardens, London SW5 0AQ;
earlscourt@yha.org.uk
Tel: 0870 770 5804 Fax: 0870 770 5805

In the heart of a young, international area full of shops, cafés, restaurants and bars, this hostel buzzes with action. Five minutes' walk from Earl's Court and Olympia exhibition centres, it's also handy for access to Heathrow Airport. Visit the Kensington museums, including the Science Museum and the Victoria and Albert Museum and, after a busy day, relax in the small courtyard garden.
Location: OS 176, GR 258783.
Great for... a busy city break.
Accommodation: 180 beds: mainly 4–6-bed rooms, plus some 2-, 3-bed options.
Family rooms: Yes. **Rent-a-Hostel:** No.
Classroom: No. **Education packages:** No.
Facilities: Reception, TV lounge, dining room, self-catering kitchen, showers, luggage room, laundry room, cycle store and garden.
Daytime access: All areas. **Reception open:** 24hrs.
Meals: Packed continental breakfast available at an additional cost.
Getting there: Leave Earl's Court Underground station by Earl's Court Road exit. Turn right outside station and take fifth street on left (Bolton Gardens).
Public transport: BUS: frequent TfL services.
UNDERGROUND: Earl's Court 0.5 miles. RAIL: Kensington Olympia 1 mile. **NATIONALEXPRESS** Earl's Court Underground 0.25 miles.
Parking: On Warwick Road (0.75 miles).
Nearest other hostels: Holland House 1 mile, South Kensington 0.75, Oxford Street 3, City of London 5.

Price Band: 🔲   **Opening category:** ❶

●● HAMPSTEAD HEATH ☆☆☆

4 Wellgarth Road, Golders Green, London NW11 7HR; hampstead@yha.org.uk
Tel: 0870 770 5846 Fax: 0870 770 5847

Enjoy a night in this busy hostel which has an enclosed garden and is a short stroll from the heath, where woods and grassland create a quiet oasis of countryside. Climb Parliament Hill for a lofty view of London or visit nearby Golders Hill park (the children will love the goats). Just don't forget that the hustle and bustle of central London is just a 20-minute tube ride away.

Location: OS 176, GR 258973.

Great for... groups who don't want to stay in the centre of London.

You need to know... breakfast is included in the overnight fee.

Accommodation: 199 beds: some 2- and 3-bed rooms, mostly 4–6-bed rooms, plus 1x7- and 1x8-bed options. Also one ground floor room specifically designed for people with disabilities. Some en-suite rooms are available.

Family rooms: Yes. **Rent-a-Hostel:** No.

Classroom: No. **Education packages:** Yes.

Facilities: Lounges with TV and video games, reception, showers, luggage/locker room, internet and email access, vending machines, self-catering kitchen, meeting room available for hire, garden and pergola area.

Daytime access: All public areas.

Reception open: 24hrs.

Meals: Breakfast, picnic lunch, evening meal, plus 'call order menu' is available 12-2pm weekdays.

Getting there: From the bus station, turn left onto North End Road. Take first left (Wellgarth Road) and entrance is past car park on right.

Public transport: BUS: frequent TfL services. UNDERGROUND: Golders Green 0.5 miles, Hampstead Heath 1.5.

NATIONALEXPRESS Golders Green bus station 0.5 miles.

Parking: Small car park. Restrictions apply on street between 11am and 12 noon, Mon–Fri.

Nearest other hostels: St Pancras 2 miles, City of London 4, Holland House 5, South Kensington 6, Oxford Street 7.

Price Band: **F** Opening category: **①**

●● HOLLAND HOUSE ☆☆☆

Holland Walk, Kensington, London W8 7QU; hollandhouse@yha.org.uk
Tel: 0870 770 5866 Fax: 0870 770 5867
Website: www.hollhse.btinternet.co.uk

Feel the history in the heart of elegant Holland Park. One wing of the hostel is a former Jacobean mansion, built in 1607 for Sir Walter Cope, Chancellor of the Exchequer for James I. In the 19th century, Lady Holland had a salon here, attended by such famous names as Sheridan, Sir Walter Scott, Lord Byron, Wordsworth and Dickens. It now offers large, comfortable rooms that overlook the park and is adjacent to the open air theatre. Just off Kensington High Street, the Royal Albert Hall, Kensington Palace and the main museums are all within walking distance.

Location: OS 176, GR 249797.

Great for... visiting the museums.

You need to know... breakfast is included in the overnight fee; use the side gate entrance when park gates are locked at night.

Accommodation: 200 beds: a few 6–8-bed rooms, mostly 12–20-bed rooms.

Family rooms: No. **FBR:** Yes. **Rent-a-Hostel:** No.

Classroom: Yes. **Education packages:** Yes.

Facilities: Reception, lounge, TV room, games room, self-catering kitchen, showers, luggage store, lockers, internet and email access, laundry facilities and grounds. **Daytime access:** All public areas.

Reception open: 24hrs.

Meals: Breakfast, lunch menu or picnic lunch, evening meal.

Getting there: Turn left out of High Street Kensington Station, head down High Street to Holland Park entrance. The hostel is at the top of walkway inside park. If arriving after park gate is closed (4pm in winter, 8pm in summer), please turn right off High Street Kensington into Phillimore Gardens then left into Duchess of Bedfordshire where signs point you to side entrance. Ring bell.

Public transport: BUS: frequent TfL services.
UNDERGROUND: Holland Park 0.5 miles, High Street Kensington 0.5. RAIL: Kensington Olympia 0.5 miles. **NATIONALEXPRESS** Hammersmith Bridge Road 1 mile.

Parking: NCP, 15 minutes' walk. Drop off/pick up at corner of Duchess of Bedford Walk and Phillimore Gdns. No parking at hostel.

Nearest other hostels: Earl's Court 1 mile, South Kensington 1, Oxford Street 3, City of London 5.

Price Band: **F** Opening category: **①**

HOSTEL MANAGERS CHOOSE...

LONDON'S BEST FREE ATTRACTIONS

Changing of the guard YHA Rotherhithe: "Daily at Buckingham Palace at 11am, mid-April to end of July, and on alternate days at 11.30am the rest of the year. When it gets busy in summer, I tell people to try the changing of the Mounted Guard in Whitehall instead."

Camden Market YHA Earls Court: "I get asked by at least 40 guests a week if there's something more alternative to do. I always recommend exploring Camden. The market at the weekend is huge and sells everything from antiques to second-hand clothes."

HMS Belfast YHA Rotherhithe: "A moored Second World War cruiser free to under-16s."

Wren's churches YHA City of London: "Within a 20-minute walk of the hostel you'll find 23 Wren-designed churches, built after the Great Fire of 1666. A monument to the fire on London Bridge has great views from the observation gallery."

The Old Bailey YHA Rotherhithe: "Arrive early to get a seat in the public gallery at the Central Criminal Court. No under-14s, cameras, video equipment or mobile phones are allowed."

Speakers Corner, Hyde Park
YHA Rotherhithe: "A great place to watch people ranting and raving. Best on a Sunday afternoon."

Lunch at Covent Garden, near YHA Oxford Street.

Purpose-built: YHA Rotherhithe is in the Docklands area.

● OXFORD STREET ☆☆

**14 Noel Street, London W1F 8GJ;
oxfordst@yha.org.uk
Tel: 0870 770 5984 Fax: 0870 770 5985**

Oxford Street is where the action is. In the middle of Soho, you can shop 'til you drop in Britain's most famous shopping street. There are pubs and clubs aplenty and the hostel is within walking distance of many theatres. If you're looking for a quiet break, don't choose this busy, vibrant hostel!

Location: OS 176, GR 294812.

Great for... shoppers, clubbers and theatre goers.

You need to know... it's self-catering accommodation only.

Accommodation: 75 beds: all 2-, 3- and 4-bed rooms.

Family rooms: No. **FBR:** Yes. **Rent-a-Hostel:** No.

Classroom: No. **Education packages:** No.

Facilities: Lounge with TV, self-catering kitchen, laundry facilities, lockers and showers. **Daytime access:** All areas.

Reception open: 24hrs.

Meals: Packed breakfast and self-catering only.

Getting there: Leave Oxford Circus Station by Exit 8. Turn left into Argyle Street; at end turn left into Great Marlborough Street and go straight ahead until intersection with Poland Street. There Great Marlborough Street changes into Noel Street and the hostel is next to a mural on the wall.

Public transport: BUS: frequent TfL services.
UNDERGROUND: Oxford Circus, Tottenham Ct Rd, both 0.5 miles.
RAIL: Charing Cross 0.5 miles, Euston 1.
NATIONALEXPRESS Marylebone, Gloucester Place, Baker Street, all 0.5 miles.

Parking: No.

Nearest other hostels: St Pancras 1.5 miles, City of London 2, Earl's Court 3, Holland House 3.

Price Band: F   **Opening category:** ❶

◐● ROTHERHITHE ☆☆

**20 Salter Road, London SE16 5PR;
rotherhithe@yha.org.uk
Tel: 0870 770 6010 Fax: 0870 770 6011**

Anyone with children will know how tiring a city visit can be for both parents and youngsters. This modern, purpose-built hostel in the newly developed Docklands area of London, on the south bank of the River Thames, offers an answer. It's a comfortable base with private bathrooms and plenty of child-friendly facilities – travel cots and high chairs are available and there is a free children's library and toy box on site, along with over 30 board games. With close public transport stops offering easy access to Greenwich Meridian Observatory and other South Bank attractions, it makes for a stress-free city break.

Location: OS 176, TQ 356 801.

Great for... families with young children.

You need to know... with 320 beds, it's a busy hostel popular with groups; breakfast is included in the overnight fee.

Accommodation: 320 beds: some 2-, 3-, 4-, 5- and 6-bed rooms, plus 3x10-bed rooms, all en-suite.

Family rooms: Yes. **Rent-a-Hostel:** No.

Classroom: Yes. **Education packages:** Yes.

Facilities: Reception, TV lounge, self-catering kitchen, laundry room, cycle store/workshop, licensed bar with games, conference rooms, library and luggage store. All rooms are en-suite.

Daytime access: All public areas.

Reception open: 24hrs.

Meals: Breakfast, picnic lunch, evening meal.

Getting there: From Rotherhithe Underground, turn left out of only exit, walk 600 metres and hostel is on left. From Canada Water station, exit beside Canada Water (keep water on right) and follow canal (left of Decathalon) to Salter Rd then cross pedestrian crossing and turn right. Hostel is on your left after 50 metres. From London Bridge Underground, exit and cross road opposite to London Dungeon and catch 381 bus to hostel. From Waterloo station, exit

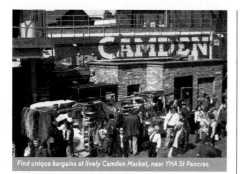

Find unique bargains at lively Camden Market, near YHA St Pancras.

onto York Road and catch 381 bus to the hostel.
Public transport: BUS: TfL 225, 381, N381.
UNDERGROUND: Rotherhithe, Canada Water both 600m.
RAIL: London Bridge 1 mile. **NATIONALEXPRESS** Victoria Coach
Station 5 miles. **Parking:** Free on-street car parking. Coaches free
(100 metres).**Nearest other hostels:** City of London 2 miles, Oxford
Street 5, Earl's Court 6, South Kensington 6.

Price Band: F	Opening category: ❶

●● ST PANCRAS ☆☆☆☆
79-81 Euston Road, London NW1 2QS;
stpancras@yha.org.uk
Tel: 0870 770 6044 Fax: 0870 770 6045

If you're just stopping for a night mid-trip, then St Pancras is the most
convenient hostel in London. Opposite St Pancras station and a short
walk from Euston and Kings Cross, it's well situated in terms of access
to transport links. If you're looking to stay longer, then lively Camden
Town is only a 10-minute walk away. Premium rooms are available,
offering en-suite bathrooms, TV and tea/coffee-making facilities.
Location: OS 176, GR 300828.
Great for... a comfortable night mid-trip or long-term stay for
exploring London.
You need to know... there's no parking; breakfast is included in the
overnight price; no groups (individuals and families only); linen
provided except towels.
Accommodation: 152 beds: 10x2-, 1x3-, 18x4-, 3x5-bed rooms, plus
7x6-bed rooms, mostly en-suite.
Family rooms: Yes. **Rent-a-Hostel:** No.
Classroom: No. **Education packages:** No.
Facilities: Lounge with satellite TV and games area, self-catering
kitchen, dining room, cycle store, luggage store, lockers and laundry
facilities. **Daytime access:** All public areas.
Reception open: 24hrs.
Meals: Breakfast, picnic lunch and evening meal available.
Getting there: From Kings Cross/St Pancras stations, turn right onto
Euston Road, cross Judd Street and hostel is second building on
left-hand side. From Euston station turn left onto Euston Road and the
hostel is opposite the British Library.
Public transport: BUS: frequent from surrounding areas.
UNDERGROUND: Kings Cross St Pancras, few minutes walk.
RAIL: Kings Cross and Euston, both few minutes walk.

NATIONALEXPRESS Victoria Coach Station 3.5 miles.
Parking: 24-hour NCP car park 15-minute walk away.
Nearest other hostels: City of London 1 mile, Oxford Street 1.5,
Hampstead Heath 2.

Price Band: F	Opening category: ❶

●● SOUTH KENSINGTON ☆☆☆☆
65-67 Queen's Gate, London
bph.hostel@scout.org.uk
Tel: 0870 770 6132 Fax: 0870 770 6133

Baden Powell House was built as a worldwide centre for scouting on
a World War II bombsite and was opened by the Queen in 1961. It is
also a conference and recreation centre. It is a short walk to
Kensington gardens and Hyde Park. Situated in central London it is in
the heart of museum land and close to South Kensington and
Gloucester Road tube stations. Conveniently located for all London
attractions and for travel within UK and Europe. After a busy day
sightseeing you can relax on our roof terrace garden or in the
coffee shop.
Location: OS 176 GR 264789.
Great for... youth and educational groups exploring London
attractions and visiting museums.
You need to know... full English breakfast is included in
accommodation rates, lunches and dinners can be pre-booked. There
are no self-catering facilities and car parking space is very restricted.
Accommodation: 180 beds: several 6x1-, 8x2-, and 3x3-, 8x4- and
10x9-19- bed rooms. Dormitories accommodate 9-19 occupants.
Family rooms: Yes. **Rent-a-Hostel:** No.
Classroom: No. **Education packages:** No.
Facilities: All bedrooms are en-suite and all except the dormitories
have TVs, tea and coffee-making facilities; coffee shop, conference
facilities, souvenir counter and roof garden. **Daytime access:** Main
entrance doors close at 11pm. Access via doorbell to call night
manager. **Reception open:** 7am-10pm. **Meals:** Full English breakfast.
Getting there: Turn left out of Gloucester Road station, cross over
Cromwell Road, turn right, keep walking for five minutes. Baden
Powell House is on the junction of Queensgate and Cromwell Road on
the left.
Public transport: BUS: 70/74/360.
UNDERGROUND: Gloucester Road 0.25 miles. RAIL: Thameslink at
Embankment 2 miles, St Paul's 4, Paddington 4.5, Liverpool Street 6.
NATIONALEXPRESS Victoria Coach Station 3 miles.
Parking: Underground car park with 4 spaces. Charged metered
parking outside hostel on Queensgate.
Nearest other hostels: Holland House 1 mile, Earl's Court 1, City of
London 2.

Price Band: F	Opening category: ❶

TRY RENT-A-HOSTEL
Many of the hostels in this
guide can be booked through
the Rent-a-Hostel scheme. For
full details, turn to page 12.

Go! *Find your hostel*

Use these street maps to locate the 21 hostels we have identified as particularly difficult to find.

Bath

From London Road, follow signs to University and American Museum. From the south-west, follow A36 to roundabout on Pulteney Road.

Beverley Friary

Follow signs to Minster and Friary. Turn down Friar's Lane next to Minster and follow to end of lane to car park.

Brighton

From Patcham village Co-op, follow Old London Road round to left past Post Office to London Road. Hostel is opposite Black Lion pub. By road, hostel is 3 miles north of Brighton city centre on London Road (A23) adjacent to A23/A27 junction.

Bristol

From London or South Wales, exit M4 at J19, then take M32. From Birmingham or South West, exit M5 at J18, then A4.

Broadstairs

From town centre and beach, head uphill along High Street, under railway bridge and left at traffic lights. The hostel is the first building after the row of shops.

Cambridge

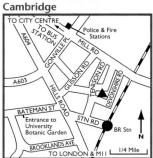

From city centre, follow signs to the railway station. Take last left turning (at hostel sign) before the railway station.

Canterbury

Follow signs for Dover. The hostel is on the A2050, 1.5 miles from the centre.

Chester

The hostel is southwest of city centre on A5104 (signposted to Saltney), 350 metres from traffic lights on right.

Exeter

From M5, J30, follow signs for city centre. Turn right at Countess Wear roundabout, then first left into School Lane. From A379, follow signs for Topsham, turn left at Countess Wear roundabout then left into School Lane. From centre follow signs for Topsham.

Lincoln

On foot from the train station turn right onto St Mary's Street. Continue to Oxford Street. Go under flyover and up steps on the right. Go along Canwick Road and over traffic lights. When the cemetery is on your left, South Park is on your right.

Liverpool

From Lime Street station follow signs for Albert Dock. Turn left onto main dock road (called Wapping). Hostel is on left after Baltic Fleet pub. From James Street station turn right then left onto Wapping, past Albert Dock on right – hostel is on left after Baltic Fleet pub.

Manchester

From bus station and Piccadilly train station, follow signs for Castlefield/Museum of Science and Industry (MSI); or take Metrolink to the G-Mex station. By car, follow signs for Castlefield/MSI. Hostel is opposite MSI, behind Castlefield Hotel.

Newcastle

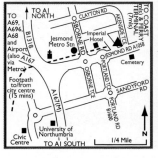

From the metro (underground) by foot, it's a 5-minute walk on left side of Jesmond Road East (A1058). By car, access the A1058 (Jesmond Road) from central motorway (A167M), which is left from the northwest or right from the south.

Ninebanks

Signposted from A686 south of Whitfield. Hostel is at Mohope, signposted from Ninebanks hamlet.

Oxford

From the station turn right and go under bridge. Hostel is on the right immediately behind the railway station.

Portsmouth

From Cosham police station, take Medina Road, then seventh turning on the right, Old Wymering Lane. The hostel is opposite the church entrance.

Salisbury

Motorists, follow A36 signposts. Follow brown signs on A36 by Salisbury college roundabout. On foot, walk east from tourist information centre following black footpath signs, leading into Milford Street and up hill.

Scarborough

From Scarborough, follow signs to North Bay attractions, then A165 to Whitby. Hostel is 2 miles north of town centre (there is a very sharp turn immediately after bridge – drive past and turn in the layby).

Stratford-upon-Avon

From Stratford-upon-Avon, at Clopton Bridge take Wellesbourne Road. Hostel is 1.5 miles on left. From M40, exit J15 and take A429 south, follow signs to Charlecote Park. Turn right onto the B4086 and hostel is 1.5 miles on right.

Winchester

From guildhall, walk over the Eastgate Bridge and take the first left into Water Lane (no vehicle entry). The hostel is the third door on the left.

York

From the Minster, take A19 to Clifton Green, turning left at Old Grey Mare pub into Water End. Hostel is on the right. From ring road, take A19 towards the city, turning right into Water End at the second set of traffic lights.

 **INDEX**

Hostel Listings

Camping Barn Listings

Go! THE GUIDE

Terms and conditions

1. General
1.1 In these terms and conditions "Camping Barns" means the accommodation in 'stone tents' as further described in our most recent brochures as published from time to time; "Customer" means any customer who makes or is making a booking with the YHA; "Group" means a group of 5 or more people staying at a Youth Hostel (in England and Wales) or a group of 9 or more people staying at a Youth Hostel outside of England and Wales under the group membership scheme; "Rent-a-Hostel" means the rental of an entire Youth Hostel by one Group; "Flexi/Explorer Packages" has the meaning given to it in our most recent brochures as published from time to time; "Writing" means letter, fax or email; "YHA" means the Youth Hostels Association (England and Wales) Ltd; "you" means the customer submitting a booking; "Youth Hostel" means a youth hostel run by the YHA;
1.2 The contract for the supply by us of accommodation and (where applicable) other related services ("Contract") will be formed when you we accept your order and we receive from you the appropriate deposit in cleared funds.
1.3 Your Contract cannot be amended unless confirmed by an authorised representative of YHA and yourself.
1.4 These conditions and any matters referred to by us form the entire

understanding between you and us and supersede any prior promises, representations (unless fraudulent) or undertakings.
1.5 Any omission or error in any sales literature, web page or site, order form, quotation, price list, order acknowledgement, despatch note, invoice or other document issued by us may be corrected by us without liability. We will advise you of any changes at the time of booking or as soon as is reasonably possible thereafter.
1.6 The provisions of the Contracts (Rights of Third Parties) Act 1999 are expressly excluded from the Contract so that no third party may claim any rights under this contract.

2. Membership
2.1 You may only stay in a Youth Hostel or other YHA accommodation (with the exception of Camping Barns) if you are a member of YHA or any other association recognised by the International Youth Hostel Federation. Where you wish to make a Rent-a-Hostel booking the nominated group leader must be a member of YHA and at least 21 years old. Where you wish to make a Group booking the Group leader must hold a group membership card.

3. Making a Booking
3.1 Bookings to stay at a Youth Hostel may be made by telephoning the bookings team at the relevant Youth

Hostel or, where directed in the YHA's brochure, by telephoning the YHA Contact Centre.
3.2 Camping Barn bookings are only made by telephoning the YHA Contact Centre.
3.3 Before your booking is confirmed and the Contract comes into force YHA reserves the right to increase or decrease prices PROVIDED THAT we will notify you in writing in good time prior to delivery of such price increases/decreases and you may cancel your order within 7 working days of this notice if you are unhappy with the price increases/decreases.
3.4 All bookings are subject to availability and YHA reserves the right to decline any booking at its discretion.

4. Payment
4.1 In order to secure your booking you must pay us the appropriate deposit, as set out below: -
4.1.1 for bookings up to and including the value of £100 full payment is required to secure your booking;
4.1.2 for bookings in excess of £100 minimum deposit of £100 is required. The balance must be paid 8 weeks before your arrival date;
4.1.3 for Rent-a-hostel bookings, Camping Barn group bookings, multi-hostel bookings, walking or activity holidays a deposit of 25% of the full cost of the booking is required. The balance must be paid 8 weeks before your arrival date;
4.1.4 for bookings for the all inclusive packages (Flexi and Explorer packages) full payment is required to

ture your booking;
1.5 for Group bookings including multi-hostel bookings) made more than six months in advance a deposit of £1 per person, per hostel is required as an initial deposit. A further deposit of 25% of the full cost of the booking is required 6 months prior to your arrival date. The balance must be paid 8 weeks before your arrival date;
4.1.6 for Group bookings less than six months in advance of your arrival date a deposit of 25% of the full cost of the booking is required. The balance must be paid 8 weeks before your arrival date.
4.2 Payments shall be made in such format as we may agree with you when you place an order.
4.3 If any payment under these terms and conditions is overdue, then without prejudice to our other rights and remedies we may cancel your booking; and/or we may suspend the supply and/or deliveries of any other services being provided to you by YHA.
4.4 Deposits payable under clause 4.1 are non-refundable in the circumstances set out in clause 8.4.

5. Group Bookings
All Groups must have a minimum leader / participant ratio of one leader for every ten participants. Mixed sex groups must have leaders of both sexes. Group leaders accompanying the Group are responsible for the discipline and behaviour of their Group. Group leaders are responsible for all damage caused by their action or the actions of those in their group. If any Group is given sole use of a Youth Hostel(s) it shall not offer for sale to the general public or publicly advertise the sale of Youth Hostel facilities or services without the prior written agreement of YHA.

6. If you change your booking – non group bookings
6.1 Changes requested within 56 days of the date of the first night of your stay will be treated as cancellations (see clause 8 below).
6.2 If you wish to change a confirmed reservation (e.g. changes in dates of visit or changes in numbers of people booked) such changes are subject to the availability of a suitable alternative and are subject to any additional costs incurred in making changes to accommodate your request.
6.3 We will inform you of the amount of any additional costs when you request your changes and shall agree such costs with you.

7. If you change a Group booking
7.1 Subject to availability, you may change a Group booking to a different location or date up to six months before your arrival date.
7.2 If, less than 6 months before your arrival date, you wish to change a Group booking such a change shall be treated as a cancellation and shall be subject to our standard cancellation charges below (see clause 8, below).
7.3 A Group booking can decrease its numbers by up to 10% up to 28 days before arrival, without incurring cancellation fees. Thereafter any additional decreases in Group numbers will be subject to our standard cancellation charges. Changes are subject to availability.
7.4 All changes shall be subject to the availability of a suitable alternative.

8. If you cancel your booking
8.1 All cancellations are subject to a cancellation charge.
8.2 Cancellations by non-Group bookings are subject to a £2.00 per person administration fee up to a maximum of £20.
8.3 Cancellation charges (whether for Group bookings or non-Group bookings) where less than 56 days

Cancellation Charges	
Number of days	**Amount you must pay**
More than 56 days	Varies according to the booking – see above
55 – 42 days	30% of the total cost of your stay
41 – 28 days	60% of the total cost of your stay
27 – 15 days	90% of the total cost of your stay
14 days or less	The total cost of your stay

notice is given are set on the sliding scale below. All cancellation charges are calculated from the day written notification is received by YHA. These charges are based on how many days before the date of the first night of your stay we receive your cancellation notice. These charges are based on the total cost of your stay.

8.4 Cancellation charges (whether for Group bookings or non-Group bookings) for cancellations more than 56 days in advance vary according to the booking. If you cancel a Rent-a-Hostel, multi-hostel booking, Camping Barn, walking or activity holiday YHA will retain the deposit paid pursuant to clause 4.1. If you cancel an all inclusive package (Flexi / Explorer package) YHA will retain 10% of the payment made pursuant to clause 4.1.

9. If we change your booking
In the unlikely event it becomes necessary to change your booking, in total or in part YHA will inform you as soon as is reasonably possible of any necessary changes. You shall have the choice of: accepting the changed arrangements; or purchasing another booking from YHA (and paying or receiving a refund in respect of any differences); or cancelling your booking and receiving a full refund of all payments made.

10. Delay or Failure to Perform
We shall not be liable to you if we are prevented or delayed in the performing of

any of our obligations to you if this is due to any cause beyond our reasonable control including (without limitation): an act of God, explosion, flood, fire or accident; war or civil disturbance; strike, industrial action or stoppages of work; any form of government intervention; a third party act or omission; failure by you to give us a correct delivery address or notify us of any change of address.

11. Our liability to you
11.1 YHA shall ensure that the accommodation and /or other services you order from us are in accordance with these terms and conditions and shall be performed by us with reasonable skill and care.
11.2 Where an element of your booking is not provided as stated in clause 11.1 you must notify us within 28 days of the alleged breach. We shall then investigate the matter and if we have not delivered the services in accordance with clause 11.1 you shall be entitled to: a full refund of the cost of your order (or, where appropriate, the relevant section of it) less any fees charged for changes requested by you; or a free stay to the equivalent value of the services complained of, where such dates are agreed in writing by us.
11.3 We will not be liable to you by way of representation (unless fraudulent), common law duty or under any express or implied term of the contract for: any losses which are not foreseeable by both you and us when the Contract is formed arising in connection with the supply

of the services or their use by you; any losses which are caused by any breach by us; business or trade losses.
11.4 Our entire liability in connection with the Contract will not exceed the purchase price of the services booked less any amendment charges paid to us.
11.5 Except in relation to death or personal injury caused by our negligence YHA's liability remains, at all times, limited to the value of the services booked, excluding any amendment charges paid to us.

12. Behaviour
If your behaviour is deemed to be unacceptable or causes damage your booking may be terminated and you may be asked to leave YHA premises. Your membership card will be retained pending further enquiry. No whole or part refunds will be made under these circumstances

13. Governing Law and Jurisdiction
The contract is subject to English law and the exclusive jurisdiction of the English Courts.

14. Your Information
We shall only store and use the information you supply to us or which is supplied to us for the purposes of carrying out our contact with you and to inform you of other services and offers which we make available from time to time. If you do not wish to receive such information, please let us know by: emailing us at contactus@yha.org.uk; or telephoning us on 0870 770 8868; or writing to us at the address noted above.